MW00612103

BETTER

FASTER

FARTHER

BETTER

FASTER

FARTHER

*How Running
Changed Everything
We Know About Women*

MAGGIE MERTENS

ALGONQUIN BOOKS OF CHAPEL HILL 2024

Published by
Algonquin Books of Chapel Hill
Post Office Box 2225
Chapel Hill, North Carolina 27515-2225

an imprint of Workman Publishing
a division of Hachette Book Group, Inc.
1290 Avenue of the Americas
New York, NY 10104

Printed in the United States of America.
Design by Steve Godwin.

The publisher is not responsible for websites (or their content) that are not owned
by the publisher.

Library of Congress Cataloging-in-Publication Data
Names: Mertens, Maggie, author.
Title: Better, faster, farther : how running changed everything we know about
    women / Maggie Mertens.
Description: First edition. | Chapel Hill, North Carolina : Algonquin Books of
    Chapel Hill, 2024. | Includes bibliographical references and index. | Identifiers:
    LCCN 2024005148 (print) | LCCN 2024005149 (ebook) | ISBN 9781643753355
    (hardcover) | ISBN 9781643756134 (ebook)
Subjects: LCSH: Running for women. | Running—Physiological aspects.
Classification: LCC GV1061.18.W66 M47 2024 (print) | LCC GV1061.18.W66 (ebook) |
    DDC 796.42082—dc23/eng/20240312
LC record available at https://lccn.loc.gov/2024005148
LC ebook record available at https://lccn.loc.gov/2024005149

10 9 8 7 6 5 4 3 2 1
First Edition

For my mom, Theresa, who never told me I couldn't.

For my aunts, my grandmothers, and great-grandmothers and all the strong women who made me.

And for every woman who was ever told she couldn't but did it anyway.

I always thought I must have been a deer or a horse in some former state, because it was such a joy to run. . . . I remember running over the hills just at dawn one summer morning, and pausing to rest in the silent woods, saw, through an arch of trees, the sun rise over river, hill, and wide green meadows as I never saw it before.

—Louisa May Alcott, *Sketch of Childhood, by herself,* c. 1880

For us, body education is core education. Our bodies are the physical bases from which we move out into the world; ignorance, uncertainty—even, at worst, shame—about our physical selves create in us an alienation from ourselves that keeps us from being the whole people that we could be.

—The Boston Women's Health Book Collective,
    Preface to *Our Bodies, Ourselves,* 1973

CONTENTS

BETTER

FASTER

FARTHER

Atalanta, Copy of Ma 52, a Roman copy by Pierre Lepautre after a Hellenistic original (Wikimedia Commons)

INTRODUCTION: WOMEN CAN'T RUN

WOMEN HAVE ALWAYS been able to run, but men have been trying to convince us for centuries that we can't.

In the first modern Olympic Games, one event epitomized manliness: the marathon. The 26.2-mile race was not an original component of the ancient Olympic Games, but a kind of tribute to the masculinity of the ancient Greeks just the same. The marathon is so named for the Athenian soldier who, supposedly, ran all the way back to Athens after the Battle of Marathon to announce "We won!" after the Athenian army beat the Persian invaders,[1] a turning point in the Greco-Persian wars that helped lead to the rise of the Classical Greek civilization. According to some accounts, this man died of exhaustion as soon as he made his announcement. Such was the difficulty of the 40-kilometer run from Marathon to Athens. What better way to honor the classic Greeks than with this: essentially the reenactment of a war story. A feat of manliness if ever there was one.

Then, a woman asked to be registered.

This woman, known as Stamata Revithi, a poor single mother, was a woman obsessed. She had been walking to Athens from Piraeus with her seventeen-month-old baby in the weeks before the marathon, seeking a better life for herself and her child. A traveler on the same path asked why she was walking so far, on foot, with her young child in her arms. "Where should I find the fare? I have no money" was her answer. When the traveler gave her some money, he also made a suggestion that she should try the upcoming marathon. Perhaps he meant it as a means of making money, gaining fame, or merely because Revithi looked like she could run, judging by her walking a 10-kilometer route while carrying a toddler.

WHEN FRENCH BARON Pierre de Coubertin wanted to revive the modern Olympic Games at the end of the nineteenth century, he framed the need for them as a way to better the world, to promote world peace. "It is clear that the telegraph, railways, the telephone, the passionate research in science, congresses and exhibitions have done more for peace than any treaty or diplomatic convention," Coubertin said at a speech in 1892.[2] "Well, I hope that athletics will do even more. Those who have seen 30,000 people running through the rain to attend a football match will not think that I am exaggerating." Coubertin wanted to build a better world through sports.

But this better, more peaceful world didn't include women. Not in the sports part, anyway. He wanted to bring back the Olympic Games "for the solemn and periodic exaltation of male athleticism . . . with the applause of women as reward."³ Later, as the president of the first-ever International Olympic Committee, he doubled down on the idea of women's (lack of) place in the Games: "Women have but one task, that of the role of crowning the winner with garlands . . . in public competitions, women's participation must be absolutely prohibited. It is indecent that spectators should be exposed to the risk of seeing the body of a woman being smashed before their eyes. Besides, no matter how toughened a sportswoman may be, her organism is not cut out to sustain certain shocks."⁴

Needless to say, when those first modern Games took place, in Greece in 1896, there were no women athletic contestants. Women, Coubertin was fond of pointing out, did not participate in the *original* Olympic Games. They were barred from even entering the stadium as spectators. Participants in those ancient games were nude so as to keep women from even attempting to disguise themselves and sneak in.⁵

Historians have found evidence that ancient Greek women held their own separate games to honor Hera, Zeus's wife, in which three separate age-groups of young women competed in a footrace, but that was no matter to Coubertin.

By the 1890s, proving *masculine* physical prowess through sport was appealing to men like Coubertin because, according to them, the very idea of "masculinity" and what it meant to be a man was being threatened at the time. Women throughout Europe and the West were beginning to organize for greater rights, for the vote, for political power, for the right to be educated and to work in the jobs they had been told were only for men.⁶ At the same time, similar organizing was happening in the US, where formerly enslaved Black people were clamoring for more rights in the wake of the Civil War and Reconstruction. In short: what many (white) men saw as the "natural order"—white men on top, women and everyone else at the bottom—was being challenged. Naturally, in the absence of mass war (since Coubertin wanted more peace), sports was the perfect stage on which to perform their masculinity and reassert their physical dominance.[7]

When Stamata Revithi's story was related many years later by Athanasios Tarasouleas, an Olympic historian who cobbled together a narrative from newspaper accounts of the time, he described Ravithi as blond, strong, and a woman with "large bones and big, clever eyes." He says that when she learned of the marathon, she saw it as her only option to try to turn her life around.

The evening before the marathon, Stamata joined some of the men at an inn in the village of Marathon, where the runners spoke to the press. Tarasouleas reports that she told the journalists there with certainty that she would run the entire distance, and that it would take her three and a half hours or maybe even less. "I saw in a dream that I had an apron full of gold and gilded sugared almonds! Who knows! My heart is in it, I suppose my feet will hold," she said.

Revithi insisted that her being poor and often going without food would only help her maintain her stamina. "So many nights I went without food while feeding my child! I had no bread to eat."

The Olympic Committee, however, tried to convince Stamata that a group of women were running the race the following week, so she should wait. She did as she was told and didn't join the men that next morning. But soon she realized she'd been lied to. There were no other women coming to race. So the following day, Stamata arrived at the starting line on her own at 8 a.m. She wrote down the time she started, and asked the school master, mayor, and magistrate to sign the paper to prove her start time.

Revithi gathered her long white slip skirt up and tucked it in at her waist to free her legs a bit. Her well-worn shoes didn't last the whole route, so partway through she removed them. Five and a half hours later, she arrived, "perspiring and covered in dust," at the finish line in Athens. She asked some officers nearby to sign her document, proving how long her marathon run had taken—proving that she had done it.

Despite Tarasouleas writing with the aid of Greek newspaper reports of the "famous marathon woman," Stamata Revithi's story is told more like a Greek myth than like a news report of a barrier-breaking athlete of the time. There is a mythical, magical air to it.[8] Her name doesn't even match in all of the accounts, some refer to her not as Stamata Revithi but as Melpomene—the name of a famous muse in Greek mythology.

There are no accompanying photographs in Tarasouleas's piece, though the games were photographed. Instead, there's a sketch of what Revithi may have looked like, long flowing skirt, hair tucked back at the nape of her neck. The drawing doesn't look all too different from the ancient Greek women illustrated in myths.

ONE SUCH MYTH begins with a baby left to die because she's a girl and therefore useless. You see, King Iasus of Arcadia had wanted a baby boy so he could pass his kingdom down. You couldn't pass kingdoms down to girls, I guess, so he ordered this baby to be taken by one of his men to a mountainside and left there, screaming and alone.

In one version of this Greek myth that I came across—it is difficult actually, to find many written accounts of this particular myth—the girl has a mother, too.[9] But the mother, the queen, though bereft at the thought of losing her child, has no power in this marriage. Women don't often have much power in these kinds of stories, do they? But the queen did make one bold statement: she named the child Atalanta. The name meant "of equal weight."

The baby was taken to the mountain and left, as ordered. But she didn't die. Instead, Atalanta was found by a bear who mothered her, or at least nursed her enough to grow. Depending on which version of the story you read, she was either raised by the bear or a group of hunters who found her and took her in as their own. Either way, being raised out in the forest with the bears and/or the hunters allowed her a form of physical freedom, certainly more than she might have had if she'd been raised in the Arcadian palace. Outside, free to roam of her own accord, she discovered she was not just an excellent hunter, she was a runner, and a fast one. In fact, she found that she was faster than any man.

One story says that she traveled to Olympia, but couldn't take part in the Olympics, since she was a woman. But there were games for women held elsewhere, where she won honors in wrestling, broad jump, discus, and of course, the footrace.

Hearing of her achievements, Iasus decided maybe she wasn't so bad after all and that he would step back into the role of her father, meaning he would marry her off.[10] In the picture book I found of the tale, the explanation is that he wanted a grandson (was still looking for a *real* heir!). Perhaps, some other accounts suggest, Iasus was just hoping for a dowry. Ovid, who first wrote down the myth of Atalanta, wrote none of the above backstory, only that she was a woman who knew she should not marry, as an oracle had once told her that marrying would be her downfall.[11]

In all of the accounts, however, Atalanta tells her father she won't agree to a marriage match unless the man could beat her in a footrace. If the suitor lost, they would be killed. She believes this means no man will even make such a risky bet and she can avoid this marriage business forever. Her father agreed, but it didn't work out so well. Many men, in fact, believed in their own ability to best this woman in a footrace and win a wife. Instead, she won, and won, and won. And so they died, and died, and died.

After some time, one man, Melanion, a known warrior, turned to the gods for help in outrunning this mortal woman, who was faster than any mortal man. In Ovid's version, Melanion is interested because she is just so *becoming* while she runs. Her pale skin blushing pink, her legs free of robes, a short white tunic the only thing covering her nakedness—that kind of thing. The children's version is not quite so salacious, but leans heavily on the romance just the same. Melanion sees Atalanta run, "her hair streaming behind her like a cloud, beautiful as a goddess," and is convinced the risk is worth it.

Aphrodite, the goddess of love, gives Melanion a trick to win. She provides him with golden apples—a symbol of heroism any person seeking greatness would seek out enthusiastically—to throw down along the track so Atalanta would be distracted from the race and lose. The feat of trickery worked, because Atalanta stopped along her race a few times to pick up the apples, which it turned out were also quite heavy and so slowed down her pace, allowing Melanion to pass her. So she wasn't beat, not really, but she married him anyway. Perhaps she respected his wit. Or she appreciated those golden apples. The stories try to make it seem like she was just a girl in love.

Later, according to Ovid, the lovers were overcome with passion in a home of the gods, (that's a no-no) and as punishment, the gods turn the pair into lions for eternity. Fittingly, because, like Atalanta, lions are proof that the gender binary in the entirety of the animal kingdom is more complex than it seems on the surface. As a lion, Atalanta wouldn't be considered strange at all to be a fast huntress. As punishments go, this one doesn't sound so bad to me.

NOW I KNOW myth is a popular place to start a story, as a way to prove that some idea has been around for a long, long time. But here I start to question myself. Is a myth about a woman who can outrun a man a confirmation of the thousands of years of stories about male physical superiority, or a challenge to them? Do myths contain a kernel of truth? Or are we meant to read them simply metaphorically?

The kingdom of Arcadia, where Atalanta was said to be born, was the seat of an ancient Greek indigenous civilization, among the mountainous Peloponnese region, a place of unspoiled wilderness. It doesn't seem far-fetched to me to believe that perhaps the ancient women of this region were strong runners, hunters, and generally took delight in a footrace. Of course, we have almost no written record of these everyday humans. Atalanta is one of the only mortal women who appear as main characters in ancient Greek myth, and even then, her story is not one of the most well known.

I'm including Atalanta here because I'm struck by how closely Stamata Revithi's story—an undeniably true story, reported in newspapers—is to Atalanta's. I see in Revithi's story proof that women like her, and thus like Atalanta, do exist. While she proves what I aim to do here—to give evidence that women have always run—the way Revithi's story has been told also perpetuates the idea that women who can run, who can beat men at a footrace, would exist only in myth, or as a wildly rare exception.

IN WHAT IS almost an aside, Tarasouleas mentions that Revithi's older child, a seven-year-old, had died a few months prior to her walk to Athens. I can't help but read this and think that perhaps it was this grief that made the marathon sound like a good idea to Revithi. Like something tangible to do in the depths of the unbelievable pain of this loss. A way to prove the seemingly impossible is, in fact, possible—like the loss of a child.

Or perhaps her run was a desperate attempt to save herself and her living child from the same fate, poor as she was. According to Tarasouleas, Revithi was asked immediately upon arriving in Athens why she would "run all that way and tire yourself?" Her response: "So that the king might award a position to my child. I am now going straight to Timoleon Philimon [the secretary general of the Greek Olympic Committee] to let him know how long it took me to run from Marathon, and tell him that whoever wishes may come to compete with me."

Or the run might have been a way to retaliate, to do something on her own, as a single mother, when society didn't think women could do much of anything without the aid of a man. Of course, there is no follow-up reporting, nothing known about this woman beyond these few days in the spotlight of history.

But perhaps wondering *why* it was that Stamata ran the marathon is just falling into the trap of myth myself. After all, do I wonder why any of the many men who completed that first Olympic marathon decided to run? Do I blame their decision on some kind of emotional heartbreak?

Perhaps Stamata just wanted to run, so she did. And we should leave her story at that, and ask instead why it is we do not hear her name as the first woman to run the Olympic Marathon—the same year that a group of men did. Instead, we hear that the Olympics didn't hold a marathon for women until 1984, giving the impression that women were merely incapable for all that time. When in fact, nearly a century before, an untrained, barefoot, grieving single mother proved it was possible.

IN SOME WAYS, it is fitting that these early stories of women runners read like myth. That they bring up more questions than answers. Women running today are similarly embroiled in questions about their bodies. The questions have changed, some, over the years, from things like: *Is a woman even capable of running? Will a woman's uterus fall out if she runs too far? How far is too far?* To things like: *Can a woman run on her period? How about during pregnancy? Will she ever run again after giving birth? How does estrogen or testosterone impact speed? Will a woman ever be faster than a man? If she's that fast, is she* really *a woman?*

For many reasons, even the most basic of these myths (*Can women run?*) would take decades and decades to address. And—though we live in a far more gender-equal world than at the turn of the twentieth century—when we look closely, the myths around women and their bodies remain hard to shake, even today.

LIKE MANY CHILDREN, I grew up running: on the soccer field, at track and cross-country meets, and all over my backyard and neighborhood, chasing my four brothers around. Since there were five of us, everything was a competition. Growing up in the 1990s and early 2000s near Seattle, and having the parents I had, meant that I was never told I *shouldn't* run or keep up with my brothers. I was encouraged, and I loved it. I was never breaking records or told I was even particularly talented, I just played sports and ran around because that's what my family and the kids I grew up with did. And it was fun.

When I got to college, a women's college on the East Coast, I was in an almost opposite gender environment than I grew up in. I no longer played any organized sports or had brothers around to keep up with, but running remained a balm. I ran through my picturesque college campus whenever I needed to clear my head or blow off steam.

I've continued to run, off and on, as a way to move my body when I feel like exercising, because it's something I can do no matter where I'm living or how broke I am. I'm no elite athlete, not even a regular racer, but running feels natural and puts me in touch with my body in a way that little else does. As a journalist, I worked early on for a women's magazine and found that I loved sniffing out gender inequality through my work. But when I began to report on equal pay and treatment for women in athletics the same I would for women CEOs, I was shocked by the angry responses I'd get. I couldn't believe how many people thought that the outright inequality for these athletes was just a matter of biology. In short, they argued that women athletes were slower, weaker, and smaller than men, so why would they ever be worth watching, let alone be paid the same as men?

Since that realization, I've begun an excavation of sorts, diving deep into the way perceived physical limitations of women have been used as an excuse for unequal recognition, pay, access, health services and support, and in some cases, devastating forms of abuse. What I learned was that running specifically, something that I grew up seeing as so simple and natural and gender-free, has been used for years and years and years to define women as being lesser than men.

WHILE WE KNOW now that women can run and jump and play sports and even run marathons, there are many things that we still don't know—or falsehoods that people want to continue on believing—about the so-called *weaker sex*. For instance, in 2006, the fastest woman marathoner in the world was pregnant.[12] A pregnancy announcement in this early twenty-first-century era was often also a retirement announcement. And though British runner Paula Radcliffe was thirty-two, and just three years out from a world-record-shattering performance in the marathon (she ran the London race in just 2 hours 15 minutes 25 seconds, a record that stood for sixteen years), the whispers about the end of her career began. Every newspaper headline I can find announcing "Radcliffe is pregnant" adds a clause something like "*but* insists she'll keep running."[13]

Doctors hardly even recommended exercise to pregnant women in 2006, let alone elite runner training regimens like a hundred-plus miles per week. In fact, a 2006 survey found that a majority of ob-gyns were still offering outdated exercise recommendations to their pregnant patients. Just half of the ob-gyns surveyed recommended exercise to most of their pregnant patients, and three out of five surveyed told their patients not to exceed a maximum heart rate of 140 bpm—a heart rate you can reach through running, biking, or other sustained cardio exercise—even though the American College of Obstetricians and Gynecologists got rid of this recommendation in 1994.[14]

Even when I was pregnant for the first time, in 2017, I received similar instructions from my doctors not to overdo it on exercise, to watch my heart rate, not to lift weights, so as to avoid the risk of miscarriage.

Needless to say, Radcliffe was in medically unknown territory when she decided not only that she would come back to running competitively after giving birth, but that she would continue to train throughout her pregnancy. For the first five months she ran for seventy-five minutes every morning and another thirty to forty-five minutes in the evening. During the last five months of pregnancy, she cut back training a bit: to *just* a one-hour run each morning, and riding a stationary bike in the evenings. She also received an ultrasound every month to monitor the fetus and her uterine lining and fluid levels. Radcliffe ran up to the day she gave birth to her daughter. And then she did take some time off—twelve days, to be exact.[15]

She had about nine months after her daughter was born before the 2007 New York City Marathon, the first marathon she would have run in two years. But her postpartum body may not have been quite ready to get back to marathon training. After a few months, she discovered her sacrum—the bone at the base of the spine—had a stress fracture, likely sustained during childbirth. Eight weeks off of running. She came back again, only to hurt her foot, setting her back another couple of weeks. Finally, by September, she was back up to 140 miles a week in preparation for the November marathon.

And though she really had no scientific insight into how her body might perform in this first big race after giving birth, Radcliffe thought she had a chance to win. She'd won the NYC marathon in 2004, after all. And nearly every other marathon she'd ever entered. At the time, medical studies had never even looked at elite athletes and pregnancy. The *New York Times* called her race "the medical unknown."[16] There were rumors that it was impossible, of course. And another rumor that running postpartum was akin to blood doping, as the amount of blood in your body increases between 20 and 100 percent during pregnancy, so she'd be sure to win.

THE MORNING OF the 2007 race was a beautiful November New York day. Breezy, but clear. The kind with that autumnal chill in the air that can burn off when the sun reaches you. But Radcliffe didn't stand still long enough to feel the warmth—she made her own. Headed down the first stretch of the race, toward the Verrazano-Narrows Bridge connecting Staten Island and Brooklyn, Radcliffe led the pack. Despite being a world record holder, however, she had massive competition. Gete Wami, of Ethiopia, had just won the Berlin Marathon thirty-five days earlier. Two-time NYC Marathon winner Jeļena Prokopčuka, of Latvia, took off at the starting gun with Radcliffe, too, as did reigning world champion Catherine Ndereba, of Kenya, and Lidiya Grigoryeva, of Russia, who had won the Boston Marathon that spring.

Radcliffe hadn't run a marathon in more than two years and she was essentially running with an entirely different body. The human body goes through massive physiological shifts during pregnancy: from that increased blood volume, to joints that get pumped full of relaxin (a hormone that makes our skeletons more stretchy), and, of course, from having the equivalent of a bowling ball or a watermelon attached to the front abdomen, pushing down on the pelvic bones and floor for months, which changes musculature, balance, and very often physically pulls the abdominal muscles into a semi-permanent or permanent separation known as diastasis recti or "mommy pooch," which can affect your core strength and stability.

And just for context, at this time—2007—there was still almost no gender-specific sport science research being done. In fact, many women athletes, from students to elite professionals, were still being trained as though they were men.

This soup of mystery about her own body was the backdrop of Radcliffe's New York City comeback marathon. Still, she stayed at the head of the pack throughout the entirety of the race. In the second to last mile, while exiting Central Park, Wami, who'd remained within striking distance of Radcliffe throughout the race, found a burst of speed big enough to overtake Radcliffe. But her lead lasted just a few seconds. Radcliffe kicked all the way up the final hill and across the finish line first.

Radcliffe, a marathon winner, still the fastest woman in the world, became a myth, too.

The photo of Radcliffe, British flag draped over one shoulder, nine-month-old wide-eyed daughter perched on one slender, sinewy arm, the other arm raised in victory, ran across newspapers all over the world. Reporters described her victory as "stunning"[17] and "surreal."[18] The

implication was that this woman must be superheroic to run so fast, to come back from what used to be considered a long-term disability and continue to be one of the fastest women in the world. But Radcliffe's race wasn't about being superhuman at all; it revealed that when it comes to women runners, we've only just begun to figure out their capabilities.

EVEN AS WOMEN were proving over the years they could also be runners, the Pierre de Coubertins of the world found ways to make those women remember they were laurel-holders, first. Running for women has remained in some ways an activity shrouded in the unknown—and it seems as though many like it that way. Why would we attempt to learn more about women's bodies and how they work, especially athletes, when men's sports are so much more *impressive*?

Paula Radcliffe and her daughter after the 2007 New York City Marathon (Alan Cordova)

It's easier, after all, to just call these women outliers, mythological beings like Atalanta herself. Women who run. How strange!

In 2011, Radcliffe's biggest victory would even be questioned. Her world-record marathon in 2 hours 15 minutes 25 seconds would be considered a "world best" instead of an official record. Why? Because there were male pace runners (who come on to run a portion of a race at a certain pace so runners can see how fast they're going) at the race. A woman running next to a man, according to the International Association of Athletics Federations, made women "artificially" faster.[19]

Another attempt at discrediting her came in 2015, when Britain's *Sunday Times* would release blood test results from thousands of "suspicious" blood scores to imply a vast doping conspiracy among Britain's track-and-field athletes, one of whom was supposedly Radcliffe.[20] This questioning, though later proved demonstrably false,[21] opened up space in the conversation for those who doubt women's capabilities. A time like that, faster than the vast majority of men (the average male runs a marathon in about 4.5 hours), must have included cheating.

Radcliffe, in other words, was—like Atalanta and Stamata Revithi—too fast, too strong, for a woman. She was artificial. Superhuman. Mythological.

Women runners, it feels like the stories tell us, are to be questioned, mythologized, accused, and most of all: doubted. Cut down to size. So that other women don't get any ideas of what they might be capable of.

How much of women's selves, our capabilities, our strengths, our speeds, have we ignored, hidden away behind this veil of myth, over the years? How do we bring the truth to the forefront? As with the story of Atalanta, I've always believed the truth is somewhere underneath the myth. We just have to dig deep enough to find it.

FUNNILY ENOUGH, THE marathon itself is a myth. Many stories of the original marathon cite the story about a soldier running to Athens after the Battle of Marathon to announce their victory. In fact, historians say now, the entire army marched the distance after the battle, back home to Athens, in all of their armor and heavy gear. Not a run, but still a feat of endurance, to be sure. But this long march became confused in legend with a separate event at the beginning of the battle, when a runner did cover a great distance, from Marathon to Sparta—140 miles—to ask for help from the Spartans.[22] Somehow, over time, the story of this lone runner merged with that of the army's march, and a tale of a great physical feat at the end of a lengthy battle became a crowning achievement.

So really, marathons should be 140 miles, instead of 26.

Ironically, if marathons were 140 miles, women would be beating men in marathons all the time.

ROXBURY GIRL FLEET HALF-MILER

Florence E. MacDonald Can Run 880 Yards in 2m 29s, Nearly Seven Seconds Under American Record

FLORENCE E. MacDONALD
Roxbury Girl, Who Recently Ran 880 Yards in Practice in Record Time of 2 Minutes 29 Seconds

Florence MacDonald
(*Boston Globe*, June 13, 1928)

1: But Not More Than 100m . . .

1928, Amsterdam, Olympics

FLORENCE MACDONALD TAKES her place in the outside lane of the track. She is the only American to have made the 800-meter final here in Amsterdam.[1] Her dark hair is cropped close to her head, swept back from her face. Her shorts hang loose, a few inches above the knee, revealing sculpted calves. Before the starting gun fires, she sets her mark, casually putting one foot at the starting line and one behind. She doesn't crouch to the cinder ground like some of her competitors, instead barely leaning forward over dark running shoes that look more like ballet slippers, her white socks rolled to her ankles.

At the starting gun, the nine women take off, propelled forward by the momentum of their own internal engines, jockeying for position along the inside of the track. Florence, just eighteen, has to work the hardest, coming from the outside. At the end of the first lap, she remains near the back of the pack. Hitomi Kinue, of Japan, who had never even run an 800-meter race before and only signed up because she'd lost the 100 and wanted another chance to run,[2] sprints hard in the first moments, from the inside lane. She then falls behind, her initial push too strong. Inga Gentzel, of Sweden, gains the lead by the end of the first lap. As the runners turn to begin the second, Hitomi changes tactics, stretching her large frame to its capacity, looking more like a distance runner than a sprinter; her arms take on the strain, seeming to join with her long legs to close the gap easily between herself and the runners in front of her. Likewise, Florence dials her legs up as she enters the final sprint, passing three other runners in the last stretch.

But Lina Radke of Germany, who held the world record for this mid-distance race, opens up her own stride in that final half a lap—so smoothly, so easily, as if she's merely jogging along a beach—and cannot be caught, even by the towering sprinter Kinue or the lanky Swede Gentzel. Radke glances back at her competitors ever so briefly before breaking the tape at the finish line. Kinue comes across second. Gentzel earns the bronze. Florence crosses in sixth. The first women's 800-meter race in Olympic history is complete. Because of what happens next, it won't be run again for thirty-two years.[3]

TWO LAPS AROUND the track—about half a mile, less than what many elementary school children in the US now run once a year to gauge their fitness level. And yet in 1928, the first year the Olympics held track-and-field events for women, the 800-meter was the longest distance women runners were allowed to run. And still there was a question hanging over the whole event: whether women would be able to finish the race at all.

According to the *Boston Globe*'s John J. Hallahan, all six contestants in the women's inaugural 800 final "collapsed after the race." "Six competitors were so exhausted that they were near collapse at the finish. All fell flat on the ground . . ." he wrote.[4]

The *London Times* claimed that "the half-dozen prostrate and obviously distressed forms lying about on the grass at the side of the track may not warrant a complete condemnation of the girl athletics championships, but it certainly suggests unpleasant possibilities."[5]

The *Daily Mail* quoted some doctors who said that those two laps around the track were "feats of endurance" that would make women "grow old too soon."[6]

William Shire of the *Chicago Tribune* noted that MacDonald was among those runners who collapsed after the race, saying she needed to be "work[ed] over" after "falling onto the grass unconscious."[7]

The *New York Times* agreed, saying that "six out of the nine runners were completely exhausted and fell headlong on the ground. Several had to be carried off the track. The little American girl, Miss Florence MacDonald, who made a gallant try but was outclassed, was in a half-faint for several minutes, while even the sturdy Miss Hitomi of Japan, who finished second, needed attention before she was able to leave the field."[8]

Harper's reporter John Tunis asserted that the fateful 800 included "Eleven wretched women, five of whom dropped out before the finish, while five collapsed after reaching the tape." If you're wondering what happened to the eleventh runner, Tunis writes, helpfully: "I was informed later that the remaining starter fainted in the dressing room shortly afterward."[9]

If you read the *Sportsman,* you would find John T. McGovern's reporting on the race. To read his story, you might not be totally sure how many women were in the final heat, but it's clear that the 800 racers were in dire shape indeed. "To see a lot of fine, young, brave girls sprawling about on the ground sobbing, convulsed, and covered with dirt, made us all feel that in 1926 we should have voted against this long race."[10]

Or perhaps you get your news from a trusted source, like Knute Rockne, former football coach for Notre Dame and apparently sometimes an international newspaper correspondent, who concluded simply: "The half-mile race for ladies was a terrible event. . . . If running the half-mile for women is an athletic event then they ought to include a six-day dancing contest between couples. One is as ridiculous as the other."[11] (Talk about a feat of endurance!)

Even now, a lifetime after the race, the first time I came across an article about why it took so long for long-distance running to be included for women in the Olympics, I saw reported with assurance that there was no race longer than 200 meters for women in all those years because of the 1928 race. The *New York Times*,[12] CBC,[13] and the *Guardian*[14] all reported nearly a hundred years after the fact that several runners collapsed after the race, and that was why the race wasn't held again for so long.

Never mind that those reporters in 1928 couldn't even agree on how many runners were in the final heat, let alone what actually happened (Did they all collapse simultaneously? Did some finish? Some not? Did they cry and convulse, or merely faint?) The myth of these women's failure to execute two laps on a track without dire results lived on in infamy.

Unfortunately for the very inventive and colorful (male) sportswriters of the time: the actual video evidence of the race tells a very different story. When I see it, I'm actually surprised it exists at all—right there on the Internet. You can google it. Video from 1928. The black-and-white silent footage is grainy, yes, but shows quite clearly nine contestants lining up on the track (not eleven, and not six).

All the women sport trendy 1920s-style haircuts. They wear varying crests and designs on T-shirts, mostly light, and loose-fitting shorts, mostly dark. There's no spandex (it has yet to be invented). No midriffs showing. No Nike swooshes or Adidas stripes on highly engineered shoes. The women look more like a group from a college gym class than elite athletes. They line up at the start, some crouch, some begin at a stand. Then a man standing behind the starting line holds one arm in the air and fires a starting gun. The women are off. I follow MacDonald as best as I can in the video footage. It's hard to keep my eye on one runner, especially in fuzzy black-and-white.

The ending, however, is clear. Radke crosses the tape first, slowing immediately to a walk with hands on hips. Kinue and Gentzel cross the line next and trot off into the middle grass to cool down. In fourth and fifth place, two Canadian runners are neck and neck coming nearer to the finish. Then the footage cuts to the crowd. Men in suits and hats and women, some in sweatshirts blaring CANADA or USA fill the rows of seats. You can see, but not hear, them cheering and jumping up and down while watching the race. The bright sunlight creates a harsh shadow across the gray-toned faces. Back to the race, where two women are crossing the finish line fairly close together. One surges to take the lead and lands in an awkward lunge. She crosses first but loses her footing, tumbling to the ground for a moment before a race official helps her back to her feet. The video cuts again, to a sheepishly smiling Lina Radke, victorious, before cutting to black.

Is this the whole thing? I wonder, watching it over and over again. This one woman tripping is the reason all of these reporters soliloquized over women's frailty for a hundred years? The reason the race wouldn't be run again for decades? They don't even show all of the finishers!

As I continue to watch the one-and-a-half minute video available on the official Olympics website, zipping back and forth from beginning to end to try to determine who the runner is that fell, I start to question what I see. I find academic papers, magazine articles, and blogs that all try to parse the same video footage. The same clip appears in a popular documentary about the marathon. Almost all of these modern-day writers cite the runner who falls as one of the two Canadians coming up in fourth and fifth place: Jean Thompson and Fanny Rosenfeld. It would make sense, given they were next to cross in the earlier frames, except that according to the official records, Florence was just 0.2 seconds behind Rosenfeld, and Marie Dollinger, another German athlete, was just half a second behind Florence. All three would have been running in quick succession at the last stretch, and in the video there are no women close behind the two who cross nearly simultaneously, with one tripping. Three more runners do come along, but not for several seconds.

On what feels like my millionth viewing, trying to decipher which runners are which as they cross the finish line, I notice something. In the frames before the woman falls, when Lina Radke crosses the finish line, the stands behind the race are packed with onlookers, the sun glares down harshly on the race and the spectators, and though the film was black-and-white (and grainy), every runner's uniform shirt in the final heat was light-colored on the film. But in the shot of the woman falling over the finish line, the stands behind her are almost empty, a misty fog hangs overhead, and a runner who clearly just crossed the finish line ahead of the fallen woman wore a dark uniform shirt. (I can't be sure but it seems to match the color of the uniform worn by the Belgian team—and no Belgian runners made this final heat.) This woman who falls clearly has tripped, lost her footing, not collapsed out of exhaustion or lost consciousness or any of the other hyperbolic things the 1928 newspaper reporters wrote. More important: this clip of the woman falling isn't even from the same race. It might have been one of the other women's races entirely, it might have been one of the heats for the 800 the day prior.

I wonder how the Olympic archives can have made this kind of mistake. I write to the archivist and they tell me no full, uncut version of the 800 final exists. But so much of the race is on film, why not the full final?

And why did they splice this other race onto the end thinking it was part of the same? Did whoever edited this together just assume it was part of the same race because of all the inaccurate newspaper reports? Or did someone back in the 1920s edit this (it certainly appears so, as the introductory frames look like those from a silent movie introducing the race, and the winner, Lina Radke), and throw in the stumble at the end to try to prove all those newspaper reports right in some way—those biggest fears about this race being simply *too much* for the frail female body? And if by some chance those newspaper reports had been right, then where's the footage or photographs of this dire moment with all the wretched women writhing on the ground? Seems like that would've made a great shot.

WHAT'S UNDENIABLY TRUE is that the race revealed that women were more than capable, not just of running the 800, but of running it far faster than previously thought. While MacDonald was frustrated with herself as she strode across the finish line in sixth place, her time broke the former world record by 1.2 seconds. Radke had bested her own 1927 record by a full 7 seconds.

More video evidence, taken seventy-three years later, in MacDonald (now Campbell's) nursing home, would show the former Olympian with eyes glinting in memory. She tells the two documentarians there, asking about the race, that not only did she not fall down unconscious at the end of the race, as one newspaper reported, she felt "fresh as a daisy" when she crossed the finish line. Her son questions her then: "The newspapers said everyone collapsed?"

"That's not true," MacDonald's voice bursts in on her son's implication with a hard edge. "They could have run another race, it seems to me that we were as fresh when we finished as we were when we started. . . . They expected the women to be exhausted and of course they weren't but this collapsing business, that was a lot of nonsense."

AND IN THAT black-and-white grainy footage from her youth, the parts that are clearly from the final race agree with her. The women, though most of them surpassed the world record in that middle-distance race, certainly do not appear as exhausted as the Olympic runners of today—men and women—who often fall to the ground after they cross a finish line, every fiber in their muscles spent on the track, then to be praised for their efforts of exertion.

As I dig into the story of that race, I find that the whole spectacle that unfolded, the video clips, the newspaper headlines—all of it—was a setup.

EVEN NINETY-TWO-YEAR-OLD FLORENCE recognized that the falsehoods reported in the newspaper in the prior century may not have seemed like lies at the time. "They didn't think the women could do so well," she said. In the 1920s, most people didn't expect women to be doing much of anything that required physical exertion.

This was the first Olympiad when women were even competing in track and field. Pierre de Coubertin, the Olympic creator, who had been adamantly against women's participation in the Games, had just stepped down as the president of the International Olympic Committee, but the mere idea of women running was still extremely controversial. Many medical doctors and physical educators did believe women should exercise for their health, but only in private (so as not to create any scandal), and should definitely not participate in competitive sports, as that would be both improper and potentially harmful to their role as future mothers. Sport and even physical exercise had only recently become popularized in the Western world in the nineteenth century, and there were strict rules about who could do what. The belief went that there were two types of bodies: male bodies, which could run and jump and compete, and female bodies, which were weaker, frailer, and built for bearing and nurturing children. To exercise, women were told they could perform "calisthenics."

The first American exercise textbook for women and by a woman, *A Course of Calisthenics for Young Ladies, in Schools and Families*, published anonymously in 1821 as a series of letters written supposedly by a concerned mother, exemplifies the exercise advice that would remain fashionable for decades. The author, who signs the letters *M*, believes girls and women need *some* exercise in order to stay healthy. "[I]t is our duty, religiously, sacredly to preserve our constitutions . . . we should increase our own firmness and vigor . . . The varied and arduous duties which woman is called upon to perform require vigorous health."[15] M believed that women should not and could not exercise the same way that boys and men do. Some dumbbells are okay, but nothing as heavy as eight pounds! She recommends instead: dancelike movements done while standing, raising the arms one at a time over the head; turning the neck from side to side; and moving the feet in a particular pattern on the floor. But, she wrote, "no circumstances could render it necessary to adopt those very vigorous exercises, which have been invented for boys."

Calisthenics became the dominant form of movement for girls and women in the US through the nineteenth century. Those movements described by M became popular during this era because they could address a desire that many doctors and educators alike had—to improve the health of the population—but without threatening "society's vision of appropriate feminine movement," wrote Jan Todd, a sports historian at the University of Texas, Austin, in her book *Physical Culture and the Body Beautiful: Purposive Exercise in the Lives of American Women 1800–1875*. And these exercises weren't enough to give women real access to their physical capabilities, Todd adds: "There was no danger when performing these exercises that women would become so strong, healthy, and self-confident that they might like to explore the world outside their homes."[16] This containment of exercise to small movements, without the threat of competition or overstrain, was a means of keeping women "feminine." In other words: focused on the domestic—even as women increasingly became interested in voting, higher education, and career opportunities outside the home. "Men had the world of business and commerce; women had their home and family. Calisthenics allowed women to be just fit enough to fulfill that limited role," Todd suggests.

Women at the turn of the century were fed a careful message about their physical bodies and what they could do: Don't run. Don't sweat. Don't get big and muscular. And definitely don't compete.

But by 1928, many women were finding that was exactly what they wanted to do, thanks to a woman named Alice Milliat.

MILLIAT—BORN ALICE MILLIONE, in Nantes, France, in 1884—might have lived a quiet life in rural France if she hadn't fallen in love with the barber's son. Joseph Milliat hadn't gone into the family business like so many children had done for generations. Instead, he'd taken advantage of the global economy's shift toward industrialization and moved to London to start his career. So when she turned twenty, Alice moved there, too— away from her small French town, her small French life as the oldest of five children, the daughter of shopkeepers—to marry him.

Then, tragedy. Joseph died just four years later, in 1908.

At just twenty-four, Alice was widowed. She had no children. She was simply a young French woman living on her own in England. Instead of returning home, though, Alice stayed. She worked for a wealthy family, likely as a tutor. Many believe the head of the house was a diplomat, as Alice traveled during this time to the United States and Scandinavia. Working in England for years meant she became fluent in English. She saw much more of the world than most of her peers had seen at that time. In England, she also saw another way of being a woman.[17]

Alice had detested the practice of moving one arm up and down in an arc over her head, or the little swaying movements such as pointing one foot back and forth in time: the calisthenics she was taught in school in France. She found them incredibly boring.

In England, however, women were finding other ways to move. Women's football clubs and rowing clubs were established in London as early as the 1880s.

The family Alice worked for lived in Chelsea, among the white plaster row houses lining prettily manicured streets. Alice likely walked those streets. I can see her dark hair bobbed in the fashion of the day, grazing her soft, round cheeks, admiring the black wrought iron gates, the bay windows, and arched doorways of the homes she passes. On a warm spring day, she might have made it down to the River Thames just in time to see one of those women's rowing clubs pulling the boats out on the water. Perhaps she went right up to the women and asked what they were doing, and if she could join. Her friends (and detractors) would remark later on Alice's outspokenness—stating that she "had a strong personality and spoke her mind firmly."[18]

IMAGINE, GROWING UP in a French village, before a feminist movement has taken hold or a murmur of suffrage has even been suggested in the country, where you've been told the purpose for your body is bearing children, that any exercise you partake in should be soft, delicate, unobtrusive, and modest. *You are not physically capable of the things men do.* Then, suddenly, you're in a foreign country, alone, and you're offered the opportunity to climb aboard a small shell, to propel yourself with two oars down the River Thames, past the geese, the tall greenery marking the waterway's edges, the steamboats. Your arms pull and push the handles of the sculls, contracting the muscles in your back and shoulders, and moving the water out of the way, for you and your boat to go through. *Your body's power is the engine.*

Later, perhaps some of the same young women you meet at the rowing club introduce you to the football clubs. And when you make it out to a game, again, you ask if you can join. You've never been on a soccer pitch before, but the moment you're given the go-ahead to run on field, you feel a jolt of energy up your legs, as though electricity is lighting you from within, your legs pump and your lungs expand as you run this way and that, following the ball as it bounces along the dirt, propelled from foot to foot as the more practiced women seem to send it exactly where they want it to go. The blood rushes into your cheeks as the cool, wet London air condenses on your warm body, your legs exposed in public beneath your shorts for maybe the first time ever. You're running. You haven't run since you were a girl. You see, for perhaps the first time, what your adult body is capable of.

ALICE CARRIED THIS feeling in her body—that she could row, and kick, and play, and compete, and run, not just stretch an arm over her head gracefully—back to France in 1910, after her father's death. Thanks to her now-fluent English, she found work as a translator, but sport was still the domain of men alone in France.

Due to the popularity of international competition like the Olympics, many countries were starting their own national sporting federations, which would help to organize national competitions and nurture talent so that their country could send athletes to the Olympics and other international competitions. In that era, the international federations organized the international competitions for each sport. So at the time, if a Frenchman wanted to compete at the Olympics in track and field, he would compete in national competitions run by the Union des Sociétés Françaises de Sports Athlétiques (the French national sporting federation), and follow the rules set by the International Amateur Athletics Federation, the international governing body for his sport. The IOC would then go to the IAAF to set the Olympic track-and-field rules and event schedule.

In France there were no women's football teams for Milliat to join. She leaned on rowing, a solitary sport, instead. I imagine her pulling a boat down the Seine, in her short bloomers and collared blouse, reminding herself of the freedom she'd found in her body in London.

Then Femina-Sport, one of the first women's sport clubs in France, was established in 1912 by Pierre Payssé, an Olympic athlete and gymnastic teacher, and a group of athletic women. Milliat joined the group and by 1917 had helped expand their offerings from just gymnastics and calisthenics to organizing the first women's football games in the nation, and a national track-and-field tournament. A year later, she and two other women's sports organizers began their own organization: Fédération des Sociétés Féminines Sportives de France (FSFSF), a national federation for women's sports. The organization came about just in time, because at the end of the war, France's national athletic federation gave up responsibility for women's sport entirely. Milliat's group took over women's sports in France, and under her guidance, they did so with gusto.

She expanded the one-off soccer games into clubs and started an annual French tournament called the Women's Cup. When Alice was unanimously elected president of the French women's sport group in 1919, she petitioned International Olympics Committee president Pierre de Coubertin to include a full slate of track-and-field events in the following year's Olympic Games, since the IAAF was only concerned with men's track and field. As Alice would write later, she "came up against a solid wall of refusal."[19] No one responded to her.

So Milliat began to reach out to the women's athletics foundations of the United States to propose an international women's sports federation, a female answer to the IAAF. The Fédération Sportive Féminine Internationale (FSFI) was created on Oct. 31, 1921.

She'd seen enough of the way men ran women's sports to know that her organization would be better off running Olympics-style games on their own. It was "likely that Milliat created the FSFI as a way of ensuring the feminist movement kept control over international competitions for women," wrote Florence Carpentier, a sports historian at the University of Rouen and a researcher at the Global Sport & Olympic Studies Center in Switzerland.

The following year, Milliat once again went to Coubertin to ask for women's athletics at the Olympic Games. And she was, once again, met by his disdainful silence. Outspoken as she was, she didn't let the wall she ran into stop her. Instead, she brought her argument right to Coubertin's door. The first Women's Olympic Games, organized by her international women's sporting federation, was held in 1922 in Paris, Coubertin's home city. The organization decided that the event would be held every four years, like the men's Olympics. Though the numbers of spectators and competitors exceeded expectations—five nations took part in the one-day event that boasted eleven track-and-field events and drew 20,000 spectators—the New York Times reported that spectators viewed the Games as "not proper for women," and feared that "they might be seriously and even permanently affected by the strains to which in the excitement of competition they subjected their hearts and other muscles."[20]

Around this time, even many doctors were making a similar argument, that women taking part in competitive sport would end up hurting the very thing that "made them women"—their fertility. One, E. H. Arnold, sums up the establishment's views at the time in a 1924 issue of the American Physical Education Review, writing that "national or international competition is a menace to womanhood." He goes on to say that women's stature, strength, weight, and wider pelvis made activities associated with sport, like running—but also walking and standing—more difficult for women. The female athlete, he concluded, "tires easier."[21]

Milliat fought back against these medical views as often as she could, even writing a column in L'Auto, a French sports magazine, often arguing for equality for women's sports. In one of her columns she called for those who stood against sports for women to prove their cases with "facts, not words." And she noted that there was no way those who were using scare tactics (like Dr. Arnold, above, and Coubertin, himself) would even know the long-term effects of women playing sports at this point. "Let us heed the opinion of our women doctors who, combining practical experience with knowledge, say that studies conducted over several generations are needed to determine, with little risk of error, which sports women can do safely and usefully," she wrote.

The strict stratification by gender of, on the one hand, sports for men and, on the other, exercises like calisthenics for women, seemed as arbitrary to Milliat as the fact that men could vote and women could not. "By what right do so-called scientific 'luminaries,' along with many ignoramuses, decree: 'these exercises are suitable for women, these exercises will do them harm'? Who can say that with any certainty at this point in time," she wrote in *L'Auto*.

When Pierre de Coubertin finally stepped down as president of the IOC in 1925, Milliat saw an opening. She started to plan the 1926 Women's Olympic Games for Brussels, as the new president, Henri de Baillet-Latour, was Belgian. At his first Olympic committee meeting, Baillet-Latour did, in fact, discuss the Women's Olympic Games, but as the meeting notes from 1925 show, the topic was raised simply to express the group's hostility toward calling the women's games "Olympics" at all. The board "was quite upset to find that the name 'Olympic' has been unrightfully appropriated by the organizers of the Women's Games and it will take the necessary steps to obtain the help of the international federations so that this designation, which is the property of the IOC, is exclusively reserved for the Games organized by the IOC the first year of every Olympiad."

Soon after, Brussels backed out of hosting duties for the Women's Games. Milliat, undeterred, moved them (now under a new name, the Women's World Games), to Gothenburg, Sweden, where the current president of the International Amateur Athletic Federation, the international governing body of track and field, lived: Siegfried Edström, her new target.

But the move, far from convincing Edström to join her team, did just the opposite. Prior to the kickoff of the 1926 Women's Games, Edström went behind Milliat's back to the IOC board to suggest allowing four women's track-and-field events at the 1928 Olympics. He never consulted with FSFI or asked for Milliat's input. Edström's aim was clear, writes Carpentier, ". . . not to promote womens' sport, rather, it was to take control of women's athletics and put an end to the FSFI."

Shortly after Edström's suggestion, he reached out to Milliat, who was completely gobsmacked by the proposal. At her next women's federation meeting she told the organization about it, without mincing words. "Mr. Edström's proposal consists simply of the dissolution of the FSFI and the creation of a commission to oversee women's athletics, the members of which would be appointed by the IAAF."

Members of Milliat's group were in agreement: they did not want the men's track governing body's proposal to the IOC to go through. Milliat wrote directly to Baillet-Latour, the IOC president, to try to strike a deal without having to go through Edström. She put forth her demands: full participation of women in Olympic track-and-field events (i.e., not the four events suggested, but all twelve events that she held at her Women's World Games) by 1932, and recognition of her women's sporting federation by the IOC at the same level as other international federations, like the IAAF.

Baillet-Latour wrote back but promised nothing. He said he would be open to her demands, but unfortunately, expanding the amount of events would only be up to the international federation for the sport: Edström's group. When Milliat and Edström finally did discuss the issue, he dangled the possibility of the 1928 Games as a "trial" for women athletes, and that they would consider the full slate once they saw how those games went. Milliat had no choice but to agree.

Edström controlled which events ended up on the Olympic slate. He suggested four events, at first, but five ended up in the 1928 Games. The 800 was added last.

By framing the women's participation as a trial, and then including a race at the last moment longer than most women were allowed to run at the time, he virtually ensured that the women runners would look unprepared, overexerted, and in danger.

Even before the Games began, Edström's gamble was paying off. *Time* magazine wrote that "the minute portion of US womanhood which is diligently muscular looks forward to a trip abroad this summer," before wondering whether the "weak women" might destroy the winning American record.[22] The chairwoman of the Women's Division of the National Amateur Athletic Federation, the US's national track-and-field federation, called allowing women and men the same athletic programs a "sacrifice [of] our school girls on the altar of an Olympic spectacle."[23]

The soon-to-be-infamous story of the women fainting after running much too far, too fast for their delicate bodies had seemingly already been written.

BUT THE WOMEN running the race didn't know about all of these back-room deals, or the men running the international sports federations who very likely wanted to see them fail. The runners, in fact, just thought about running.

In 2001, all those years after the 1928 race, MacDonald stated that she believed she probably could have won the whole thing if she'd actually known what she was doing. "I was so young and so dumb," she said bluntly. "The race was okay. I could have done better, but I didn't, so that's in the past."

MacDonald wasn't expected to win the race, not by any means. In fact, she wasn't even the American girl that anyone expected to make the race's final. She was an eighteen-year-old high school senior. Her diploma came by mail while she was at the Olympics. She'd run her first 800 just two months before the Games were held.

A Gaelic speaker whose Scottish family, including her father, sister, and stepmother, had immigrated from Nova Scotia to Boston when she was a child, MacDonald ended up at the Olympics because of a footrace at a neighborhood festival less than a year earlier. The Scottish Highland Games were held each fall in her neighborhood in Roxbury, a section of Boston, by the Caledonia Society. Macdonald's sister, Christine, was a prizewinning Highland dancer. In September 1927, perhaps she was looking for something to fill the time at the festival while her sister danced. Perhaps she'd always wanted to run. Either way, her performance in the sprint that day caught the eye of someone from the Boston Swimming Association, which had recently started a running division for girls, as national competitions had just begun for women and girls in track and field a few years prior.[24]

Thinking she was going out for a swim team, MacDonald was surprised when she was sent to Eddie O'Brien, the track coach.[25] He put her on the BSA 4 x 100-meter relay team. That January, her team won a New England title. Though the papers rarely covered these women's races, I find one mention of another relay her team won, in May. Then, in early June, MacDonald won the 50-yard dash at a New England regional championship held in Boston.[26] Her coaches were curious about her stamina, about her ability to (according to one newspaper reporter) "run at a fast clip around the Franklin Field track many times without becoming exhausted."

O'Brien had a plan to get MacDonald to the Olympics in an event that was a bit of a wild card: the 800. Even though national championships had been held for women in track and field in the US since 1923, they hadn't held a running event longer than 220 yards. First, Coach O'Brien set up a time trial for MacDonald to run half that distance: a quarter-mile, one lap around the track. She did it in less than a minute. O'Brien then had her checked out by a medical doctor, Dr. Charles C. Parker, Jr., who "declared her physically fit to run for miles at a time."

With the doctor's approval, about a month before the Olympic trials in Newark, O'Brien set up a time trial with the Boston Parks Department for a distance MacDonald had never been timed at before, 880 yards, or about 800 meters. The current American women's record for the race was 2:35. She finished her first lap in 1:00.2. By the end of the second lap, "three different watches," the *Boston Globe* reports, "showed her time as being 2 minutes 29 seconds, six seconds under the American record."

The newspaper's account of the time trial is effusive. ROXBURY GIRL FLEET HALF-MILER, the headline blares. While the story mentions that MacDonald's time bested the current American women's record, it doesn't mention the probable reason for this time trial, or why the newspaper was covering a high school girl running 880 yards with two coaches in a park not for competition: to qualify her for the Olympic trials coming up the following month. "Followers of women's track athletics in this section are overjoyed with the future possibilities shown by Florence E. MacDonald," wrote the *Boston Globe*. Accompanying the article is a black-and-white photo of the eighteen-year-old in a crouched starting position. Her hair is pressed flat, worn just below the neck. She's not wearing running clothes, but what is probably a school uniform or Sunday outfit, and her long-sleeve Peter Pan collar and pencil skirt look lightweight and wrinkled. Kitten heel Mary Janes adorn her runners' feet. She looks forward, her face at an angle to the camera, eyes pointed up. I wonder what she thought, wearing her nice clothes to meet a newspaper photographer, who then asked her to kneel on the ground as though she ran while dressed that way.

Less than a month later, MacDonald, Coach O'Brien, and five other women's track-and-field stars of the Boston Swimming Association headed to Newark, NJ, for the National Women's Championship in track and field, which, given the recent addition of the athletics events to the Olympic Games, would double as Olympic qualifiers. Though the women's championships had twelve events total, the five events the women would compete in at the Olympic Games were the 100-meter race, the 800-meter race, the 4-x-100-meter relay, the high jump, and the discus throw. The men's national championships, held at the same time, though in a different place, would send American men to the Olympics in twenty-two track-and-field events altogether. The running events alone included the 100, 200, 800, 1,500, 5,000, 10,000, and, of course, the marathon.

ON JULY 4, 1928, the sun baked the cinder track of the Schools Stadium in Newark. Invited to compete were 250 young women, from around the country.[27] As the mercury rose into the nineties, the races went in heats. MacDonald ran with one goal likely top of mind: a trip to Europe. The opportunity for a girl like her to take a ship to Amsterdam? To compete in the Olympic Games? That was practically unbelievable. And all she had to do was pump her arms and legs faster than the other girls.

She left behind no letters, no diaries. No one still living knows what was in her head as she stood on the starting line.

What we do know is that she won her heat.[28] And her time that day, 2:36 for a half a mile, was seven seconds slower than in the time trial she'd run by herself in Boston, but still good enough for third place overall. The top four finishers in each event qualified. Florence MacDonald—a working-class immigrant girl who spoke English as a second language, a high school senior who was missing her last days of school and had only joined a track team because someone saw her run at a neighborhood festival—was going to the Olympic Games.

As the women ended their races that day, the skies opened up in that way the summer sky in the Northeast sometimes does when a day starts off too extreme—after baking heat in the morning and early afternoon, suddenly dark clouds enter the space, as if seeking balance, and rain pours down.

SEVEN DAYS LATER, MacDonald and the other 18 young women, the first ever US Women's Olympic track-and-field team, prepared to board the SS *President Roosevelt* steamship in New York Harbor. A band played. Chants rang out. And 2,000 onlookers crowded pier 86 as 268 Olympians made their way to the ship that morning. MacDonald and three other girls from the Boston Swimming Association who had made the Olympic track-and-field team boarded that day. The foursome already knew each other, and would become close over the next few weeks, months, and years as they competed first in Europe and then around the country. Nearly all of the photos I can find from the time show them as a group: Florence MacDonald, Olive Hasenfus, Mildred Wiley, and Rena McDonald (no relation to Florence). They even posed for a photo before boarding the ship. The girls stand shortest to tallest, at an angle to the camera, each holding their right hand high in the air. Perhaps they're gesturing at the ship. Perhaps they're waving goodbye. Perhaps they're raising a hand in celebration. Florence MacDonald, the shortest, wears flat oxfords and bobbed socks, a drop-waisted sweater over a knee-length pleated skirt. Her dark hair is cut short, just below her ears, and parted over her right eye. She clutches a handbag. The other three girls are all dressed up in Sunday best, too, in heavy-looking skirts and jackets. Mildred Wiley, who was favored to medal in the high jump, stands tall at the end of the line, a white cloche hat perched on her head. All four women have a flower corsage pinned to their lapel. All four, too, look a little uncomfortable in these skirts and hats and flowers and shoes.[29]

On board the ship, a track was erected on the deck so the athletes could keep up their training on the nine-day voyage to Amsterdam. Though training on the boat was difficult, MacDonald threw herself into preparation as best she could. She'd only been running a short time, but there was quite clearly something in her of the competitive spirit. Nearly a hundred years later, her son, John Campbell, eighty-one years old himself, would tell me he didn't know of his mother "the athlete." By the time he was born, her running days were long forgotten. But he thought the trip to Amsterdam was probably his mother's greatest motivation for racing well at the Olympic trials. I have to imagine, though, that—to make it to the Olympics, to the *final*, in a race she had hardly run before, and to remember it all those years later and vow that she could have done better—she must have had a competitive fire inside.

When I see the group of Boston girls again, in a photo at the Games, they stand side by side, arms around each other's backs, hip to hip. This time the two runners, Florence and Olive, stand on the outside. The two taller women—Mildred, the high jumper, and Rena, the discus thrower— are in the middle. The quartet looks far more comfortable in this photo, far more themselves, wearing their official USA uniforms: a white V-neck T-shirt with a USA crest on the left chest and a red-white-and-blue stripe running diagonally from right shoulder to left hip.[30]

THE AMERICAN MEN were disappointing the press. Near the end of the track-and-field events in Amsterdam, they had just one gold medal, in the men's 400. The ultra-competitive news media that exists today during the Olympics, breathlessly counting up medals as emblems of national pride, appears to have begun this tradition in the 1920s, and each article I read makes it clear that the US men's track-and-field team was definitely cramping the reporters' boast of American exceptionalism. The American women, however, were offering a different narrative.

In the first women's track event, a nearly unknown young American woman, Betty Robinson, just sixteen years old, stunned everyone by winning gold in the 100.

MacDonald, too, wanted to represent her country well: but perhaps more than that, she wanted to represent her Boston club well. The day before her first qualifying race, she wrote to her coach at the Boston Swimming Association, Ben Levias: "I train morning and noon and believe I am improving a lot. Jack Ryder [her Olympic coach] thinks I will run away with the works and if I don't it won't be because I didn't do my very best, for you know we must put the B.S.A. over the top."

MacDonald's competitive spirit was known back in Boston. One local reporter said that those who had been following her New England races "declare she is one of the grittiest and gamest track athletes that has ever appeared around here."

MacDonald ran in the third and final heat. She was in fourth coming down the back stretch, but her kick came just in time, pulling all the way to second place and qualifying for the final.

With their successes, newspapers began to fawn over the American women track-and-field stars. Speculation about a one-two USA punch in the 100- and 800-meter women's races was everywhere. Photos of a smiling Florence with the other young women appeared in newspapers all across the country as a means of advertising the team, drumming up reader interest, and filling sports pages. But the images, like that first photo that ran with news of her record-breaking first 800-meter run, weren't ever action shots of her running, nor even in that crouched starting position in her Olympic uniform. Instead, they showed Florence's mouth lipsticked, her dark hair combed and set, dark eyebrows filled (whether via makeup or nature or printer's ink, I can't be sure), and teeth sparkling white: they were headshots.

AMONG THE MEDIA cheering for MacDonald and the other girls, many of whom brought home team points for the USA, there were consistent caveats regarding their athletic performances. Even in the laudatory profile noting her "grit" after her sixth-place finish, the reporter goes on to say: "According to dispatches Miss McDonald [sic] was near collapse at

the end of her trial heat, but had enough stamina left to beat out an oppo-
nent 20 yards from the tape to land a place in the finals." This mention
of exhaustion is repeated in the sub-headline of the article, so that the
headlines read:

BOSTON GIRL SHOWS GRIT IN THE OLYMPICS
Florence McDonald, Only Yankee Girl in 880, Inside World's Record

RAN FOR HER TEAM
Girl Near Collapse at End of Trial Heat, but Rallied Next Day.

Reading old newspapers can be confusing. There were no cell phones,
of course, no Internet, no means of getting information quickly from
one side of the world to the other beyond the telegraph. Photographs
and video recordings existed, but getting them broadcast across an ocean
took time and equipment few had access to. So the capital-*T* truth according to most newspapers was some version of whatever the reporter said
happened, or heard happened from somebody else, who heard it from
somebody else who was there, or had a better view of the race. Again and
again, as I read the newspaper articles about the 800-meter race, I found
these conflicting reports right up next to each other.

The women finished the race.

And: The women collapsed.

The women broke world records.

And: They are not capable of the race.

They all finished.

And: The race should be dropped.

Of course, running is taxing on the body. When men first began to
run long distances, some similar concerns were raised about whether this
kind of visible physical exhaustion could possibly be healthy. A medical ailment in the late 1800s known as athletes' heart was thought to be
caused by *too much* physical exercise or exertion. Starting in 1897, the first

The 1928 800-meter women's final. Florence MacDonald, far left (USOPC)

year that the Boston Marathon was run, there were medical papers and articles written on the health risks of such extreme sport.

But instead of keeping men from ever running another marathon in order to protect their health, the medical community studied this problem. In 1899, researchers at Tufts Medical School began examining nearly all the men who completed the Boston Marathon course before and after the race, noting their pulse rates, heart sizes, and beat patterns. In 1903, a summary of three years of marathoner research was published, according to James C. Whorton, a professor of medical history and ethics. The paper concluded that "there was no evidence of permanent injury. In this instance, blistered feet comprised the most serious type of injury."[31]

IN THE 1920S, the role of women in society was being very carefully observed and controlled, and running became a symbol of freedom that was one step too far. As Carpentier and her coauthor Jean-Pierre Lefèvre put it in their paper *The modern Olympic Movement, women's sport and the social order during the inter-war period:* "[O]nce the women's emancipation movement was perceived as a threat to institutional domination by men, thereby throwing into question the social order, significant reactions on the part of sports leaders in general and Olympic leaders in particular were not long to follow." In other words: allowing women to run in international competitions, especially in long, grueling distances that only the most masculine athletes could perform, was dangerous to the world order.

NOT *all* WOMEN athletes were seen as deviants. In 1920, the same year women in the US won the right to vote, the American Olympic Council had first allowed women to join the US Olympic team, sending fifteen swimmers and divers to the Games in Antwerp. The US women swept all the medals in four out of five swimming and diving events. They were treated like national heroes. They got a ticker-tape parade, and the press treated them like they did the men, as symbols of American superiority over the rest of the world. And yet, the press made sure to note these young women's (and in most cases teen girls') sex appeal at every opportunity. And with the swimmers and divers, being the scantily clad and lithe young women they were, there was ample opportunity. One newspaper referred to one of the swimmers as a "blond New York mermaid."[32] The idea of the swimmers as "mermaids" took off, an easy way to remind everyone that though these were elite athletes, they were also just *pretty girls.* Even during the Olympics, the women appeared in the sports pages largely in alluring poses in their swimsuits—and for the most part, there would be no text accompanying their images. No stories of their accomplishments or interviews about their training practices appeared. "Instead of perceiving sport as an arena for the exercise of women's rights, this view [which flourished in the American media] promoted exercising women as an erotic industry," wrote Mark Dyreson, in an article in the *Journal of Contemporary History.*[33] When male Olympians were featured, however, the photos were often of them in action shots, while swimming or diving or running, and always, a story ran by their photographs.

So when track and field opened for women at the Olympics in 1928, the sports sections of most newspapers tried to stand astride the same fine line: these women were doing their national duty by proving American exceptionalism in sport, and they were doing so while remaining proper women: beautiful and alluring, and definitely not masculine. Take those head shots of MacDonald, for instance. This photo came up in so many newspapers around the country as I searched desperately for her voice, her records, her history. Instead, I found again and again: her face. She looks up at the camera directly with her piercing eyes, under the headline:

MIDDLE DISTANCE STAR FLORENCE MACDONALD
Miss Florence MacDonald, of the Boston Swimming Association will represent Uncle Sam in the middle distance runs of the Olympic Games at Amsterdam, Holland.[34]

She's not running in the photo. There's no accompanying article about her background or her best times.

Despite being portrayed by the media as sexy mermaids, some of the swimmers were outspoken about the fact that they saw themselves as strong, capable beings, and that sport could be their way into societal power. Ethelda Bleibtrey, a swimmer and three-time Olympic gold medalist at the 1920 Olympics, wrote in *Ambition* magazine in 1923 that "sundry members of the so-called weaker sex, having obtained the vote . . . are making herculean efforts to overcome the vaunted superiority of their brothers in games requiring physical skill and prowess."[35]

When it came to running, however, the media had more trouble creating the same narrative that they did for swimmers. After all, running women were more easily photographed with strain on their face during competition (and less scantily clad). Grantland Rice, famed sportswriter of the generation, wrote of the 1928 track-and-field controversy that the

French were worried these runners would become an "Amazon race." And, it seems, Rice agreed. "There is something to be said on the side of the critics. Golf, tennis, swimming, diving, the shorter sprints and other forms of competition are fine things, but women are not yet ready for marathons, football, boxing and wrestling."[36]

Another sportswriter, Paul Gallico, cut to the heart of the reason the women's 800-meter race was so often described as impossible for women: "If there is anything more dreadful aesthetically or more depressing than the fatigue-distorted face of a girl runner at the finish line, I have never seen it."[37]

In other words, whether the women in the 800 collapsed or not, they did not finish their race while looking beautiful enough to sell home on their sex appeal. Lurking behind the story was the assumption many medical professionals were still spouting off as the truth: that running long distances would ruin the reproductive organs of women and threaten their ability to become mothers. Even among the Women's Athletic Association, a club in the US specifically for women runners, this belief existed. In 1925, they'd sponsored a doctor to medically appraise track and field. Here's part of what he wrote:

> Even if one does not see any ill results at the time from too strenuous devotion to athletics, the final result may be very deleterious to the girls' health and natural functions. As one great authority has it, "it is only when children begin to come or ought to begin to come, that many women find they are having to pay a pretty heavy price for a very temporary period of athletic enjoyment and glory."[38]

It's likely that Edström, the president of the international track-and-field governing body, imagined that when he allowed women's track-and-field events into the Olympic Games this would become the media narrative: that women who run too far are selfishly trading in mother-hood for athletic glory. The more the story was repeated, the quicker the 800 faced its doom. In fact, before the 1928 Olympics had even held their closing ceremonies, Edström's International Amateur Athletic Federation was ready to cut the 800 for women from future Games, and possibly even athletics for women at the Olympics altogether.

Just four days after the women's 800-meter final, Edström's group—the men's international governing body for track and field—met to vote on the fate of women's track and field in the next Olympics. While Milliat's organization suggested increasing the women's slate to ten events, citing the success of the women, the IAAF council submitted a majority report favoring just six events, "provided the gruelling 800m race be eliminated." A fight ensued, not in favor of keeping the 800, but over whether to abolish women's events altogether. A representative for Finland suggested the "injurious effects of competition" were "unwom-anly" and reported that Finnish girls "desired to leave track-and-field efforts to men."[39] Indeed, Finland sent only two women to the Olympics that year, a swimmer and a diver. Five other countries' IAAF delegations (Canada, England, Italy, Ireland, and Hungary) joined with Finland to vote against including any of those "unwomanly" track-and-field events at all going forward.[40] Clearly these delegations weren't representative of the athletes of these nations, many of whom made the immense effort to compete, not just in the 800 but the other four track-and-field events as well. Canada's women athletes brought home seven medals in the five events, and while Britain's women's team had boycotted because they wanted *more* events, their IAAF delegation voted against their partici-pation at all.[41] Lady Mary Heath of Great Britain, vice president of the FSFI and a famous aviatrix and former high jumper and hurdler,[42] gave an impassioned speech arguing for their inclusion as a matter of ethics. "We are now your comrades and co-workers in industry, commerce, art and science—why not in athletics?" she asked the council. "If you approve of athletics for women at all you must approve of participation in the Olympics, for women need the stimulus of matching their prowess against others of the world's best athletes quite as much as the men."

In the end, the council voted 16 to 6 to retain women's events, but banished the 800 outright, and even Milliat's group's suggestion to include broad jump, shotput, and the 200 (apparently half a lap was also too grueling!).

The next Olympics in 1932 wouldn't force anyone to watch a woman run farther than 100 meters.

THE 800 WOULD not be run by women at the Olympics again for generations. The idea that women were simply incapable of running more than a quarter of a lap, or that a longer race was too risky to women's fertility, was international, especially as the fight for suffrage for women was splashing like a wave over much of the Western world. The silver medalist in the 1928 800, Japan's Hitomi Kinue, had been an athlete since she was a girl, and had previously won the prize for outstanding overall athlete at the Women's Olympic Games in Gothenburg in 1926 after winning the long jump, standing broad jump, discus throw, 100-yard dash, 60-meter dash, and the 250-meter race. When she failed to medal in the 100 at the Olympics, she begged her coach to let her run in the 800, where she pulled off her incredible silver medal performance as the only member of the Japanese women's track-and-field team. But the glow of her achievement faded quickly in the media, replaced with questions about Hitomi's body. One printed interview shows a reporter probing about Hitomi's height and weight. Hitomi answered that she was around five feet seven and weighed 119 pounds, and the journalist scoffed.

"Well, that is a bit surprising! So, since that is about the same weight as most men, haven't people said that they are doubtful that you are really a woman?"[43]

Hitomi would continue on in her athletics, anyway, even while the press questioned her gender and called her a "giantess." When she was twenty-three, however, and still competing as an athlete in international competitions, Hitomi contracted pneumonia and never recovered. Even in her obituary the following year, which appeared in one of Japan's largest daily newspapers, her gender was questioned because of her size, because of her body's shape, because of what she was capable of.

"At 168 cm and 58 kg, this magnificently muscular, swarthy giant was asked by one female reporter at the Women's Olympic Games in Sweden, 'Are you *really* a woman?' . . . When Hitomi saw a younger teammate fall in love with a man and leave athletics to pursue life as a housewife, Hitomi reportedly said that she was firmly resolved against having any sort of romantic affairs—an interesting episode that shows a rather manly side of Hitomi."[44]

MacDonald, too, though petite and pretty enough to have her headshot grace newspapers around the nation, was asked whether she'd be able to become a mother after all of that running.

After the infamous 800, she continued to race. While I'm sure she was aware of the 800-meter race being struck from the Olympic program almost immediately after, I don't know what she thought of it. I found more mentions of her running as a national competitor in the 220-yard dash and as a coach of a relay team. She attended banquets regularly to be feted as an Olympian.

Her son sent me a photograph of her, a dress covered in medals, a table next to her covered in cups and trophies—all winnings from her track days after the Olympics, he says.

I wonder if she—a woman who stayed in the Boston area her whole life—ever watched the Boston Marathon. I wonder how she felt during all those years that women weren't allowed to race. I wonder if she ever considered trying to run it herself. Her son, John, tells me she never mentioned it, not to him. In 1930 she married an old family friend, Peter Campbell. Her first child, a daughter named June, was born in 1936; John was born in 1941. The last newspaper article I find about MacDonald is about her as a mother of then three-year-old June.[45] Look, here, it seems to say: A baby! There is also a photograph of her in her running days (not running, of course, but the pretty headshot of her smiling at the camera), and another of her pulling a baked good out of the oven while her tiny daughter looks on. Finally, the raison d'être of the article, a photo of little June in a dance outfit.

It may be recalled that Florence Macdonald ran in the 800-meters in the 1928 Olympics and it may also be recalled there is no longer competition in races of this distance for women in the Olympics or any AAU girls' track meets. At the time the 800 was run there were reports of girls collapsing in this event and women's organizations raised a cry that competition at this distance might be detrimental to motherhood. But Florence MacDonald ran in that last 800 meters . . . And Florence Macdonald is the mother of that three-year-old girl who is to dance on June 12 and June 21 in recitals at Jordan's Hall. And that little girl, June Marie, is entitled to win all kinds of prizes as one of the nation's healthiest children.

Two years after the IAAF saved women from the grueling 800-meter race in the Olympics, more than 200 women athletes from seventeen countries arrived in Prague to compete in three days of athletics events. The Third Women's World Games, still organized by Milliat, included the 60-, 100-, 200-, and 800-meter races.[46]

After the 1932 Olympic Games, where women only competed in six athletics events (and nothing longer than 100 meters), Milliat went to the IAAF once again to ask for a complete track-and-field program for women at the 1936 Olympic Games. She told them if they didn't want to support a full slate of events for women, then they shouldn't hold events for women at all, and her group would focus on building up the Women's

Alice Milliat, in her boat (Agence Rol, 1920)

World Games as an alternative to the Olympics. The IAAF stalled. "The International Olympic Committee was neither willing to allow women a full program in the Olympic Games nor to let the FSFI [run their own games]," wrote Mary H. Leigh and Thérèse M. Bonin in a 1977 article in the *Journal of Sport History*. "It would seem, then, that the IOC made deliberate attempts to rid itself of the troublesome thorn in its side."

In fact, Edström wrote to a colleague in 1935 about how irksome he found the women's federation: "I suppose you know that Mme Milliat's Federation has caused us so much trouble that we certainly have no interest at all to support it. We should like the whole thing to disappear from the surface of the earth."[47]

And disappear, it did. In 1936, the IAAF, who had previously been cooperating with the women's federation's jurisdiction over international competition, voted to take total control of women's track and field. They took over what would have been the fifth Women's World Games in 1938, turning them instead into a European Championship competition. Because the IOC recognized only one international governing body per sport, IAAF held all the power—once they decided to host women's international competitions, they trumped the women's federation. Instead of continuing the uphill battle for a separate international competition, Milliat's pioneering organization never met again, and she receded from public life. The Olympics, with its anemic roster of women's track-and-field events, went on.

In the 1940s, then-IOC president Henri de Baillet-Latour died, and Milliat's fiercest critic, Edström, became president of the IOC, remaining so until 1952. Avery Brundage, his good friend, would take over then, and "would carry forward the Olympic tradition of stringent control over women that had occurred during the period between the two wars into his presidency, much to the detriment of women athletes," wrote Carpentier and Lefèvre.

During this period, women's track and field would face immense growing pains. As the public received the message from the sporting world's highest stage that women athletes weren't quite *natural*, the demographics of who was given the encouragement to participate changed considerably.

Milliat's public story ends here, her life's work essentially undone by men who thought they knew best. Historians have sought clues as to what she did after 1936 and not found much. She exists today in a few photographs that live on the Internet. She is heralded in a few short articles as the force behind women's track entrance to the Olympic Games.[48] Yes, and yet she wanted so much more, I think, reading the headlines.

She is in her boat in so many of these images: a vessel she could control entirely by using the power of her own body to take her where she wanted to go.

Tidye Sails Over Top

Tidye Pickett, 1932 (Northern Illinois University Libraries)

2: But Only White Women . . .

1932, A train car, somewhere between Denver and Los Angeles
TIDYE PICKETT WAS far from home. Tucked away in the bottom bunk of a sleeper train car somewhere between Denver and Los Angeles, she might have been thinking about what it had been like for her teammates to be feted and doted on at the Brown Palace, the Denver hotel they had just left. They'd all been invited to speak with reporters and eat an elaborate multicourse meal at the hotel's large banquet hall. But she and Louise Stokes, the only other Black girl on the US track-and-field team, hadn't been included. The hotel's dining room was only for whites. It was just

a rule—one that no one had seemed to question, not a teammate, not a coach, not a chaperone. Instead, she and Louise ate in the room that they shared up near the attic, while their teammates each had their own separate rooms in the grand hotel that had played host to US presidents and other dignitaries.[1, 2]

Her coaches and teammates were mostly wonderful. Tidye liked them. It felt like some kind of miracle, really, that she was on her way to the 1932 Olympics, she'd tell an interviewer years later. After all, she was only seventeen years old, just a high school student from Chicago who had started beating all the other neighborhood kids at the park in races a few years ago. Then she caught the eye of a future Olympic track star, who asked her parents if he could train her. Suddenly, she found herself at the Olympic Trials in Evanston, Illinois, and then here, on this train on the way to the biggest sporting competition in the world, to participate in the second ever Olympic Games to have track-and-field events for women.[3]

Thoughts must have been tumbling through her head: the Olympic trials, meeting the rest of her team, being fitted for a USA uniform, and all that was to come, as she lay on the bottom bunk of her train car. Maybe she wondered whether Louise, in the bunk above her, was awake, too. Almost certainly, Tidye had one ear out for that big girl on the team, Babe, who was always pulling pranks. Babe Didrikson, who had been the star of the Olympic trials for her multiple first-place performances, may have been a media darling, but to the rest of her team, she was a nuisance. She liked to grab pillows out from under her teammates' heads as soon as they fell asleep or drop an ice cube down their shirt when they weren't looking, just for laughs. When it came to Tidye and Louise, the pranks seemed to have an extra edge to them. Babe was from Texas and made no secret of the fact that she not only disliked the two Black girls on the team, she didn't want them there at all.

Perhaps it was just as Tidye was succumbing to the sway and hum of the train car, lulling her eyelids to sleep, that a flash of light snapped her awake. Before she realized what happened, she was soaking wet, freezing cold. Babe hadn't just gone for the ice cube trick this time, she'd dumped an entire pitcher of ice water on Tidye while she lay in bed. Tidye was up faster than if she'd heard a starting gun fire. She unloaded on Babe, letting the anger that had been simmering the entire train ride release in her voice, and Babe returned fire. She was known to throw around the N-word when speaking to Black people. Needless to say, the 1932 US women's track-and-field team was anything but united when they arrived at the Olympics.[4]

ONCE IN LOS Angeles, the team had a couple of weeks to prepare for the track events: there were just three this time around, the 100, the 80-meter hurdles, and the 4 x 100-meter relay. There hadn't been a specific event at the Olympic trials for the 4 x 100-meter relay team. Instead, the results of the 100-meter race were supposed to have given the coaches a pool of options. According to press reports at the time, the first three finishers of the 100 would qualify for that race at the Olympics, and the next three would be on the relay team, along with one other member to be named later.[5] At the trials, Tidye Pickett had come in sixth, and Louise Stokes, of Malden, Massachusetts, in fourth, tied with Mary Carew, a white runner from Medford, Massachusetts.

But even though all the reports before the Games, from the *Boston Globe*[6] to the *Los Angeles Times*,[7] cited Pickett, Stokes, and Carew as relay runners, Pickett and Stokes didn't run in the relay race held at the Olympic Games on August 8.[8] Why coach George Vreeland made that decision isn't clear. As they do today, Olympic coaches often made their decisions behind closed doors. According to historian Doris Pieroth, who interviewed several members of the 1932 Olympic team decades later, the athletes who made the team were all in contention for the relay spots, and time trials held during the two weeks in Los Angeles chose the final entrants.[9] The official Olympic program listed eight sprinters eligible for the team. Vreeland was obsessed with winning the relay after the US failed to capture gold in the 100-meter race. "He sought the four fastest runners while looking for the quickest start, the strongest finishing drive, and the surest baton handling. For two weeks, all eight ran trial sprints," Pieroth writes. The final Olympic relay team included Carew and Wilhelmina von Brevman (who'd placed second in the Trials), as well as Evelyn Furtsch and Annette Rogers. Furtsch and Rogers hadn't placed in the 100-meter race at the trials. Rogers had lost a shoe in an early heat, and Furtsch had tripped before the finish line.

Perhaps it was proof of just how little attention women on the track team, and especially the Black women, received in the first place that several newspapers didn't even mention the fact that neither of the Black members actually appeared on the track during the games, after initially reporting that they had qualified. Most simply reported that the US relay team won gold in a tight race against Canada, setting a new world record.[10, 11] But some of the Black newspapers asked questions. The sports page of the *California Eagle*,[12] for example, devoted an entire story to the missing women runners. "First surprise then indignation swept through the minds of Negro spectators and fair minded whites last Sunday when Tidye Pickett and Louise Stokes, speedy colored sprinters on the American girl track team, did not trot out on the field for the relay race,"[13] they wrote.

A white newspaper editor, Don Roberts of the *Los Angeles Evening Post-Record*, the article notes, called for an investigation into why Pickett wasn't put on the team in an editorial. "We are still wondering why Tidye Pickett, the game little colored girl who qualified for the American team at Chicago, is going home without having run. She was sidetracked in favor of another young lady who DID NOT qualify," Roberts wrote.[14]

Years later, Pickett would talk about how she and Stokes deserved to be on the relay team. "But times were different then. Some people just didn't want to admit that we were better runners," she said.

By the time Pieroth interviewed the Olympic runners in the 1990s, Pickett and Stokes had both died. She found the stories of the selection process told by the rest of the team all agreed that there was never a set relay team to begin with, suggesting that this wasn't a race-based conspiracy but an athletic decision. But this was 1932, twenty-two years before *Brown v. Board of Education* abolished legal segregation in public schools. Lynchings were still common modes of vigilante justice in the South. Black people were still routinely turned away from jobs, polling places, and colleges simply due to their race. A white member of the team had been harassing the two Black members for the weeks they were all training and traveling together. Prior to Vreeland's decision, the NAACP had sent a telegram to the US team, expressing their hope that Pickett and Stokes would be fairly treated in selecting the relay team. I can't say for sure what went into Vreeland's decision, but four years later, a similar story played out.

IN 1936, ONCE again, Tidye Pickett and Louise Stokes qualified for the US Olympic team. Once again, they were the only two Black women to do so.[15] This time, instead of traveling through their own racist country, the two young women, now twenty-one and twenty-two years old, respectively, boarded the USS *Manhattan* for a weeklong journey to Berlin, Germany, where Hitler's Nazis were in charge. The games would become famous for how Jesse Owens won four gold medals, securing a place as the winningest individual athlete in a single Olympics, much to Hitler's chagrin. Owens would also become a symbol of hope for Black Americans, that perhaps sporting excellence in the international arena could lead to newfound respect and equality at home. The success of Owens, and his fellow Black American runners Ralph Metcalfe, Archie Williams, and Cornelius Johnson, "challenged assumptions of white superiority and further popularized track and field among black sports fans and young athletes, including girls,"[16] wrote Susan K. Cahn, a historian at University of Buffalo, in her 1994 book *Coming on Strong: Gender and Sexuality in Twentieth-Century American Sport.*

While many Americans heatedly debated a boycott of the games when it became clear Nazi Germany would not allow Jewish athletes to compete, and after the enactment there of laws restricting the rights and citizenship of Jewish and Black Germans,[17] the discrimination coming from Germany's government was far from unusual for the Black American athletes. In fact, as journalist Isabel Wilkerson reports in her 2020 book *Caste*, Nazi Germany borrowed some of their own ideas about eugenics from laws in the American South.[18] Jim Crow laws were still prevalent throughout the South, and more casually ingrained racism (though often just as denigrating) was rampant throughout the nation. Black women had to deal with that as well as the degrading sexism of the period, and with the way these two forces interacted, aka misogynoir. Cultural and legal sexism kept women's wages low if they did work outside of the home and forced them to live in subordination to their husbands or fathers, either way prohibiting their own bank accounts or purchases of property. Although the NAACP pushed for a boycott of the Games held in Germany, many Black newspapers supported the Black athletes going to prove their physical capabilities on a world stage.

Offensive and unfounded stereotypes about sex and race were such a normal part of daily life at the time that they appeared even in the more lighthearted coverage of the journey to the Olympics. The *St. Louis Post-Dispatch* sports columnist reported on the difficulties of the weeklong journey by sea, singling out the Black athletes for what he called a "racial weakness" of seasickness. "The group most seriously affected by the water journey undoubtedly were the Negroes. There isn't much doubt that they are racially sensitive to seasickness, for mal de mer was confined almost entirely to the dusky athletes. The two Negro girls were out for the greater part of the trip—Tidye Pickett and Louise Stokes. The Negro boys also suffered but not so severely."[19] In later years, Pickett would remember that she did experience seasickness the entire trip, as did at least one other Black athlete, Archie Williams. But even if the reports weren't largely speculation or hyperbole, I wonder whether perhaps this was more due to the fact that the eighteen Black athletes' quarters on the ship weren't as cushy as those for the white athletes—the two groups were segregated on the boat.

While the Black male track athletes, like Owens, were at least allowed to shine on the track, Black women would again be nearly invisible in the 1936 events. Pickett had markedly improved as a runner since the 1932 Games and qualified in the 1936 trials in all three women's track events: the 80-meter hurdles, the 100-meter race, and again, in the 4 x 100-meter relay. Stokes was once again set to run the relay.

In Berlin, as Pickett prepared to run in her first race, the 80-meter hurdles, she was under pressure from her team. "They were sure I'd win—and I was too. Nothing ever excited me in those days, so I wasn't nervous, I just wanted to run." The main thing on her mind as she finally started her race was to remember what Jesse Owens had been helping her with on the ship ride over: to keep her trailing foot high instead of letting it graze the hurdle. In the US, it didn't matter if you knocked a hurdle down on your way over, the L-shaped hurdles tipped to the ground and you kept going, but this was not the case in the Olympics. Though Pickett was becoming an expert hurdler, she had developed a bit of a habit of letting her back foot knock them down as she ran, which could slow you down. In her first heat, Pickett placed third, good enough to move to the semifinals. In that moment she also made history: she became the first Black American woman to compete at the Olympics.

But instead of writing her name in the record books, Pickett's semifinal race brought only heartbreak.

The Olympic hurdles were heavier than the ones she was used to. They stayed upright. As she leapt over the second hurdle on the short track, her trailing foot smacked the wooden bar. Pickett fell to the ground. She couldn't finish the event she was finally able to start, and she wouldn't be able to run in the other two she had on her schedule. She was carried off the track. Her foot was broken. "I'm heartbroken," she said en route to the hospital. "I felt I could win another victory for the United States."[20]

Then three days later, as the women's 4 x 100-meter relay started heats, Stokes stretched with her teammates, readying to take the track. She'd vowed, as Pickett was carried from the stadium, to win a gold medal for her friend. Instead, the track coach called her over and replaced her with a white athlete without explanation. She would never run another race.

SINCE 1923 THE Amateur Athletic Union in the US, the national governing body for track and field, had held national contests for women. The first had been inspired by the growing interest in women's athletics, thanks to Alice Milliat's Women's Games, and as World War II canceled two Olympiads, these events became one of the only ways for America's track-and-field women to compete at a national level. Most teams at the national championships were made up of community associations, like the one Florence MacDonald ran with in Boston, but by 1947, when the competition was held in San Antonio, Texas, there was one team that dominated. Tuskegee Institute's 4 x 100 relay team crossed the finish line in 50.5 seconds, winning first place. Alice Coachman, one of Tuskegee's team members, won first place in the high jump, with a jump good enough to qualify her for the Olympic trials the following year, and she came in second in the 100-meter dash.[21]

When all the results were in, Tuskegee Institute (today's Tuskegee University in Alabama) ran away with the team win, earning 107 points in the senior division competition, far above the next closest team: the Polish Olympic Athletic Club of Cleveland, which had just 55 points. The win was a notable one, not because it was surprising, just the opposite: it marked Tuskegee's tenth national championship in eleven years.

Despite the dominance on display, the US governing body of track was tempering expectations about its women runners for the next Olympics. "Officials of the Amateur Athletic Union were gloomy today over prospects of the United States winning the women's track-and-field championship of the 1948 Olympic games," wrote the Associated Press in recapping the 1947 AAU tournament. "They found little to encourage them as they took stock of America's chances after the national AAU junior and senior meets held here over the weekend."

To believe this reporter: the meet's results were dire, resulting in no "record-nearing performance on the part of any woman athlete." All of the winning times and event highlights are reported, but the reporter degrades all of them. Stella Walsh's 200-meter run was "slow." The Tuskegee Institute's relay team finish was "fair." The winning baseball throw (because women weren't allowed to do shot put) was "a good, though not outstanding mark."

Despite the fact that one team dominated both the senior and the junior competition, and had been doing so for a decade, and that the meet had hosted more women athletes than it ever had before, the sec- retary-treasurer of the AAU told the Associated Press they were not expecting any good results at the following year's Olympics from the US women track athletes. "There has been a big fall-off in interest in women's track . . . We do not have enough big, rugged girls to expect to win the Olympics. The other countries have them."

There was something the article wasn't saying outright: interest in women's track may have been falling off, but only for white women. Black women, like those who made up the entirety of the Tuskegee Institute team, weren't just taking up track in great numbers, they were outcom- peting their white counterparts time and again; but they were being sum- marily ignored by the white governing body.

THERE ARE SEVERAL photos of the 1936 women's track team, including one of Tidye Pickett and Louise Stokes aboard the USS *Manhattan* on their way to Berlin. These images are joyous and posed. Pickett would say later in her life that she and Stokes were treated much better at the 1936 Games than they had been at the 1932 Games.[22] (Likely, at least in part, because by then Babe Didrikson had left amateur track for a professional golfing career.) In another photograph, the athletes are all in their opening ceremony outfits, cream-colored below-the-knee skirts and dark matching blazers. Six of the athletes sit on a bench on the deck of the ship, alongside their coach and chaperone, Dee Boeckmann (who had competed in the 1928 Games). The other six are standing above them, bending down awkwardly with their hands on the shoulders of the girls in front of them. The women are mostly wearing hats. Stokes's smile looks forced, as though she's been caught a bit off guard. Pickett is looking straight ahead, hands on the shoulders of the women in front of her, as though crouching at a starting line; her mouth is a flat line, her eyes staring off at something in the distance. A finish line, maybe?

These team photos tell stories—more stories than any of us today could know—but the clearest story is told when you compare the 1936 team photo to that of the next US Women's Olympic track team.

After two canceled Olympics, twelve years later, twelve different women pose on the deck of the SS *America* in New York harbor preparing to head to the Olympic Games. The young Americans stand side by side, in two rows. They're all dressed in stark white T-shirts and shorts. The only decor on the white outfits is the US crest on the left side of the chest, and a sashlike stripe going from the right shoulder to the left hip. The shorts are plain. Plain white socks and sneakers on all twenty-four feet. But the black-and-white photo is almost an inverse from the 1936 version: of the twelve women, three are white and nine are Black. These women would not be left in the grandstands to watch their white counterparts take home Olympic medals; they would represent their country themselves.[23]

The reason the gloomy AAU bigwigs hadn't been excited about this team is because it showed that they hadn't really been doing their jobs: to nurture prospective American track talent. While they had been under-investing in women's track in recent years only to complain that there was no talent, a few organizations were showing that when women track athletes were given the opportunity to train and compete, they could run, and run well.[24] Thanks to a couple of Black colleges in the South, a shift had occurred in how women runners found their way to the Olympics.

MORE THAN ONCE, I tripped up or down the stairs on my way to class in college—not because I was clumsy, but because the stairs weren't right.

The main academic hall at Smith College appeared, at first glance, similar to many buildings at small Northeastern liberal arts colleges: brick with ivy crawling up the outside, grand high ceilings inside, and of course, a magnificent staircase that wound its way up the middle of the building. But it was impossible not to notice one particular design element, the height of the stairs. These slick gray stairs were shallower in height and longer in depth than a typical stair, so they created a gentler slope, one that was nearly impossible to climb using a normal gait.

I distinctly remember heading to an Italian class on the third floor one day alongside a friend, skipping stairs two or three at a time—it was the only way not to feel like you were taking tiny stutter steps—complaining about how awkward the stairs were. A classmate overheard us and laughed, "Well, they had to make them this way, so that our uteruses didn't fall out."

We all laughed.

Old myths and rumors were normal at Smith: like most old colleges, much of its allure lay in the legends the campus held. The ghosts haunting certain houses, for example, or the places on campus where Sylvia Plath, Julia Child, Gloria Steinem, or Barbara Bush supposedly slept, studied, and ate. And many of the stories of Smith's past included some reference to the quaint notion that, in 1875, when the campus first opened, and for decades after, women college students were thought of as needing more accommodations, niceties, and guidance than male students. Housemothers, for instance, and weekly candlelight dinners, and Friday afternoon tea were all traditions that, even as students in the twenty-first century, we often heard about and even continued participating in in some way or another, even though many of them were rooted in the outdated idea that women couldn't have the same independent, freewheeling college experience as men.

So, when I first heard the story about the stairs being short possibly because the all-controlling men of yesteryear believed our reproductive organs couldn't handle normal-sized stairs when the building was constructed, I didn't think too hard about it. But the reality is that, just as those stairs built in 1899 are still standing, so, too, are the lies about women and education that built them in the first place.

FOR MANY OF us today, our first taste of running for sport or competition happens in gym class at school. From there, if you fall in love with it or a teacher notices you're especially fast, you might join a track or cross-country team. But physical education for women today has come a long way from where it was in the previous century.

While half of the 1948 Olympic team were young Black women who had trained by competing for their college teams, the few white athletes who made it came to track and field via community organizations or ethnic clubs, much like Florence MacDonald had in 1928. Young women in the US in the 1940s attended schools that might not have had physical education at all. And unlike today, where successful sports teams can be a marker of a good college, for the vast majority of women who attended college, there were no competitive school sports to speak of.

This can be traced back to the way American higher education was designed in the late 1800s. At that time most men and women alike believed that attending school itself—forget playing on sports teams—would take an extreme physical toll on female biology. "Today the American woman is, to speak plainly, physically unfit for her duties as woman, and is, perhaps, of all civilized females, the least qualified to undertake those weightier tasks which tax so heavily the nervous system of a man,"[25] Dr. Silas Weir Mitchell, an American physician and a pioneer in the fields of physiology and neurology, is quoted as saying in an 1873 book.

Mitchell goes on to make it clear that women were so weak as to barely survive their limited domestic lives, so how should we expect their bodies to handle anything more? "She is not fairly up to what Nature asks from her as wife and mother. How will she sustain herself under the pressure of those yet more exacting duties which now-a-days she is eager to share with the man?"

These quotes appear in a book so popular it published seventeen editions in just thirteen years. *Sex in Education; Or, A Fair Chance for Girls,* was written by another esteemed medical doctor of the day, Dr. E. H. Clarke. Clarke argued, with several "case studies" of young women who pursued higher education and then experienced disastrous health effects, that women simply cannot be educated in the same way as men and boys.[26] He wrote that women's bodies cannot handle the strain caused by things like studying, writing papers, reading—and yes, standing or walking too much.

Clarke's working theory in *Sex in Education* is that women can't possibly go through intense periods of education during puberty and the onset of menstruation without *disastrous consequences.* The problem with this theory is that what was actually understood about the female reproductive system and the menstrual cycle at the time was, well, lacking. Here's how Clarke—a graduate of and professor at Harvard Medical School—describes female puberty's effect on the reproductive system, apparently completely incapable of settling on the right metaphor: "No such extraordinary task, calling for such rapid expenditure of force, building up such a delicate and extensive mechanism within the organism—a house within a house, an engine within an engine—is imposed upon the male physique at the same epoch. The organization of the male grows steadily, gradually, and equally, from birth to maturity." Ostensibly, he is writing about the onset of periods, though it sounds more like he believes adolescent girls must spend long hours engineering complex structures inside of their bodies.

He writes that "our methods of female education" must recognize this intense "peculiar demand for growth" so that girls can adequately develop their ovaries and start their periods. Clarke argued that if a young woman's body was overtaxed by her methods of learning during puberty, she will never have a functioning reproductive system as long as she lives.

His expert advice was for colleges to accommodate women and girls by requiring that they rest during their periods for at least one day but perhaps up to a week, without attending class, standing, walking up and down stairs, or even reading. "The sustained regimen, regular recitation, erect posture, daily walk, persistent exercise, and unintermitted labor that toughens a boy, and makes a man of him, can only be partially applied to a girl," he writes.

These differences meant that women needed institutions that catered to their special needs and should absolutely under no circumstances ever set foot in *male* universities like, say Harvard. (It's probably not surprising that Clarke was a staunch opposer of allowing women into the Ivy League universities.) And while he may very well have believed that education was hurting the health of American girls and women, his concern clearly had nothing to do with protecting those girls and women for their own sake. His concern was for the uteruses of rich, white women. Or, as he put it: "the cradle of the race."

Meanwhile, most Black women weren't allowed, or accepted, into many of the white women's colleges, nor were books being written about how to protect *their* fertility from the strains of higher education. Just 500 Black women graduated from all the Seven Sisters colleges (the informal all-female answer to the Ivy League) combined between 1880 and 1960.[27] But during the same period, Black women were graduating at higher rates than Black men from many of the historically black colleges and universities.[28] Many such HBCUs were started by white benefactors in the wake of the Civil War, as industrial, agricultural, and trade schools that would give formerly enslaved people what these white benefactors considered to be employable skills. This was seen as an act of charity, and often was steeped in racial discrimination, such as in the case of the founders of Hampton Institute in Hampton, Virginia, who wanted to educate a corps of Black school teachers who would "model particular social values and transmit them to the Afro-American South," according to James D. Anderson, an education historian, so that Black people would become comfortable with their "subordinate social role in the political economy."

In other words, Black and white women, though in distinctly unequal ways, were both educated in a manner that would maintain their lower status in the white, male-dominated United States. While it might seem that women at Black colleges would have fewer opportunities than those at white schools when it came to things like competitive sports, the story was actually the opposite, especially for track and field.

When we look at the history of physical education, for instance, we'll see how, thanks in large part to stereotypes about Black and white women, women at Tuskegee Institute were dominating women's track and field by the mid-twentieth century, while students at Smith weren't even allowed to participate in interscholastic sports.

WHEN SENDA BERENSON, the director of Physical Education at Smith College, set up a match between the classes of 1895 and 1896 to play a new game, invented by a male physical education teacher up the road in

Springfield, Massachusetts, just a year earlier, she didn't expect it to be so popular.[29]

Instead, the school's gymnasium was full to the rafters on that spring day in 1893. The entire student body had turned out to watch the first ever basketball game played by women. The students in the balcony dressed in their class colors, with long, thick skirts of the day and light-colored blouses with draping sleeves. Ornate hats covered most of their heads. The spectators waved banners and cheered on their classmates on the gym floor below—never before had women played a sport like this, in teams. "The cheering and screaming of the spectators was a high-pitched sound I do believe no one had ever heard before and was deafening," Berenson remembered later.

The whistle blew. Nine women on each team stood on the floor, wearing bloomers, billowy pants that cut off below the knee, dark stockings pulled up below. Some rolled up their long sleeves to the elbow, the thick, dark fabric of their blouses covered by a square sailor-style collar. Just after tipoff, *pop*, one of the players fell to the ground, her shoulder dislocated from its socket. Berenson and another teacher took her to the office and maneuvered the joint back into place before the game continued.

For two fifteen-minute halves the women played—as per the rules of the game at the time—without dribbling or running, just passing. They used a soccer ball to shoot through one of two peach baskets pinned to a backboard made of chicken wire. The local paper covered the momentous occasion: THE GLADIATORS APPEAR, ONE DYING, read the headline.

The students were hooked.

For decades to come, each year the championship basketball game between the best two classes turned out almost the entire campus. Berenson would become known as the expert on women's basketball. She changed the rules slightly from those originally established for the men's game, ensuring that her students retain their femininity while playing, and edited multiple editions of *Spalding's Official Basket Ball Guide for*

Women. But despite the enthusiasm from the student body for competitive team sports, Berenson put her foot down about one aspect, refusing any and all invitations for intercollegiate play. Like many women physical educators, she believed that allowing women to play sports as men were beginning to do at men's colleges would threaten physical education for women altogether by stoking the biggest fears society had at the time about women and physicality: that *too much* of the wrong kind of movement would turn women *mannish.*

But Berenson, for her time, was actually on the progressive side of things, at least for the faculty of a school educating white women. Before she arrived at Smith, one of the first Seven Sister colleges, physical education on campus had consisted of a style of gymnastics that was essentially stretching and marching in unison. Classes met in the social hall and were taught by the elocution teacher. "Little stupid dancing steps to music,"[30] as Berenson would later call the system.

Many students didn't participate at all, thanks to the fears spread by men like Dr. Clarke. Her biggest challenge was the ignorance of the parents of the students and the faculty "who quite honestly believed either that physical exercise was injurious to the delicate mechanism of the female body or that gymnastics should not be taught in a college," wrote Edith Naomi Hill in a biography of Berenson. Women like Berenson wanted to protect physical education for women, which they considered to be so important for health and well-being as well as for academic success, and in that era this meant keeping it as feminine and nonthreatening as possible.

The rest of the Smith faculty didn't agree with her on its value. Some tried to overturn the college's physical education requirement shortly after Berenson arrived. At the faculty meeting where this vote took place, Berenson gave an impassioned speech that convinced her fellow faculty members to keep the requirement, which mandated two years of physical education for each student.

Like many women physical educators at the time, Berenson was a tightrope walker of sorts, balancing the extent of her goals with the dictates of the power structures she was operating within.

On the one hand, Berenson and other like-minded people showed just how wrong some of the misogynistic lies about women's frailty were by showing what women *were* capable of. And yet they were content to uphold strict rules governing what was proper and natural for women: fun, noncompetitive, undemanding sport, such as basketball without the running. In contrast to what was natural for men: intercollegiate team sports and masculine enterprises like track and field and football. Berenson would remain at the school for nearly twenty years, and the school would hold on to her vision for decades after. While intramural sports were always popular with Smith students, intercollegiate games would not be allowed until 1971.

AT SOME ALL-BLACK institutions, there was a different sort of hand-wringing going on about what physical education and sport could and should look like. The Tuskegee Institute had had a men's running team since the turn of the twentieth century, but it wasn't until 1929 that the women of Tuskegee formed a competitive track team.[31] Founded in 1881 by Booker T. Washington, Tuskegee remained, almost fifty years later, one of just a few colleges for Black students started by a Black founder and employing Black faculty. Washington organized the college as a trade school, believing that the best way to prove racial equality to the world would be to give the Black population living in the Jim Crow South specialized skills, all while maintaining respectability that would ensure they were inoffensive to white Americans, some of whom happened to be major funders of the school. In the many Black colleges set up by white people, sports were shunned based on concerns that athletics would further cement the stereotypical ideas about Black people being especially brutish, violent, and animalistic, instead of promoting the kind of image these white people wanted to portray, that of refined citizens who could contribute to white society.

But as men's intercollegiate sports grew more important to white America, Cleveland Abbott, Tuskegee's enterprising athletic director, bet that sports done in the *right way* could earn respectability for Black students. If Tuskegee started turning out world-class athletes, it would be harder to treat Southern Blacks as second-class citizens, he believed. In 1927 Abbott founded the Tuskegee Relays, a track meet for Black schools, advertising it from the beginning as a nationally influential event.

For Black women, however, earning societal respect was far more complex. The pressure to present a proper, gender-divided student body had stifled earlier attempts at women's track and field at Tuskegee, but by 1929, the Relays had become such a massive event that the school's female students voted to begin a women's track team, too. Abbott was soon promising that his women's team would produce Olympians, a sure way to demonstrate the worth of Tuskegee's students to the country.

Because of the various social pressures on them, the women athletes needed both to perform at an elite level *and* appear appropriately feminine. Abbott thus made sure that, in addition to intense training on the track, they took lessons in proper attire, etiquette, and manners. He had to combat the racist stereotype that Black women were inherently more inclined to brute strength and masculinity. Even the school administration and some male athletes disapproved at first of Abbott's attempt to nurture women's track superstars, for fear that this would masculinize them, and perhaps just as important, emasculate their male students. The boys' team actually tried to discourage the girls from participating.[32]

Abbott and his women athletes pushed ahead. There were at least twenty women on the team every year throughout the 1930s. Outside of the Tuskegee Relays, Tuskegee began to send a school team to the AAU national championships every year (where they mostly competed against runners from ethnic and community groups, since most schools didn't have women's track). The women won their first national title in 1937.

Abbott was hoping his women would grab Olympic slots in the 1940 Games, but since World War II canceled both the 1940 and 1944 Games, the Tuskegee women just kept competing at the national level, and winning. Between 1937 and 1948 their dominance essentially shifted the balance of athletic power away from the predominantly white women's national team that Tidye Pickett and Louise Stokes had been on in 1936. Alice Coachman, Tuskegee's all-around star, nearly beat superstar Stella Walsh in the 100-meter race in 1944 and never lost a national high jump competition.[33] Soon, other Black Southern schools were following in Tuskegee's footsteps. Majority white colleges, meanwhile, were doubling down on keeping women out of competitive sports, track in particular. In the 1930s, white women's groups had rallied against the US national track governing body, the AAU, and Olympic women's track altogether. "They argued vehemently for the elimination of public track-and-field competitions on the grounds that they subjected women to debilitating physical, emotional, and sexual strains," wrote the historian Susan Cahn. By 1936, AAU women's track and field no longer existed in most regions of the country. "Unable to shake its masculine aura, women's track and field by the late 1940s occupied a marginal, denigrated position within American popular culture," she wrote.

In the years after World War II, gender roles were in flux, and this changed college campuses. Midwar, in 1940, women in the US were earning more than 40 percent of all bachelor's degrees. Postwar, by 1950, this share dropped to less than 25 percent.[34] The necessity to fill the jobs men had left vacant during the war had ended, and women's education came to be viewed by many as a hindrance to a woman's ultimate duty: to become a wife and mother and help rebuild the traditional American family. This wasn't exactly the case for Black women.[35] Even after the war, women were still taking up 58 percent of spots at historically black institutions, likely because in the Black community women were much more likely to have to work outside of the home for financial reasons, and a college education would at least put them on the path to becoming, say, a teacher, instead of a housekeeper.

And because higher education was seen as having different purposes entirely—professional versus marital—for Black women and white women, the opportunity to do something like run track while at school remained just as segregated as did the schooling.

LESSONS OF DIFFERENCE are especially potent when they're taught in our schools. "When a schoolboy in the early 1900s participated in military drills and his sister practiced calisthenics, both performed a gender system that associated power and status with manhood," writes historian Martha Verbrugge in *Active Bodies: A History of Women's Physical Education in Twentieth-Century America.* "When white-dominated school districts showered resources on white pupils and shortchanged black programs, physical educators and their pupils experienced racial privilege and subordination." Similarly, when Black women college students were encouraged to compete in sports like track and field and white women college students were told physical education had to remain noncompetitive and feminine if done at all, this left a lasting impression on our society.

When schools, the places where we learn what we are capable of, are different for people based on their sex or their race, and those differences are said to be because we have different physical capabilities, young people are set up to believe that these differences are inherent. Though our schools today are not subject to state-mandated segregation by race or sex, many beliefs about inherent biological differences endure, in large part because physical education remains separate and unequal. Some of this is due to opportunity, some to tradition. Black girls play basketball. White girls play volleyball. Girls play softball in gym class. Boys play baseball. In my middle school PE class in the early 2000s, the boys did a wrestling unit while the girls did yoga.

Lessons learned in our own bodies at the time when we're figuring out our places in the world remain deeply ingrained. "This naturalization of difference becomes self-perpetuating once displayed for all to see, apparent disparities are then inscribed directly on the body. By practicing difference in the gym, people embody powerful lessons of body, self, and inequity, in literal as well as symbolic ways," writes Verbrugge.

And so the women competing in track and field at midcentury all had something in common: they were largely Black women and working-class white women, people who didn't have the option of being *just* a wife and mother, people who saw their bodies as useful in other ways, outside of gender norms. "White women who competed in track and field [during the mid-1900s] seemingly forswore the privileges of white womanhood," wrote historian Cat Ariail, in her book *Passing the Baton: Black Women Track Stars and American Identity*. "Black and white track women thus together competed, cooperatively and copacetically, on the margins of American sport culture, seemingly irrelevant and summarily ignored."

WHILE THE AMATEUR Athletic Union, the national governing body of track, downplayed the women's track talent ahead of the 1948 Olympics, Black newspapers like *Chicago World* portrayed the upcoming Games in overwhelmingly positive terms. "Negro men athletes of superb ability are no novelty on United States Olympic teams. . . . But this year, too, for the first time, Negro women athletes seem certain not only to win places on the American team, which they have done in the past, but to win their events when the Games are run in London," declared an article in the *World* in June 1948.[36] Though Alice Coachman, Tuskegee's all-around track-and-field all-star during the war years was twenty-four years old and no longer in peak running form, the *World* assured readers she was "not to be overlooked," in the high jump. Coachman had won the national title in the event for a decade straight.

At the same time, a star from Tennessee State was piquing Olympic interest and showcasing that Black Southerners with track talent had more options for school than Tuskegee. Audrey "Mickey" Patterson grew up in New Orleans. She'd been running since she was a child, even though her mother said running was "bad for a lady."[37] Her father said it was okay, however, so she played sports in the neighborhood. At Gilbert Academy, a private Black high school in New Orleans, Patterson was the only girl on the track team. "In those days, black women didn't compete against white women in New Orleans. . . . I was the only one interested," she'd remember later. She entered her first track meet at sixteen, and won the 100- and 200-meter races, two jumps, and also anchored the winning relay team. "Cinders have been my diet ever since that day,"[38] she'd tell a New Orleans paper, referring to the cinders that used to make up dirt-track surfaces.

So when Jesse Owens, who had run his way to fame and thus become a credit to Black Americans everywhere, visited Gilbert Academy her senior year to speak, she paid attention. "He shared his experiences in Germany at the 1936 Olympics with us," she told a *Los Angeles Times* reporter later in her life. "He said someone here should think about trying for the Olympic team, and that's when I decided I would like to be that person."

She learned how to sprint from her high school coach, with her eye on the goal of following in Owens' running steps. In her first year at Wiley College in Texas, she shocked everyone at the Tuskegee Relays by winning the 100 and 200, beating all of the Tuskegee Tigerettes on their own turf.[39] Then her parents made her transfer her sophomore year, and she chose Tennessee State, which was in the process of building a women's track-and-field program in the model of Tuskegee.[40]

The TSU president, Walter S. Davis, hired Jessie Abbott, Cleveland

Abbott's daughter and a Tuskegee alumna, as the first head coach in 1943 and made it clear he wanted what Tuskegee had, even for women. "We knew that there was nothing to prove that competitive sports was harmful," Davis said. "And we decided to go into it . . . We had seen Abbott win the AAU with Negro girls, and being a geneticist I know that individuals are born equal . . . and it's the environment that makes the difference."[41]

The Nashville school wasn't wealthy. Practicing in a grass field, instead of on a real track, became a problem after a few years. One day during practice, new coach Tom Harris, a former Olympic athlete, convinced a pair of dump trucks carrying gravel and dirt near their training area to unload some into an oval. The supplies only covered three-quarters of a track. Even so, it was an improvement. Harris believed in his athletes and began to enter the students into more competitions. Patterson would compete at the AAU National Indoor Championships in 1948, winning the 100 and 200 and the long jump. From there, she and her TSU teammate, long-jumper Emma Reed, were driven out to Providence, Rhode Island, where the women's Olympic Trials were taking place at Brown University's football stadium, a towering cement structure built in the 1920s. While the men's track trials were held in Evanston, Illinois, over two days of competition so athletes could rest between competing in heats and finals, the women's trials were all held on one day.

On July 12, the day of the trials, Patterson would have to race five times to qualify for two events: the 100- and 200-meter races. In the 92-degree sweltering heat of that Northeast summer day, before a wall of spectators in the stadium seating, Patterson took her mark for her first race, the 200 heat. She crossed the finish line a full 1.5 seconds ahead of the second-place finisher and the crowd in the stands burst into applause. They took a liking to the tall, lanky girl with the mischievous smile.

During the 200 final, Patterson again sprinted into the lead, finishing a half second ahead of Tuskegee's Nell Jackson, who took second place, and 0.6 seconds ahead of fourteen-year-old Mae Faggs, who ran for the

New York Police Athletic League. Again, the spectators went wild for the New Orleans native, who wasn't shy about flashing them her smile when she realized she'd qualified for the Olympic team. But she was used to winning, she hadn't lost a race in nearly four years.

Then came the 100 heats. Again Patterson crossed first, again the crowd seemed to zero in on her, bursting into applause as soon as she crossed, and growing louder as she came closer to the stands on her walk back. In her semifinal heat, she again sprinted out in front of the rest of the pack, finishing in just 12.4 seconds.

Getting set for the finals, Patterson must have been tired, but the crowd was on her side now. As she waited for the starting gun to go off, she looked ahead to the finish line. Maybe it was the heat, maybe it was the five races in a row she'd just run, maybe it was the weight of realizing she was going to the Olympic Games in London. Whatever the reason, she got off her blocks more slowly than usual. Mabel Walker, a Tuskegee runner, shot to the front of the six-woman pack instead. And for the first time in four years, Patterson felt what it was like to run from behind. She pushed her legs to work harder, if only for a few more seconds. The crowd seemed to join in on the race, pulling for Patterson, cheering in surprise and delight as she nearly caught Walker in an uproarious twelve seconds. The two crossed nearly simultaneously but Walker had the win by one-tenth of a second. Patterson's second-place finish was good enough to qualify for a second Olympic event, but it was the first race she hadn't won outright since she started running competitively.[42]

JUST TWO DAYS later, the twelve women who qualified for the US track team boarded a train to New York: Patterson and Reed, from Tennessee State, plus four others—Mabel Walker, Nell Jackson, Theresa Manuel, and Alice Coachman—who were also all current or former students at Tuskegee.[43] In other words, half the team was made up of women from HBCUs. It was a whirlwind experience for Patterson. "We had little orientation," she said later. "They gave us a piece of paper that told us what to bring. We had no spending money. Our per diem was $10 a day."

While the men's swimming and water polo teams flew to London, the rest of the US Olympic team boarded the SS *America* in New York Harbor to make the long journey by boat. Patterson found the giant ship a bit frightening as it shuttled the group over an ocean, though the athletes tried to make the best of it. They enjoyed the rich food available on board, served in a formal dining room with white tablecloths and flower arrangements each evening. Alice Coachman even performed a dance to the "St. Louis Blues," in front of hundreds of other athletes and coaches at a ship's concert they all put together. The group of American athletes was joyous, relaxed, and happy.

Once they arrived in England, the war wasn't far from anyone's minds, however. "The team stayed at a college in the southern part of the country," Patterson remembered. "They kept prisoners there during the war and we stayed in the same rooms. Nothing much had changed in three years."

In contrast to the outright hostility Pickett and Stokes had experienced in 1932, the twelve women on the 1948 team seemed to get along just fine. The team called one of the three white women on the team, shot putter Frances Kaszubski of Cleveland, Ohio, "Granny," because, at thirty-two, she was the oldest in the group. [44] Later, Patterson would say Kaszubski acted as the "mother hen . . . She looked after us," she said.

IN THE GROUP portrait of the team aboard the SS *America*, Mickey Patterson stands on the left-hand side. She's thin and tall, with a proud posture, hands clasped behind her back, chest up, neck straight. [45] One reporter would say she seemed to be built specifically for sprinting. Her slight frame seemed made up of "whip-cord sinews," and structurally he wrote that she was "as streamlined as a human can be. Even her eager face is cast as if designed to offer no wind resistance." Her short, dark hair is neatly pinned up so rows of curls seem to stand on end from her forehead to her crown. Patterson was one to speak her mind. During her first few days in London, she blew two whole dollars to go see her favorite British actor, James Mason, at the movies. A United Press International reporter asked her how she was liking the city. "'Whew. Two dollars for a couple of murders and a suicide,' groaned Audrey. 'Back home in New Orleans we pay 25 cents for a double feature.'"[46] Her comment made me wonder how else Patterson compared her Olympic experience to her life back home.

From being the only girl in her high school to join the track team, she had gone on to become a national champion who wasn't allowed to even compete in the South against white women, then a college student accepting a work study scholarship at one of the only programs for Black women runners in the country—where the campus didn't even have a track.

She had come so far on her own two legs, competing at the Olympics just like Jesse Owens had suggested at her high school just two years earlier.

THE AMERICAN TRACK girls arrived at a disadvantage, however. Their major competition was the beautiful, ultra-feminine star from Holland, Fanny Blankers-Koen, or as the media dubbed her, the Flying Dutch Housewife.

In the first women's track event, the 100-meter race, Patterson and the other American women failed to make it through to the semifinals. Blankers-Koen won her first gold, much to the delight of the media covering the event.[47] The fair, tall, lithe, blond, Dutch married housewife with two children epitomized the white feminine ideal that American society held in such high regard. The Associated Press called Blankers-Koen "a slender girl with tossing blonde hair." The International News Service's Bob Considine wrote: "She ran like a modern goddess with her blonde hair streaming behind her to win the event."[48] Her orange shorts, tapered at the bottom so they clung to her muscular thighs while adding a ruffled texture, and her demure white polo with cap sleeves were distributed as the Dutch national uniform, but they seemed to emphasize her feminine image, especially compared to the other countries' more athletic uniform tank tops and T-shirts. Her blond, coifed hair, pulled back in perfect 1950s housewife-esque pinned curls, as though she were ready for a dance or some housework once she slips on a dress, only added to the effect.[49]

By the time the 200-meter race came around, Blankers-Koen had become the face of women's track at the Olympics, even in the United States. She'd run away with the gold medal in the 100 on August 2. Two days later, she earned her second gold medal, despite a slow start, in the 80-meter hurdles.[50] So on August 5, the day of the 200-meter heats, Blankers-Koen had already won more gold medals than any of the men in the track competition had yet that year and seemed on track to break a record for most gold medals ever in one Olympics by a woman athlete. (American Babe Didrikson, the Belle of the 1932 Games who had terrorized her Black teammates, had won two golds and one silver that year.)

IN THE FIRST heat of the evening, at 3:30 p.m. Blankers-Koen finishes first, as usual. The top two runners of each of the seven heats would move on to the semifinal race later that evening. Because this is the first time the 200 has taken place at the Olympics for women, Blankers-Koen's 25.7-second performance sets an Olympic record. Patterson, running in heat five, finishes in a commanding 25.5 seconds, faster even than Blankers-Koen's heat performance. An hour later Patterson faces Blankers-Koen directly in the semifinals, where the top three from each of two heats will go on to run in the final the following day.

The Dutch Housewife opens a massive spurt of energy in the semifinals, blazing ahead of the field to finish in 24.3 seconds. Patterson crosses behind her, in 25 seconds flat. The final would be held the following day.

Of course, the press didn't pass up the opportunity to comment on the question of the 200-meter race being run by women for the first time, too. According to the Associated Press, the distance "looks strenuous for the fair sex."[51] Stop me if you've heard this one before.

THE FOLLOWING AFTERNOON, the day of the 200 finals, it poured. Images of the crowd that packed into Wembley stadium appear more like an oil painting than a photograph or movie still. The Londoners' clothing, trench coats buttoned high and suit jackets pulled close, are deeply saturated blues, grays, and browns, so dark you can feel the wet wool on your skin when you look at the scene. Pops of black sheen appear throughout the packed stands, where umbrellas protect a few heads from heavy rains. Hats or improvised hoods cover other spectators, while some, having clearly just given into their fate of sopping hair, stare intently at the track through the falling droplets.

PATTERSON IS NERVOUS before the race begins, and when she's nervous, she can't stop talking. Her teammate and competitive veteran, Coachman, lets her talk, to release the nervous energy before she takes her place on the rain-soaked track.

As the racers take their marks, Patterson kneels down into the starting blocks at lane 5, the second from the outside, waiting to hear the starting gun. She begins with her right knee down on the track, her hands lightly touching the ground, her back flat. As the starter marks "set," the six racers lift their knees, waiting for the gun. While the other runners all seem to push their heads down and butts up, bending into triangles, Patterson keeps her back flat, her eyes ahead, her body an arrow pointing toward the finish line. The gun fires and she's off the blocks first, catching and passing the Australian runner to her right in her first few strides. Every tiny movement in her body seems to be propelling her forward. For a moment, she seems to have the rest of the field beat. But at the halfway mark, Blankers-Koen pushes into the lead in a blur of orange shorts up the inside lane. Her muscular legs stride seemingly twice as far with each step than those of the other racers. There's no catching her, not for Patterson, not for anyone. When she crosses the tape, she's seven yards ahead of the next runner, Audrey Williamson, of Great Britain, who is followed closely by Patterson, in third. The American women have won their first 1948 medal in track and field, a bronze.

Mickey Patterson became the first ever Black American woman to win an Olympic medal.

INSTEAD OF FANFARE and reporters mobbing Patterson to trumpet the details of her story back home, Patterson was merely a footnote, one tiny mention, if anything, in the American press coverage at the time. In the most descriptive stories of those that ran that day, she is merely a "tall Negro girl from New Orleans," who took third.[52, 53] A member of the US Olympic Committee praised Patterson, not for her tough race or her grit and excellent training despite attending a school that didn't even have a full track, but for her "thoroughbred stride,"[54] citing a harmful trope of comparing Black athletes to animals, as though her body's capabilities weren't hers at all, but mere genetics.

When Patterson's teammate Alice Coachman won first place in the high jump, the smidgen of attention that the press was willing to give to the Black American women medalists went to Coachman's gold, outright ignoring Patterson's bronze. Not that it was much coverage, of course. Blankers-Koen ended the Games with a record-breaking four gold medals and was evidently the kind of athlete white Americans wanted to see and celebrate, given the press coverage. "She made it possible for mainstream American sport culture to imagine a laudable woman athlete, one who resembled and therefore reinforced the image of an ideal American womanhood defined by wifehood and motherhood," writes Ariail, the historian.

100-meter Olympic race, 1948. Mickey Patterson, far right (USOPC)

   In all of my newspaper archival searches, I don't even find one photo of Alice Coachman or Mickey Patterson holding their Olympic medals or standing on the Olympic podium in the coverage from the time.

   From my perch in the twenty-first century, where photos and videos of athletes, especially at the Olympics, are nearly impossible to escape, thanks to all types of media coverage and athletes' own social media accounts, I wonder how more photographic evidence of Patterson's and Coachman's victories might have changed the historical record. If more Americans had *seen* just how striking their presence and success on the international stage was, would we have learned different lessons from the 1948 Olympic Games? Ariail suggests that Patterson's presence in the 200 final, the only Black woman against five white women, made her hyper-visible. "Although the majority of the spectators in Wembley likely focused attention on Blankers-Koen . . . they couldn't help but see Patterson . . . Considering the pre-Olympic rhetoric about the inadequacy of American track women, the combination of Patterson's racial and national identities made her presence surprising and significant." But without these images making their way overseas,

Patterson's hyper-visibility existed only at Wembley itself, for just a few moments.

Even in the official Olympics video of the final race, in the shot of the three medalists on the podium, Patterson is hidden entirely behind Blankers-Koen's tall frame in the angle they used—she isn't even visible. I seek out a photo of the podium in which you can see all three medalists, and I'm struck by the emotion on Patterson's face. None of the three athletes are smiling, but there is a tension in Patterson's face not evident on the faces of the other two competitors. In marked contrast to the image of her on the SS *America* on the way over to the Games, where she seems joyous and relaxed, here her jaw is held tight, mouth flat and gaze laser-focused on something ahead of her, as if to confirm to anyone who might question the USA emblazoned across her chest, "Yes, this is what an American runner looks like."

I can only guess what Patterson was feeling in that moment. She died in 1996. But she told *Essence* magazine in 1984, "At the time I competed, you know, we were still sitting at the back of the bus and eating at separate lunch counters. Just imagine what it was like for me."[55]

DESPITE COACHMAN AND Patterson's medals, the women's 1948 track team was considered a big failure by the AAU. On their return to the US, the response would become clear: Black American men were a credit to their race—Jesse Owens was proof Black men could be just as good, masculine, and powerful as white men. But the success of the two Black women medalists in the 1948 Olympics was nearly forgotten before it could even be celebrated.

When Patterson came home to New Orleans, bronze medal in tow, she was met at the airport by her all-Black high school's marching band, playing their school victory song. They presented her with a celebratory silver cup. But that was about it for the city celebrating its first-ever Olympic medalist. The mayor declined an invitation to a party her neighbors threw for her. The *Times-Picayune*, her local paper, never mentioned that she was a New Orleans native in their Olympics coverage. "I think I'll always be a little hurt about the way New Orleans treated me," she would say in 1976. "It was heartbreaking, really."[56]

Coachman, gold medalist, did receive a parade in Albany, Georgia, her hometown, but the white mayor refused to say her name, shake her hand, or congratulate her on her achievement during the festivities.

The success of Patterson and Coachman and the powerful track programs at the Southern HBCUs may actually have turned popular opinion against expanding such athletic programs to schools for white women. "White observers may have tacitly dismissed black women's accomplishments as the inevitable result of 'natural,' 'masculine,' prowess," historian Susan Cahn writes. "By this logic black women's very success could appear to provide further evidence of track and field's unfeminine character."

Because the governing body of track and field failed to hold up Tuskegee and TSU as models of successful track-and-field programs after the 1948 Olympics, other schools missed an opportunity to follow in their footsteps. Though women's running in the US would begin a dry spell at the international level, Tennessee State would carry on its pursuit of nurturing female track talent, becoming the home of the lone Olympic bright spot for American women runners for decades: Wilma Rudolph, who won three gold medals in the 1960 Olympics. Tuskegee's storied program, however, would fall prey to the gender ideals pushed by white institutions.

Cleveland Abbott died in 1955. Tuskegee's next athletic director was less enthusiastic about women's track. He worried the dominance of the women's team was outshining the men's. In 1965, Tuskegee's track program was cut altogether. Administrators provided a bigger budget to the football team, instead, to enhance their male students' standing in the white-centered world, where football had become a status symbol of American pride and masculinity.

Patterson was named AAU Athlete of the Year in 1949 for her

continued dominance in sprints. At Tennessee State, she wanted to major in everything, and said in 1950 she was preparing for many potential futures: "Maybe coaching, maybe I'll go to France and work; maybe I'll dance or do lab work or be an actress. I'm getting ready for any and all of them. I'm studying like nobody studied before. Nobody excepting Socrates or even Leonardo, who could put his wonderful hands to anything." After she won her Olympic medal, she and some others on the team had competed at a meet in Paris, where she won the 100 and 200. As a prize, she was given two quart-size bottles of perfume: Jean Patou and Chanel No. 5. She loved them both so much that she said part of the reason she wanted to make the 1952 Olympics in Helsinki was so she could return to Paris and get a refill,[57] but she failed to make the team.

After that, Patterson married a classmate, Ron Tyler, and finished her degree in education. Like many talented women athletes before her, she went into teaching and coaching, but she was annoyed by the fact that no one in her hometown wanted to hire the first Olympian the city had ever turned out. Instead, she had job offers from athletic clubs and playgrounds in several other states. Though she wanted to continue to live in New Orleans, she ended up moving with her husband and four children to San Diego in 1964 to accept a teaching job. There she started a track team for underprivileged girls. She called them Mickey's Missiles.

Later, she would coach both boys and girls, but her focus was always on expanding opportunities for the Olympics to those who might not otherwise have access. In 1983 she told the *Los Angeles Times* she was planning to build a program for the underprivileged kids of color in San Diego County to give those who had the talent access to better training and to competitions to get them to the 1984 Los Angeles Olympics. "I've looked for the last ten years in this city at many prospective Olympians, talents gone down the drain simply because of a lack of knowledge of what's really going on with our Olympic program," she told the reporter. She said many children, especially youth of color, weren't even aware of what kinds of races they needed to run or organizations they needed to join to be invited to the Olympic Trials.

By this time, years after the passage of Title IX, schools were seen as the incubators of future track talent for boys and girls alike. But making schools the epicenter of sporting culture for young American women hasn't resulted in the erasure of sex- and race-based inequality in sport, it's exacerbated it. Inequity caused by vastly differing local education budgets, often along racial lines, continues to flourish in schools, and therefore in sports—and Black girls and other girls of color are the least likely to have access to sports equal to their male peers.[58]

As was true for Tidye Pickett and Louise Stokes, Alice Coachman, and Mickey Patterson, the vast majority of us are still taught how to be a person in a system where some talent is seen, and nurtured, and other talent never gets the chance to even be exposed to daylight.

Decades after her history-making Olympic medal, Patterson felt as though the lessons she had to impart on the younger generations were in danger of becoming lost. Ahead of the 1984 Olympics in Los Angeles, she told the *Essence* reporter who interviewed her that she felt like a "forgotten woman." The reporter said Patterson "burns with anger to tell her story." But Patterson held tight to the idea that she could still make her story count. She said she was headed out on the lecture circuit because she knew that her story mattered. Because when stories about proving the impossible aren't seen as important enough to write down, we're stuck in a cycle of untruth.

Like, for instance, when the governing body of track and field wouldn't even bother to keep most women's running records over the next several decades, even as women kept breaking them.

Diane Leather crossing the finish line in an 880-yard race, May 12, 1956.

3: But Not a Mile . . .

May 6, 1954, Oxford, England

BEFORE 1954 HUMANS couldn't run a mile faster than four minutes. Then—suddenly—we could.

We had steadily been getting faster. The very first officially recognized world record in the mile was set in 1913, by American John Paul Jones, in 4:14.4 seconds. This doesn't mean that no one had ever run anything faster than this, just that when the International Amateur Athletics Foundation, the international governing body for track and field, officially recognized the mile distance, Jones was the first to hit this fastest recorded mark. Twenty years later, the *official* record was about seven seconds faster, at 4:07.6.

During the 1940s, two Swedes, Gunder Hägg and Arne Andersson, bumped the record back and forth—from 4:06.2 to 4:04.6 to 4:02.6 to 4:01.6 to 4:01.4. But like the points of a parabola the seconds shaved off the record went from whole numbers to decimals, to, well, no noticeable progress. That x-axis of 4:00 seemed to be untouchable for nearly another decade.

Experts wondered if humans were simply stuck. Perhaps we'd hit our limit.

But on May 6, 1954, we learned something new about ourselves, thanks to a young Oxford medical student named Roger Bannister.[1]

A runner all through his college years, he was good, but not great at first. He made it to the Olympics in 1952 in the 1,500 meter race but didn't medal. As his medical training got more intense, the time he had to train lessened, but his mile pace began to hover closer to a tempting mark. Something in him drove him to attempt the impossible: the four-minute mile. "My running had become something of a crusade," he wrote later in his autobiography. "This was the goal that athletes and sportsmen had talked of and dreamt about for so many years, since the days of Paavo Nurmi, the great Finnish runner. Everyone used to think it was quite impossible, and beyond the reach of any runner. Then gradually the world mile record had been lowered."

Soon the question began to haunt him. "Whether as athletes we liked it or not, the four-minute mile had become rather like an Everest—a challenge to the human spirit. It was a barrier that seemed to defy all attempts to break it—an irksome reminder that man's striving might be in vain."

Looking ahead to the end of his medical training, Bannister realized that his competitive days were numbered. He thought the summer of 1954 would be his final racing season. Bannister convinced two of his training partners to run with him, and go for the record attempt, at a race between Oxford University and the Amateur Athletics Association of England (AAA).

There, on May 6 at this obscure university race—not at the Olympics, not at an important national or international competition—Bannister overcame what he describes as "a mental" problem. Three hundred yards from the finish, he says, his mind took over.

> It raced well ahead of my body and drew my body compellingly forward. I felt that the moment of a lifetime had come. There was no pain, only a great unity of movement and aim. The world seemed to stand still, or did not exist. The only reality was the next 200 yards of track under my feet. The tape meant finality— extinction, perhaps. I felt at that moment that it was my chance to do one thing supremely well. I drove on, impelled by a combination of fear and pride. . . . I leapt at the tape like a man taking his last spring to save himself from the chasm that threatens to engulf him.

Since that moment, Bannister has been a celebrity, embraced in the arms of all those who saw in him the miracle of human potential. He'd gone from obscurity to a household name. A young medical student to an athletic hall of famer. That day, the British House of Commons adjourned the House for 3 minutes, 59.4 seconds in honor of his record mile. The press hounded him so much that he began leaving his home through the garden, using chairs and ladders to climb the fences of his neighbors' yards. He received a suitcase full of fan mail and invitations, and the British foreign office sent him on an all-expenses-paid press tour to New York City. Before he left, he was mobbed by fans at London Airport. When he landed in New York, he had a police escort from his flight into the city.

Bannister became a symbol of man's ability to overcome the seemingly impossible. Emphasis on *man's*.

DIANE LEATHER LOOKED down from the bus window at Alexander Stadium in Birmingham, seventy-five miles north of Oxford, and saw a group of girls on the track running hurdles.[2] The nineteen-year-old university student was always looking for something else to do when field hockey wasn't in season.[3] When she showed up at the Birchfield Harriers training grounds in 1952, she met the women's coach, Dorette Nelson Neale. She found a lively group of runners there, who soon welcomed her wholeheartedly. The club had existed since before the turn of the century, though women had only been involved since the 1920s. By the time Leather arrived, they were well known throughout the country for winning major titles each year.

Legend has it that, Nelson, as the runners called the women's coach, first appeared at the Harriers track in 1929 as a young runner, dropped off by a chauffeur who was driving a Rolls Royce. She stepped out of the car wearing a fur coat. She ran the half-mile race at a time when British women were starting to show up internationally as runners. She wasn't the star of the team, but she had that thing that good coaches had: she could see what worked, and explain it to others. As a coach she doled out advice and training schedules to her runners while wearing glamorous sunglasses, heels, and yes, often a fur coat.[4]

Nelson put Leather into training as she did with all of her girls, four evenings a week at their training fields.[5] Leather came to practice after she finished up schoolwork at the University of Birmingham, where she also worked as a microanalyst in the chemistry department.[6, 7] Before long Nelson could see that though Leather was not a natural hurdler or sprinter, she was a gifted middle-distance runner. Her long frame—she was five feet ten and all legs—could carry her quickly through cross-country races, and she barely even seemed winded after running half-miles and miles in practice, even at some of the fastest speeds ever recorded for women. The Birchfield Harriers club, which usually had between 200 and 300 runners, prided itself on not pushing anyone too far too fast, instead focusing on athleticism and physical fitness to maintain long athletic careers.[8] Leather added trophies to the club's shelves as soon as she began to race. In her first cross-country season, she won the regional cross-country championships, then went on to the nationals and won that, too. Paradoxically, even while women's track events in the Olympics were still restricted to 200-meter races or less, in England, women were allowed to run up to three miles in cross-country races, though the sport would remain in its infancy and international championships were considered unofficial until 1967.

Then, at Leather's first ever mile race, in September 1953, less than a year after she first started to run, Leather set a record—5:02.6—the fastest mile ever officially recorded by a woman. By January, the British athletic association had certified Leather's time as a new English record. But it was not a world record.[9] There was no world record at that length for women. The international federation for athletics did not keep *official* records for women's races for any distance above 1,000 meters.[10]

Leather didn't compete again in a mile until the next spring, just as Bannister was breaking the four-minute mile story wide open, and the papers picked up on her potential. "It is confidently expected that she will be inside the 5min. mark before the end of her second year," wrote the *Birmingham Weekly Post* the day after Roger Bannister broke the four-minute record. "Opinions may be divided as to whether or not women should take part in competitive athletics, which undoubtedly make heavy demands on physical attributes, but Miss Leather had no hesitation in saying that, far from feeling any ill-effects from her efforts she feels all the better," the same news article went on to say. "And, as the daughter of a distinguished surgeon, it may be taken for granted that she would not have been encouraged to go on with the sport if there had been any reason to suppose it would do her any physical harm."

On May 26, 1954, twenty days after Bannister's accomplishment, Leather would run in the Midland Counties women's one-mile team race at Perry Barr. Although the sports pages rarely devoted much energy to covering women's track, mentions of her upcoming race appeared in newspapers up and down the United Kingdom,[11, 12] as well as in wire stories that showed up in hundreds of papers in the United States.[13]

THE MILE WAS supposed to begin at 8:25 p.m. that Wednesday evening, but it had been delayed. There was the weather—the rain had turned the track to mud—which made the six-mile men's race that had just occurred more difficult than normal to clean up. As the minutes ticked by under the floodlights, the stadium crew raked the track, attempting to get it back in shape for the women's mile.[14] Leather stuck close to her Birchfield Harrier teammates, all dressed in black sweatshirts and pants. The wind pushed her cropped hair off her face as she walked up and down the track with her teammate Dilys Williams. She often wore a beanie on the crown of her head, behind her ears so that it stood up a bit in the back. She paced to pass the time, probably to keep her legs warm, probably also because she couldn't sit still under all that pressure—and most likely, because she was just itching to run.[15]

Her week had been a busy one, with university exams. So instead of her usual four training runs a week at Birchfield, she hadn't trained since Sunday, after a competition on Saturday. She'd sat for an examination the night before—no time to run. And all day she'd been stuck at work in the university lab.[16] She confided in Williams before the race that she was nervous, because so many people—2,000 spectators—were there to watch, expecting that here, in just her second ever mile race, during a week when she hadn't been focusing on running at all, that she'd "do a Bannister," as the papers had been hyping all week.[17]

On her way into the stadium that day, one of the dozens of reporters there to cover her race asked if she thought she could break the five-minute mile that night. Naturally quiet, Leather offered: "Wait and see."

FINALLY, AT 8:45, the track has been raked and rolled and the girls are called to line up for the mile. Leather strips down to her black shorts and Birchfield top, with its square neck and a Birchfield stag patch she'd sewn on the front herself, with the club's motto, "Fleet and Free," in script beneath. As usual, Leather towers over the rest of the field by at least a few inches. Standing at the starting line, she takes the inside lane of the crowded field. She digs her spikes into the dirt and sees that, despite the delay, the track remains a bit bumpy from the huge field of six-milers tearing it up in the prior race. There's still some light in the late spring sky. Before the gun goes off, she looks toward her coach while pulling nervously on her shorts. Nelson, standing just inside the track, covers her mouth with a hand, perhaps giving Leather some direction. Her friend, Williams, lines up beside her, seemingly whispering a word of encouragement under her breath without making eye contact.

As the race begins, Leather, Williams, and two other Harriers take off at a jog in a small group at the lead. Her teammates are trying their best just to give Leather some comfort with all the hubbub around. But Dilys was a race-walking champion, not a miler. So after the first lap, Leather pulls ahead of her competitors, heading right into the increasing crosswind with no one to break it for her, for the last three-quarters of the race.

As she comes down the final stretch of her fourth lap, the time keepers, tape-watchers, over a dozen reporters, nine photographers, and one camera crew train eyes, lenses, and flashbulbs on Leather's long loping legs.

The camera shutters click and stopwatches stop and eyes stare as Leather strains her neck muscles in a grimace and her jersey hits the tape.

"ONE STRIDE. TWO-TENTHS of a second. The time it takes to blink an eye. That's all there was between 21-year-old Diane Leather and a piece of history at Alexander Stadium last night. That is by how much she failed to be the first woman to run a mile in five minutes," wrote Dick Knight, the *Birmingham Despatch*'s sports columnist the following day. At 5:00.2 Leather had set what was another unofficial world record for the mile. Despite all the continued concern about whether women could run long distances, Leather was reportedly "quite fresh, and with a pleasant smile," after her race.

Nelson grasped her hand just after she saw the time, the fastest mile a woman had ever run in a race, even though it hadn't broken the five-minute barrier. Nor would it be an official record, because, you know, women simply couldn't set records at this distance.[18] "Everything was against Diane. I'm quite sure if it had been put on earlier in the evening she would have broken the five minutes," she told Dick Knight.

An avid chronicler of her life via her scrapbooks, sometime later Leather placed a print of a photo of herself crossing the finish line of this race on a full-page spread. The judges seem to stare her down as she crosses mid-stride, dark gray clouds loom over her in proof of the poor weather. Underneath, in her neat cursive, she doesn't betray any inner thoughts or feelings either, writing simply: *Finish, with time of 5 minutes 0.2 seconds.*

Nelson, however, didn't shy away from her thoughts on the matter after the race.

Leather was blunt in at least one assessment—running out in front for the entire mile was no easy task. "I could do better if I had somebody to pace me," she said. And to see the race, you believe her. In a video captured of the event, she doesn't seem as though she's running as fast as she can at all. But then, how would you know what your fastest speed is if you're told you're the fastest woman in the world at a distance women shouldn't be able to run anyway? But that was as far as her own analysis went. "And now, I'm going home to bed for a night's solid sleep. I have to sit for an examination tomorrow as part of my work in the Birmingham University laboratory."

Nelson went on to remind the reporters present in Birmingham, obsessing over Leather's mile time, that, yes, she will likely try it again, but probably not for a few months. In October, there would be another race opportunity. But remember, Nelson emphasized: Leather does not even train for the mile, she trains for the half-mile, because that's the race she can *officially* set records in. And she has a competition coming up in just four days, where she very likely will set an official record—so, she'll be focusing on that one for now.

WEEKS AFTER BANNISTER had completed his feat, a story ran in several American papers, claiming to tell the "Scientific Story" of how he ran his historic mile.[19]

"It is the story of how he slowed his heart and changed its very structure, how he built up a giant supply of oxygen and finally how he ran on nerve alone to the point of absolute collapse," the reporter states.

The article claims that Bannister used his own medical knowledge to make himself a better runner—that his experiments on athletes and oxygen levels gave him some edge to enable him to lower his resting pulse. "Blessed with a barrel chest with a large rib cage for his powerful lungs, the 25-year-old Bannister began boosting his chest measurements even more. He altered the very structure of his heart, his blood vessels and his muscles by severe training methods. And all the time he was keeping close scientific observation of himself in the coldly detached way of a medico."

These "severe" training methods were what we'd now call interval training—mixing bursts of sprinting, jogging, and walking to increase speed and endurance instead of simply increasing the distance of long runs at the same pace. It was not a common training method back in the

1950s, but it wasn't unheard of. And intervals enabled the busy medical student to keep fit in the one hour a day he had available to him. Yes, he did do physiology experiments on oxygen's effects on an athlete's performance in medical school, but this had little to do with his own training beyond knowing that more training meant more oxygen uptake in his body, as it does with any athlete.

Though the idea of Bannister as some kind of mad-scientist medical student experimenting on his own body in order to complete a feat no one before him had done is an appealing one, it isn't true. Oxygen and muscles and training do of course very much matter when discussing how fast a person can run, but what matters just as much—especially when we are talking about how to shave off the mere seconds and milliseconds needed to set running records—are our brains. Specifically, our expectations for ourselves based on what we believe to be possible.

In his 2018 book *Endure,* Alex Hutchinson, a writer, runner, and researcher, describes how this impact of belief on running records happens. "This sort of earned, transferable belief—if he can do it, so can I—also plays out at the very highest levels of sport. Why is it that world records in virtually every test of human endurance keep edging downward? You might think it's our ever-advancing knowledge of training, nutrition, hydration, recovery and so on, along with fancy technologies like cryosaunas. But all of this knowledge and technology is applied with equal enthusiasm to nonhuman sports like horse and dog racing." And, Hutchinson explains, horse racing times "have remained stagnant since about 1950," while human times continue to drop. The difference? "[O]nly humans can make the abstract leap to virtual competition: if you know that someone, somewhere, has covered a given distance in 1:59.4, you know that it's *possible* to cover that distance in 1:59.3—and you can guide your training and execute your race plan accordingly."[20]

Even Bannister knew that he wouldn't have broken the four-minute barrier if it weren't for two of his competitors in the race he ran that day, who were also his training partners and friends: Chris Brasher and Chris Chataway. Bannister had this theory that to beat the four-minute mile—which translates to four laps around a track—each lap should be as even as possible. In this case, as close as possible to one minute. He had a scientific mind, after all, and he liked that there was a neat solution to this math problem. So Bannister trained in intervals, getting his quarter mile pace as close to 1 minute as he could. But in order to sustain that pace throughout, he knew he needed help.

So during his record-breaking run, Brasher paced his first lap, running out ahead of Bannister, making sure he was not only blocking the high winds blowing that day, but setting a pace that would achieve the world record. They finished the first lap in 57.5 seconds. Brasher took him around the second lap, too, finishing the half-mile in 1:58 seconds. Around the next bend, Chataway took the lead, and led Bannister to a 3:00:0.7 three-quarter mile time. They knew they needed a fast final lap to finish the job, and Chataway pushed them all the way until the final stretch. Then in the back straight, 300 yards from the finish, Bannister finally took the lead himself, crossing that finish line in the storied 3:59.4.

WHILE THAT FOUR-MINUTE barrier had seemed to be a concrete wall for decades, Bannister was only able to crash through it thanks to the Chrises. Together, they enabled Bannister to cross the line two whole seconds before Gunder Hägg had nearly nine years earlier, with no human (not *officially* anyway) going faster in the years between.

Various studies over the years have tried to pin down the reason why humans can run faster in competition than they typically do in training, and why running with faster competitors speeds up a whole field. Because running is actually a complex physiological task, there are lots of answers, really. (Sorry, even with all the sports science in the world behind you, you can't just multiply someone's VO_2 max by their resting pulse rate and divide by their glute strength or something to figure out how fast they will run a race.) Getting a slight advantage in speed by drafting—aka keeping the front runner from tiring themselves out by blocking some of the headwind[21]—helps, as does the boost from a psychological need to beat a rival.[22] But we do know pace setters push elite runners to go faster than they can on their own. Although what many see as the next limit of human running, the sub-two hour marathon, has never been *officially* completed, Kenyan runner Eliud Kipchoge did complete a marathon distance on a track in 2019 in 1:59:40, thanks to the aid of forty-two rotating pacesetters.[23]

After the record mile time was stagnant for years, Bannister's mile world record was broken just forty-six days after he set it, by Australian John Landy, who had been beating at the door of the four-minute mile for years without being able to break through. Finally, Landy found the way when he raced against (who else?) Chris Chataway, who pushed him to a 3:58 mile—a new world record.

AFTER THE 5:00:0.2 mile attempt in the middle of her long week of lab work and examinations, Leather had been too tired to train on Friday. By Saturday, May 29, when the individual races of the Midland Women's Athletics Championships (a separate competition from the team events days earlier) were held, she only had to focus on the 800, and without all the pressure the mile race had had.

Early in the day, she raced the course she'd been training on for the past nineteen months and crossed the line 2 minutes and 14.1 seconds later, beating the previous British women's record by 1.5 seconds.

Given all the media coverage and her new official record in the 800, one might think she'd be done then. But instead, Leather had come up with a plan of her own—she wasn't waiting until October to run the mile again. She wanted to try again "without fuss or bother." So, not long after her win in the 800 that day, with just half an hour to go before the mile race began, she said she'd enter. As usual, she stuck close by her friends in the Birchfield Harriers after her first race, remarking that she felt fine. "I am going to have a shot at the double," she told them.

Despite feeling confident about her chances, since she'd missed the five-minute mark by just a stride earlier in the week, she wouldn't have an easy run. A cross wind of eight miles per hour blew over the final straight, and once again, no Chrises were on hand to pace her laps appropriately. She didn't get the help from a person drafting her, she didn't get the psychological boost of trying to beat a rival, or of even seeing someone else nearby to help her believe what was possible. She had just her own lungs, her own legs. She was chasing herself. After one lap, the clock read 68.8 seconds, after two: 2:27. After three, she clocked 3:46.3. The record was in her reach then, as she opened her stride to beat that crosswind in the last stretch. She crossed the line, at 4:59.6. The judges read the time out to her. "Oh! Good. At last," the famously soft-spoken runner betrayed just a smidge of excitement in her initial response. Later, when asked to expound a bit, she told a reporter: "Of course I am thrilled," she added. "But so glad it's over."

A photo taken of her just after the race, and carefully placed in her scrapbook later, confirms the sentiment—she looks perfectly calm, smiling with her left dimple pinched and her teeth open. She confidently faces the camera, looking as though she's ready to head out for a coffee, not like she just ran a faster mile than any woman on earth ever had—unofficially.

Her father, a surgeon who did his rounds in a top hat and tails throughout the posh neighborhood of Staffordshire where she grew up, watched from the stands with a much smaller crowd than had attended the previous race a few days earlier. He kept repeating "Marvellous."

THEY BECAME INTERTWINED, Leather and Bannister. The narrative, after all, was just too perfect. Two young Brits, both students, breaking minute records in the same distance, just weeks apart. But perhaps most important to the lore is that their stories helped maintain a hierarchy. Even though she was pushing the boundaries for what women should properly do with their bodies, Leather's feat could still be painted as secondary to Bannister's, inspired by him, even. Newspaper after newspaper state that Leather had "Set Sights on Record After Roger Cracked 4:00"[24] or that "a 5-minute mile in womens track and field has been looked upon as the sport's greatest goal,"[25] and that her ambition was to emulate Bannister "in a feminine way."

An ocean away, the *Buffalo Evening News* reported: "It is the 5-minute mile that has beckoned women distance runners for as long as the four-minute mile has beckoned males. Diane Leather, a Birmingham University co-ed, chopped 2.4 seconds from the world's mile record for women."[26]

Except that Leather wasn't trying to be the next Bannister. That was only the third mile race she'd ever run, and she'd started to train just a year and a half earlier. She was simply running. Despite the shared country, and the shared distance—they existed in completely different worlds. The five-minute mile wasn't a beckoning force in women's running because the race—let alone a real record—barely even existed.

The shadow of the 1928 800-meter Olympic race hung over Leather's unofficial race, and her whole life, really. When she did break that five-minute mark, headlines spread all over the world. They were sure, again, to caveat her accomplishment: this was not an *official world record*, instead, it was a *world best*. The IAAF, the international governing body of track and field, still did not even see this distance as something women should be competing in.

The wording is important, because it keeps Leather's feat from being in the same category as Bannister's. The media attention on her accomplishment ended there. But Leather didn't. She kept running, and breaking records.

By the end of 1954, she set a new world record in the 880 yards, another world record in the 3 x 880-yard relay, a British record in the mile relay, a British record in the 440-yard, and got second place in the European Games 800-meter race. The following year she retained her national championship status in cross country, and set a new world best in the mile, lowering her time by nearly 10 seconds, to 4:50.8. By the end of the year, she'd lowered it even more, to 4:45.0. In other words, in the space of one year, she'd lowered the "world best" in the mile more than fifteen seconds—a feat that had taken the world's best men forty-one years. And she'd done it all without pace runners or even training for that particular race.

Perhaps Leather's name would be more widely known had she been able to attend the Olympics that following year, to run in the event in which she held the world record. But the 1956 Olympics continued the tradition set in 1928: they had no running events for women above 200 meters. This is a good time to recall the media misrepresentation of the 800 final in 1928 and its "collapsed" women.

That kept Leather from racing three decades later.

Perhaps it's also a good time to point out that Bannister describes the moments after he finally broke the four-minute mile this way: "My effort was over and I collapsed almost unconscious, with an arm on either side of me. It was only then that the real pain overtook me. I felt like an exploded flashlight with no will to live; I just went on existing in the most passive physical state without being quite unconscious. Blood surged from my muscles and seemed to fell me. It was as if all my limbs were caught in an ever-tightening vice."

Bannister's collapse is proof of his masculinity. His toughness. His bravery. His physical prowess. He pushed his body to the limit. And so we celebrated him, then and now. Sixty-four years later, *Smithsonian* magazine would remember the photos of Bannister's achievement, particularly his exhaustion, as "a testament to what humankind could achieve."[27]

Leather, though a runner who held more records and titles than Bannister, was described by the press as "slender" and "good-looking."

After the photos of Leather's 1954 record-breaking race in her scrapbook are some of the few of her not wearing running sweats, a reminder that she was feted a bit for her accomplishment. She was invited to tea with Birmingham's Lord Mayor and Lady Mayoress.[28] After that there aren't many news clippings or photos of big celebrations, just photos of her friends and more races, unseen by the rest of the world.

Bannister, who retired shortly after setting the mile mark, was *Sports Illustrated*'s first Sportsman of the Year in 1954. In 1975, he was knighted by the Queen.

SEVENTY YEARS AFTER Leather had seen Alexander Stadium the first time from her bus ride through Birmingham, I look down on the track from a bus window at the same track where she trained and competed—where she nearly broke the five-minute mile, and then did, in a surprise to nearly everyone, four days later.

The dirt track is still there. It's still used for racing, but for greyhounds, not humans. Compared to the modern Alexander stadium, rebuilt to host the 2022 Commonwealth Games, it is small, old and tired. But I could see how it was welcoming back in its day. It reminded me of the small dirt tracks at my elementary and middle schools growing up, when everyone was encouraged to run in gym class, or join the track or cross-country team after school. I would gleefully run around with the boys in my class.

On the bus with me is Stuart Paul, whose mother had run with Leather and later worked for the track club. He's remained active with the Birchfield Harriers and offered to ride with me to the new Alexander stadium, where the club is now based, from my hotel in Birmingham. Just up the road from where Leather broke the record, the bus drops Paul and I off at Perry Park. I walk across the grounds with the tall, lanky, retired high school teacher and he tells me that he basically grew up on the track.

His mother was always running or officiating races, and he was along for the ride. As he points out the fields in the park where the cross-country team performs, and the small chapel where war veterans are buried in the yard—the graves of former club members marked with the Birchfield Harrier stag—it's clear that he takes his role as heritage director of the club, seriously. Under a bright blue January sky, with a bitter English wind blowing, I can picture myself running through the grounds, too, following in Leather and many other women runners' footsteps, joyfully loping along through the green grass. How strange that Paul's mother and Leather had to blaze trails that seem so natural for anyone to take up today, running for fun.

At the parking lot of the track stadium, we meet Lindsey Armstrong, Leather's youngest child and only daughter. Armstrong and Paul have never met, but he grew up hearing stories about Leather and he's clearly excited to meet the daughter of one of the Harriers' most famous members. Though Armstrong and her brothers had donated all of Leather's scrapbooks and memorabilia to the Harriers archive after she died, she's never been here before to see the old stadium where her mother broke the infamous mile mark, nor the new one where her club is now based. Armstrong clearly inherited her mother's height and athletic genes, though she tells me she was better in the field events than on the track, growing up.

Together, we walk through the inner workings of the stadium. Behind the stands are locker rooms and offices, some still used by the Birchfield Harriers. The track club continues to win medals and titles and raise champions, as well as encourage young people in Birmingham to get involved in athletics.

When we arrive at the room with the archival materials, Paul put on an electric kettle, and he, Armstrong, and I sip tea while sifting through the boxes. This is where I see Leather's own photo albums, and those belonging to her coach, Nelson. As we read through club notebooks, with minutes of each regular meeting held by its officers, and pamphlets and magazines that list track-and-field record-holders and Olympians of decades past, we'd call the others over to see what we found when it appeared important, or just amusing. Paul was almost always able to name all the other people in the images—women athletes from nearly seventy years ago—as though they were today's superstar athletes. As I frantically scribbled notes and took photos of as much information as possible, I wondered whether Leather would have gotten as much attention for all she did had Bannister not set the new men's-mile record the same month.

There were so many other women in these notebooks, albums, and newspaper articles. Leather was just one—to be sure, one very impressive—athlete at one club in one country, who had gotten a glimmer of recognition because her accomplishment came at a moment when the press was already primed to care, and because it was done in a manner that didn't threaten men's standing in the world.

LIKE MOST PEOPLE living through the mid-twentieth century, Leather and Bannister's early lives were shaped by World War II, a time when traditional gender roles were turned on their head. Bannister's family left London after the war broke out, moving to the historic city of Bath when he was ten to avoid the bombings. He writes in his autobiography that he had a difficult childhood as a war evacuee. He was "not very strong physically" and was often bullied by the other boys in school for being small, and interested in his schoolwork. But when he discovered he was good at running, winning the first school-wide junior cross-country race he entered, he won some attention from his peers. "It wasn't easy to win, but I was conscious of accepting the discomfort as the price of freedom to work, and gain the toleration, if not the respect, of the other boys for the rest of the year." In other words, he was allowed to show interest in academics, theater, and music without getting beat up by the other boys, so long as he could also prove his masculinity through being a good runner.

Children in Britain at the time attended single-sex schools throughout their education, which made sense given the vastly different expectations for women and men in both home life and the workplace before World War II. Just one-third of British women—most of them unmarried[29]—worked outside the home, prewar, nearly all in domestic, assembly, clerical, or administrative work. The professional and technical industries were completely male-dominated. Women's wages reflected society's ideas about them: they were paid around half what men were, no matter their work, and most jobs that allowed women in their ranks required them to resign if they got married, as then they were expected to have babies and stay home to raise them while their husband earned the family's income.[30]

When Leather was seven years old, however, and London was being blitzed by the Germans near daily, Britain, like the US, suddenly saw women as physically capable of much more than just raising children or doing the household chores. While in the US, a propaganda campaign built around a burly Rosie the Riveter convinced women all across the country to get their newly discovered muscles into factories to build some airplanes, Britain drafted women into the war effort. Every unmarried woman between twenty and thirty was conscripted to join either the Auxiliary Territorial Service, Women's Auxiliary Air Force, Land Army, Women's Royal Naval Service, nursing services, or to take up an industrial job in a factory to keep the country running.[31] By 1943, nearly 90 percent of single women were working for the military or in the war industry, as well as 80 percent of married women in Britain.[32]

Though Leather and her three brothers saw more traditional gender roles in their own home growing up—their father as a successful surgeon, and mother as a homemaker—her formative years were spent in this new world, seeing women given wholly different opportunities in the working world and in the military. Perhaps this is why Leather attended the University of Birmingham, where she studied chemistry, working in a lab there. After all, during the war, working women had become the norm, even in previously male fields like science.

This window began to close in the 1950s.

Social analysis carried out by Anna Freud (Sigmund's daughter) during the war on the importance of the mother-child bond—she wrote of the trauma inflicted on those children who were separated from their parents in the evacuations—was used to convince Britain's government to reconfigure the social welfare system after the war to encourage the return of traditional gender roles. Government-run daycare centers were closed, and policies allowing employers to deny married women jobs were reinstated.

At first, women who could afford it went back to their homes, to have more children and do housework, and the birth rate increased dramatically between the end of the war and 1960. But as it turned out, opening the door for women to work outside of the home had already changed the way people saw what women could do.

"[A]fter an initial trend toward full-time motherhood, such attitudes gradually faded into obsolescence during the postwar era," wrote historian Ann Taylor Allen, in *Feminism and Motherhood in Western Europe 1890–1970*. "An influx of married women transformed the labor force." By 1967, half of the married women in Britain were in the workforce, whereas prewar they'd almost all stayed home. British sociologist Judith Hubback wrote at the time that re-entering the labor force after the war meant women must "evolve from exclusive femaleness towards the fulfillment of a wider personality."

As little girls saw Leather's race in the newspapers and felt they, too, could be runners who ran the mile, so women after the war knew they could be more than just wives and mothers, if they'd like to be.

LEATHER MARRIED JUST before the 1960 Olympics, where, for the first time since 1928, there was an 800-meter race for women. "Diane Leather has been grabbing the titles this year but will take a new and permanent title when she gets married early in July!" wrote *Modern Athletics* in announcing the news. Diane Leather Charles, as she would become known after marriage, was beyond her peak years by the time she went to the Olympics, but she was appointed vice-captain of the British team. She didn't make it out of the first heat in the 800 (there was still no mile race, which had become her specialty),[33] but proclaimed she was proud all the same to wear the British uniform on the international stage.

She retired from running then, and went on to have four children. But as soon as they were all in school, she, too, went back to school. To go to work. While about half of married women were working again in Britain by the 1970s, most of Leather's peers didn't work full-time. "It was quite unusual for us to have a mother who wasn't at home full time," her daughter, Armstrong, told me. "[My parents] very much believed that women should be able to do exactly what they wanted to do." Leather went back to school for social work. After graduation, she first worked in bereavement therapy, then became one of the first social workers in the nation to focus on child welfare and protection.

Bannister, on the other hand, similarly married and had children, but he continued in his medical profession as a neurologist. He didn't take a break when his children were young. He specialized in research of autonomic nervous system responses, publishing more than eighty papers in the field, and edited five editions of the neurology textbook: *Brain and Bannister's Clinical Neurology.* He also never stopped being recognized as the man who first broke the sub-four-minute mile, called up for comment by the BBC whenever something happened in the track world.

WHILE WOMEN WERE seeing themselves on the track, and in the workforce, they were still separated by sex in these new realms. There was *women's* running, and *men's* running. *Women's* work, and *men's* work. And in many ways, that separation has remained intact. Throughout the end of the twentieth century and into the twenty-first, the working world remained so segregated by sex that even today, half of all workers world-wide are in occupations that are at least 80 percent one sex.

Female-dominated fields are often those that conform to the ste-reotypes of women's skills: patience, caretaking, service. While male-dominated fields, even today, are those that are seen as requir-ing heavy physical labor, or significant time investment. We know that women are capable of things like factory jobs, and construction, and driving garbage trucks, and we know men can make excellent nurses, social workers, and administrative assistants, but these unofficial bound-aries remain.

Scientists have been trying to understand for decades why this level of segregation continues to exist in workforces. Karen Messing, a biologist who researches the ergonomics of work, at the University of Quebec at Montreal, studied the way that a group of hospital cleaners in Canada separated their work by gender in 1994. The cleaners assigned the men "heavy work," such as mopping with a large mop, using a polishing machine, and washing vents and windows, and women "light work," such as mopping with a smaller mop, dusting, washing toilets, and fill-ing dispensers. Most of the workers, men and women alike, perceived that the "heavy work" was simply impossible for women to do. It also paid better.[34]

However, when Messing's team actually went in and analyzed the physicality of the jobs, they found that even when they were assigned to "light work," the women were doing 30 percent more physical operations per hour than men did, and were more often working alone. In other words, scrubbing a vent can require more physical work than operating a machine, but we perceive these activities differently. Some of the hospital workers themselves didn't believe women could operate the big machines that the men used, even after being presented with the data, because the stereotypes about the kind of work they did were so deeply ingrained.[35]

When I speak with Messing, she's eighty years old. She says when she was young, the newspaper Help Wanted ads were literally split into two sections: Help Wanted Female, and Help Wanted Male. But when discriminating by sex in hiring became illegal, they just changed terminology: "so they call the men's jobs heavy work, and the women's jobs light work." But what she found was inconsistency in terms of what heavy work really meant. For instance, she told me, "lifting an inanimate object from the floor to the waist, or the waist up high in a relatively uniform way," would be considered heavy work. But if the object being moved was a human body, such as in the case of a health care aide, or a daycare teacher, who are both lifting heavy, moving, nonuniform weights around consistently, the work isn't even typically considered physical labor, it's considered "caring" labor, in other words: women's work. Women's physical labor is often less visible than men's, but that doesn't mean they don't do it. Whether it is the repetitive picking up of babies or the standing all day that bank tellers (mostly women) or grocery clerks (mostly women) do.

Messing has found that in most jobs that have a physical component there is no biological aspect that would keep all women or all men from doing a particular job. But physical jobs are often set up for men's bodies, making them more dangerous for women because of this, or are so male-dominated that women who break into the field are more likely to experience harassment or abuse to the point that they leave, which can contribute to the idea that women simply can't hack it. And this perception keeps segregation intact.

Even in jobs that used to be seen as male-dominated but aren't seen as physically laborious at all anymore, Messing says there has been an interesting shift in perception. Take doctors, for instance, which used to be considered one of those professions women simply didn't have the stamina or strength for. In Quebec, where she is based, medicine is becoming a majority-female profession. As a result, though, women aren't being seen as necessarily more capable, just the opposite. The medical profession has become perceived as not being as rigorous, the doctors themselves as not working as hard. "People get on doctors all the time, because they're not doing enough. They're taking all this time off to have children. They're not working the number of hours they used to work in the olden days."

Messing says that, as someone dedicated to ergonomics, she just wants everyone to be able to do the jobs they want to do safely, regardless of their sex. Yet she sees the continued sex segregation of the workforce as a consequence of "some very rigid ideas about human potential"—ideas that some people attribute to ancient history.

IN DAVID EPSTEIN's popular 2013 book, *The Sports Gene: Inside the Science of Extraordinary Sports Performance*, he and the researchers he speaks with try to pin down just exactly why men are so much more athletically gifted than women.

"So male-typical hormone patterns . . . skeletons . . . and genes . . . can confer certain athletic advantages. An interesting evolutionary question, then, is: Why are women athletic at all? Like our male forebears, our female ancestors needed to be athletic enough to walk long distances, carry kids and firewood, chop down trees, and dig up tubers. But women were far less likely to fight, to run, or to push the capacity of their upper body strength with strenuous activities like tree climbing. Part of the reason that women are as athletic as they are, Geary and several other scientists told me, might be because men are," writes Epstein.[36]

He goes on to compare a woman's ability to run to a man's reason for having nipples. "Nipples are absolutely essential for reproductive success in women, and they are not so harmful in men that there has been significant natural selection pressure to get rid of them. As Harvard anthropologist Dan Lieberman, who has studied the role of endurance running in human hunting and evolution, told me, 'You can't program males and females totally separately. You can't order us like a car in red or blue. Our basic biology is mostly the same, with a little difference. If women didn't need to run, you could argue that they don't need the Achilles tendon for springs in their legs. But how would you do that? You would have to have a sex-specific loss of the Achilles.' Instead, nature has left humans with a system whereby—instead of great numbers of genes changing—hormones can selectively activate genes to different effect."

If women didn't need to run, he says. The idea he is gesturing to is that early women and men were so sex segregated, that men would do something so basic and human as *run* to survive—the natural extension of walking, an essential human trait—and women just *never* did.

This stereotype is a common way of explaining away women's physical capabilities when it comes to work, sport, or really for anything other than bearing and birthing and rearing children. The excuses can be applied to so many things, why women can't be construction workers, or big-wave surfers, or soldiers, or run a mile as fast as men: *if it were natural, early humans would have done it! We evolved this way. It's not discriminatory, it's just biology.*

But this story simply isn't true. As anthropologists discover more and more evidence about early humans, they've found that roles were not so sex-segregated as we might have previously believed. Even in hunter-gatherer groups many women were hunters.[37] Anthropologist Kathleen Sterling, who focuses much of her field research on a Paleolithic-era archaeological site in the French Pyrenees, has written that even in hunter-gatherer cultures "universality of gender roles as we know them does not exist."[38]

To begin with, early humans were not all barbaric and animalistic with time only to focus on survival. Neither were all of them hunter-gatherers! What we call the Stone Age, Sterling says, was actually a time period 2 million years long, and so included many, many various groups of early humans who all had different ways of living. "It seems unlikely

that during the over 100,000 years of *homo sapiens sapiens*'s early existence there was less diversity of practices and beliefs through time and
space, from culture to culture, than there has been within the last few
thousand years," Sterling writes in her chapter in the book *Ideologies in
Archaeology*. Even if there were some groups in which men hunted big
game, and women stayed close to their homes and raised children and
foraged for vegetables, this was far from universal.

Also, she writes, "human populations continue to evolve. While overall human genetic makeup may not have changed much over the last
40,000 years or longer, the environment certainly has. We are a species
of infinite variety, with each body creating and inhabiting its own unique
environment."

SO WHEN LEATHER ran a mile in under five minutes, just after Bannister
ran one in under four, it feels like a simple way to say, look how giant the
gap is between men and women at the basic physiological level. But that
was one moment in time, one distance run, and in very different contexts.

Men had been encouraged for decades to run for sport, and were at
that time even told by society that by running they were fulfilling their
natural, biological role. The record mile time for men had been watched
carefully for a century. At the same time, women were still told that a mile
wasn't even an appropriate distance for them to run at all, let alone something to train significantly for just to push the limit of human potential.

Today, the mile world records between men and women are less than
25 seconds apart. The 100-meter records are less than one second apart.
The winner of the 2023 Boston Marathon women's division finished
ahead of more than one third of the professional men's field (and more
than two hours before the average marathon-running man).

But we have been trained to see women's running as "less than."
Women's work as light, men's as heavy. Men's running as natural, as
human. Women's as divergent.

Dr. Roger Bannister, Diane Leather, Chris Chataway and Sylvia Cheesemen (right to left) are presented with plaques for record-breaking runs by the Duke of Edinburgh, May 7, 1955.

We've been trained to see two distinct buckets, instead of a long, overlapping line of diverse humanity with various traits and talents.

AT THE END of our day together, Armstrong was simmering with frustration. Part of it was sitting in Birmingham traffic for the prior half hour—and she was anxious to head home to her son, who was heading back to university shortly. But she had more she wanted to tell me about her mother, as she stirred the foam of her flat white coffee in the coffee shop where we'd gone after our morning at the archives. Speaking about her mother all day and digging through the archival records of her achievements had brought something up for her.

She remembers being surprised when she finally discovered the extent of her mother's accomplishments. Armstrong was eleven when she found some scrapbooks on a shelf and asked her mum about them. "She just said, 'Yeah, I used to run.'"

There was a modesty to her mother, Armstrong said, a quietness. But she wondered if it wasn't something more, too. Something about the way the world perceived her accomplishments that kept her quiet. "Because, imagine you did something that was so far beyond anything anyone had ever done before. And you weren't even allowed to call it a world record? You know that's just extraordinary and ridiculous. So, I don't know. I guess that must make you feel slightly less proud of it."

I had had a similar feeling that morning as we'd been sifting through the photos and documents about her mother's running club, as though we were seeing something we weren't meant to see. Something that wasn't meant to be remembered. After all, those distances Leather had run were unofficial. They earned a gray mark in history books, not the bold, black, outline of an official record or an Olympic medal.

When Leather died in 2018—strangely enough, in the same year as Roger Bannister—some of the coverage surprised Armstrong and her brothers. "Suddenly people were emailing me obituaries from the *New York Times* and the *Washington Post*," she says. And at first they were proud, and then another emotion snuck in, in the form of a question: "Why didn't you make a fuss about her while she was alive?"

The following year, when Armstrong met Bannister's daughters at the World Athletics Heritage Mile Night in Monaco, where both Bannister and Leather were to be honored posthumously, she was struck by the difference of their upbringing. While she hadn't known about her mother's running feats until she'd stumbled upon the evidence herself, Bannister's daughters remembered hearing about his accomplishments on the news, and around the dinner table, and from their friends at school when he'd show up to their athletics contests. "That was their life," Armstrong said.

She shook her head, remembering the last, perhaps most painful, oversight. The BBC Sports Personality of the Year, an annual television program and award, is "a massive thing every year," she told me. She and her brothers grew up watching each year. In 2018, as Armstrong and her brothers watched, they hoped to see a nod to their recently departed mother. Before the program begins, there's a montage of great athletes who have died that year, the in memoriam section. She and her siblings weren't together—their adult lives have brought them all to live in different parts of England—but they were texting, keeping an eye out for their mum's moment of glory.

But she never showed. "Roger Bannister was included. Mum wasn't included," Armstrong said, an edge of anger to her voice. "And there were people no one had ever heard of, like an obscure darts player from somewhere." She had turned off the program in anger.

Armstrong asked her mother once if she thought she was Bannister's equal. "And she said, 'Well, you know what? He had all of those pace makers and they prepared for it and it was this big thing. . . . I just went out and did it by myself. So do I think I'm his equal? No, I think I'm better than he is.'"

Bobbi Gibb running the Boston Marathon in 1968 (Jeff Johnson)

4 : But Definitely Not a Marathon ...

March 1966, San Diego, California

BOBBI GIBB'S BODY was screaming. Not screaming in the metaphorical sense, like when her muscles and bones and joints ached after a long run through the forest. No, her voice was filling her small house.[1] She had just read the letter she'd been awaiting impatiently for for weeks, from the Boston Athletic Association. In it, the race director, a guy named Will Cloney, had informed her that not only was she not allowed to register for the Boston Marathon that spring because it was a men's division race, but that the longest sanctioned women's race was just one and a half miles.

Then he made a point of adding that she was not "physiologically able to run twenty-six miles," because she was a woman, and the organization "would not want to take on the medical liability."

She screamed into the emptiness of her home, where the husband she had recently married was legally considered the head of the household because of his sex, which meant she couldn't open a credit card in her own name, or be listed on the mortgage, even though he wasn't home most of the time as he was in the Navy, deployed in Vietnam. She kept screaming as she pulled her nurse's shoes onto her feet, put a T-shirt on over her black bathing suit and shorts, and left the small house where she'd only lived for a couple of months, since making the somewhat rash decision to get married and leave Massachusetts.

Turning onto the street, Bobbi channeled the weight of the blind fury she felt in her chest into her legs, letting them lead in the familiar loping gait of a long run. She didn't run with a watch or with mileage planned out. She typically just ran on trails through woods, or on the beach, letting her body move and her mind percolate. After running for several hours, the feeling of outrage now eased, she found herself on the beach, jumping into the Pacific Ocean to stare up at the blue sky, an image that always calmed her.

GIBB FELT A calling the first time she'd been a spectator at the Boston Marathon two years earlier. Watching the field of runners, their feet nearly silent as they moved along in sync like fish swimming in a stream, she knew she, too, would one day run the race. Even though she knew it was supposedly impossible for a woman to run so far. In 1966, marathon running was still niche, thought to be nearly impossible even for extreme athletes. But she had to try.

By the time she got the letter explaining her incapability, Gibb already knew she *was* capable. She'd been training for two years, running longer and longer distances. She already could run the length of a marathon.

She'd run forty miles at a stretch earlier that year, and then twenty-five miles the next day! But she also knew that her running, just like her interest in science, math, medicine, and philosophy, made her different, and not exactly in a good way.

Two years earlier, her parents had had enough of her running to and from her classes at the Tufts School of Special Studies, or taking off when she was upset to jog through the woods with the neighborhood dogs for a few hours a day. Her mother liked to remind her: "When I was your age, I was engaged to be married!" And to ask: "How are you going to find a husband running in the woods with the dogs?" She'd called the family psychiatrist, a man who worked in a stuffy office in Cambridge, and booked Gibb weekly appointments. She didn't feel she had a choice, so Gibb would sit in the psychiatrist's plush office and tell him all about how much she loved running, and how fascinating she found her science classes, and how she felt at one with the Earth when she slept outdoors, something she did most nights.

"Do you like to inflict pain on yourself? Is that why you run?" he'd ask her. And: "What about these pathological feelings of oneness with the universe?"

Gibb would respond with her typical enthusiasm, explaining how running didn't hurt, it actually felt great—it relieved that itchy feeling in her legs, and the outrage in her heart when she thought about all the things women were told they couldn't and shouldn't do. And she told him all about how a oneness with the universe wasn't pathological, it was a fact. "Where do you think the atoms in your body come from?" she'd say. "They come from the cores of stars. Isn't that incredible? . . . That's just miraculous!"

He'd just shake his head and scribble in his notebook.

When Gibb agreed to marry her old friend Will, in a spur-of-the-moment decision while he was home on leave from the Navy, she saw it as an opportunity to escape the psychiatry appointments, her

overbearing parents, and maybe even a traditional marriage arrange-
ment, as Will had been the one to introduce her to long-distance running
in the first place. When she left her home in suburban Boston to join
him in San Diego, where his ship was based, she thought she'd outwitted
them all. They probably thought those sessions with the doctor had paid
off, that she was cured of her delusions and was settling down to a proper
woman's life.

So when Gibb called her parents from the bus station in Boston a
few months later, the night before the Boston Marathon, to say she came
home to run it and could she have a ride back to the house please, they
told her to *sit there and just wait*. She imagined they'd called the family
psychiatrist, that they figured that, this time, she'd really gone off the
deep end.

IN 1966 RADICAL change was marching through the streets. Martin
Luther King, Jr. had led more than 200,000 protestors to gather on the
National Mall for the March on Washington for Jobs and Freedom just
three years before. The fight for civil rights for Black Americans was in
full swing. Young Americans of all races were becoming vocal opponents
to the draft and the rapidly escalating war in Vietnam, which was killing
thousands of young American men and Vietnamese people each year.

But women's rights were still "the problem that has no name,"[2]
according to Betty Friedan's groundbreaking 1963 book *The Feminine
Mystique*. Friedan described the longing and dissatisfaction of those
women of Diane Leather's postwar generation, who had largely gone
back home, leaving wartime jobs and college degrees behind, convinced they were helping to heal the broken family bonds of wartime.
Friedan got some people talking, but the movement that would come
to be known as second wave feminism, or more radically, the Women's
Liberation Movement, was still quiet as Gibb was planning her marathon
run, even as the discrimination they faced became unbearable. Women's

rights were seen as the *next* project, according to the activists at the time. Women who were civil rights pioneers and Vietnam War protestors, or who sat alongside them as allies, were told to wait their turn.[3]

Young women like Gibb weren't just told they couldn't run long distances, they were coming around to realizing how little had changed since the 1920s, when women had constitutionally won the right to vote. Women were still simply not allowed to enter Ivy League universities, and many professions were actively and legally discriminatory, only hiring women as secretaries or typists and requiring that they quit or be fired if they got married. As Gloria Steinem, then a young magazine journalist and not yet a feminist icon, put it in a *New York* magazine article in 1969, "women's opportunities expanded greatly for about 15 years after they won the vote in 1920 (just as Negroes had more freedom during Reconstruction, before Jim Crow laws took over where slavery had left off), but they have been getting more limited ever since."

Take medicine, for instance. While the first woman in the US to earn a medical degree did so in 1849,[4] in 1960 the percentage of doctors in the country who were women was 6 percent, a percentage that hadn't changed since 1910.[5] Medical schools could legally refuse admission to women simply on the basis of sex—and most would limit the number of women they accepted each year to fifteen or fewer.[6] So medicine—the discipline that informs how we as a society understand bodies and what they need, what makes us sick or well, what we can and cannot do—was a domain much like running: almost entirely male.

In fact, the way Gibb was treated, as though she were mentally ill for wanting to do things like run and not get married, would have been eerily familiar to a woman of similar ambition nearly a century before her.

FOR ONE MONTH, Charlotte Perkins Gilman, a physically healthy twenty-six-year-old woman, was not supposed to leave her own bed, let alone the room. Instead, she lay in the dark, unmoving, muscles deteriorating, fed milk and other fatty foods to soften her body. Isolated from her family, friends, books, journals, or any stimulation of any kind, day after day. A nurse came now and then to massage her limbs, rearranging her body to avoid bedsores, as though she were an invalid. A doctor came from time to time to make sure she was being obedient, fattening up, not thinking too hard, and definitely not moving her body.[7]

This wasn't a torture chamber, nor a nightmare, this was a medically prescribed "rest cure," in 1887. The belief held by the medical establishment at the time was that women like Gilman suffered mentally because they had stretched their physical selves beyond their natural roles of cooking, cleaning, caring for children, and the like. So, doctors like S. Weir Mitchell, who prescribed Gilman and many other women a rest cure, believed they needed a hard reset, like we might treat a fussy modem today. "Have you tried unplugging her?"

In her early twenties Gilman had devoted her time and energy to drawing and painting at art school, as well as organizing meetings for women's groups, and securing funding for a women's gymnasium in her hometown of Providence, Rhode Island, so she could expand her physical training repertoire. One of her first loves was the women's gymnasium. While upper-class white women like herself were encouraged to perform calisthenics for exercise at the time, German immigrants were importing the idea of the "gymnasium" and gymnastic exercises designed to increase strength, fitness, and overall health. Gilman discovered a book in her teens that became her bedside bible, William Blaikie's *How to Get Strong and How to Stay So*, which recommended specific strength exercises, and Gilman, a deeply disciplined soul, took them to heart. She attended the gym regularly. "Going twice a week, each day I ran a mile, not for speed but wind," she wrote later. "I could vault and jump, go up a knotted rope, walk on my hands under a ladder, kick as high as my head, and revel in the flying rings. But best of all were the traveling rings, those wide-spaced single ones, stirrup-handled, that dangle in a line the length of the hall."[8] (If you have ever, as an adult, gone back to a jungle gym with monkey-bar-style hanging rings and attempted them, you know how much strength these rings take—they are absurdly difficult.)

Later in life, she reflected: "I never was vain of my looks, nor of any professional achievements, but am absurdly vain of my physical strength and agility." But like Gibb, this strong woman ended up in a room with a doctor who believed she needed to be restricted from her own bodily power.

She received a fashionable diagnosis of the time: neurasthenia, or "nervous prostration," an affliction meaning, essentially, that she'd worn herself out, brain and body. Gilman quips in her own autobiography that those treated for the disease at the time were "the business man exhausted from too much work, and the society woman exhausted from too much play." Gilman, however, was neither. Her "exhaustion," as she described it, came upon her quite suddenly after her marriage—a union that she put off for two years while arguing with her future husband about how she could possibly get married and still live an independent life and have a career [9]—and intensified after the birth of their child.

The nausea, fatigue, and depression that came along with her pregnancy left Gilman unable to focus on anything outside of the home. She wrote in her journals of hope that the fog would lift once the baby was born and she could go back to more of a normal life. Instead, the opposite occurred.

Once the baby came, Gilman was overwhelmed by grief, tears she couldn't stop, and a general feeling of dread. Motherhood and the wifely duties expected of her simply didn't permit the work she wanted to be doing, and as this became clearer, her emotions spiraled still deeper into a depression. She complained to her husband about her loss of strength and identity and about an emotional state that she couldn't seem to control.

Her husband, for his part, found her obsession with changing the world, as opposed to caring for their new family, disgraceful. He'd hoped that becoming a mother would end his wife's quest for independence and instead stir up her innate need to provide domesticity and caretaking.

He attributed her inability to cope to "some uterine irritation." Because of course he did.

If Gilman were my friend today, I'd urge her to talk to her doctor, to seek treatment for postpartum depression, to find a good therapist. I'd also be concerned that her mood had changed so much at the start of a relationship—especially one with a partner who seemed bent on controlling her life.

But health care, medicine, and marriage in the 1880s were not then what they are today. Women of Gilman's class and race were expected to let go of their own ambitions in service of their marriage and children. If they did not, they were often sent to a doctor.

When Gilman sought help from Dr. S. Weir Mitchell for what was likely depression, whether caused by postpartum hormonal imbalance or her dashed attempts to live an independent life while a wife and mother, Mitchell decided that Gilman had done too much, and to heal her, he would attempt to put her body back in what he saw as its rightful place: a weakened, servile state. When women wanted more power than they had in their own homes, the medical community told them they were sick. Then, to "cure" them of this disease, told them they needed to be cut off from the rest of the world, from seeing how capable they truly were—literally, weakening their bodies. The doctors' prophecies fulfilled, many of these women then believed their own weakness and adjusted their ambitions accordingly.

Keeping upper-class white women like Gilman as perpetual patients, pathologizing those who stepped outside the strict boundaries put on gender—and especially womanhood—was in fact, intrinsic to medicine's design.

MARY PUTNAM JACOBI, a doctor who disagreed with S. Weir Mitchell's methods and would later treat Gilman for her anxiety and depression using vastly different ones, found herself in conflict with the medical establishment by her mere existence: Jacobi, an American educated at École de Médecine of the University of Paris,[10] was one of the first women medical doctors in the United States.

It didn't matter that Dr. Mitchell was a central figure of medicine in the 1870s: Jacobi took him on just the same. Whereas Mitchell did not feel the need, in his hugely popular book *Fat and Blood: And How to Make Them,* to go into *why* the rest cure supposedly alleviated anemia, hysteria, and general nervousness, Jacobi published a small volume three years later that detailed a specific treatment for anemia, which she saw many women suffering from at the time. In her book, she detailed eight different cases of anemic women and showed how they reacted to a treatment of a "cold pack," or wrapping a patient in cold, wet sheets. Before and after the treatment she measured the composition of the patients' urine, their heartbeats and temperatures. She concluded that the use of the cold pack could improve their blood supply and help treat their anemia. Her careful experimentation and strict focus were revolutionary, and far more in line with medical research practices of today, but it was difficult for this kind of academic-style writing to make a splash like the work of Dr. Weir Mitchell or Dr. E. H. Clarke's *Sex in Education,* both of which which included huge misleading blanket statements with no scientific proof, just anecdotal evidence.

Perhaps it's not surprising that Jacobi would so specifically take aim at the men in her field whose theories tried to make the case against her becoming a doctor at all. After all, Clarke's *Sex in Education,* which argued that women's menstrual cycles made them too fragile for the kind of education undertaken by men, was growing popular *after* she'd proven she could attend college and medical school, study pharmaceuticals, chemistry, and biology, attend autopsies, work in labs, and write columns in American newspapers about the advancements being made in French medicine. Not to mention that she sat for and passed the four oral examinations required by L'École de Médecine—the last of which she took in the midst of the bloody siege known as the Paris Commune, a radical socialist uprising suppressed by the French army after a few months—all, in fact, without breaks during her periods.

Upon her return to the US in 1871, Jacobi was invited to chair a department at the Woman's Medical College of the New York Infirmary. Though Jacobi would do her utmost to use her scientific mind to ease the way for those who came after her, the path for other women doctors in the US—and for more woman-conscious medicine—would be a long, difficult one.

Jacobi may have been a rebel for the time, but in some ways, she was reconnecting medicine to its roots. Before the formal institutionalization of medicine in the West, women were the traditional healers and midwives in many societies, offering healing techniques and herbal remedies to ill patients. Nearly all women were expected to have at least some working knowledge of medicine in most traditional societies.[11] According to Barbara Ehrenreich and Deirdre English's book *For Her Own Good: Two Centuries of the Experts' Advice to Women,* in the twelfth century St. Hildegard of Bingen showed just how scientific these women already were. In her 1160 book *Liber Simplis Medicinae*, she detailed an encyclopedia of the knowledge of women healers of the twelfth century in Germany, including a list of the healing properties of 213 varieties of plants, 55 trees, including those used to aid in digestion, help ease pain, and treat inflammation and contractions during birth.

But in the fifteenth and sixteenth centuries in Europe, deep religiosity that centered around men as superior beings started to declare these women's work as "witchcraft." Thousands of women were executed, many burned at the stake, in countries like Germany, Italy, France, and England. The charges against them included the ways that these women could actually heal ill people, or that they could offer contraception, or drugs to ease the pain of labor. Meanwhile, men took it upon themselves to become doctors in a way they saw as more appropriate: by studying Christian theology and Plato and Aristotle and, in so doing, often *not* healing the sick. They didn't dissect bodies, experiment, or even see patients while training. As a result, one Oxford-educated doctor tending to King Edward II in the 1300s would treat a toothache by writing on the jaws of the patient "in the name of the Father, the Son, and the Holy Ghost." Another treatment? Touching a needle to a caterpillar, and then to the tooth. "Such was the state of medical 'science' at the time when witch-healers were prosecuted for being practitioners of satanic magic," write Erhenreich and English. "It was witches who developed an extensive understanding of bones and muscles, herbs and drugs, while physicians were still deriving their prognoses from astrology, and alchemists were trying to turn lead into gold."

In the colonial US, formal education lagged, so women healers who brought their own traditions from their European countries often continued sharing this knowledge among women in the new country. They combined knowledge from other immigrants, from Indigenous women who knew the properties of the native plants, and from the enslaved African women with their own healing traditions and knowledge. Even in the 1800s it was common for men and women alike to seek help from women healers when they were ill in America. That is, until mid-century, when men in the US realized that medicine was a potential capitalist venture.

Men who wanted to make their own way financially started to offer medical services, but without the same kind of knowledge of actual healing methods. Instead, they, like the men in Europe who depended on Christian theology for medical wisdom, largely made it up. But in order to outdo women healers, these early "doctors" used drastic measures on patients. Their goal was for their treatments to be shocking enough that patients and their families would be willing to pay for prescriptions.

These totally unhelpful and often harmful treatments—including blood-letting, purges, vomiting, blistering, and enemas—became standard measures of care.

Women were shut out of this system entirely because male doctors determined that the only way to become a doctor was to intern with one, and they didn't take on women. They even pushed to pass laws banning midwives from assisting with births. In some states, similar laws still stand today, banning licensure for certified professional midwives. As this bold new medical institution in the US grew and matured, women were few and far between in medical schools and associations. Women made up just 2.9 percent of medical school graduates in 1915, and by 1930, just one women's medical school remained open.[12]

Soon a problem arose: only treating the elite white upper-class meant a fairly small clientele. Doctors realized they needed to find more ways to treat patients so they could keep their customers routinely coming back. What they needed was a clientele that always needed them, but who could also afford to pay. This clearly precluded the people faced with ill health caused by overwork and rampant disease, predominantly in the lower classes. Instead, these doctors took aim at one group: upper-class white women. After all, they were already convinced these women were innately fragile, a good synonym for "chronically ill," and also they could afford ongoing treatment. Everyone who bought into Dr. Clarke's theories of menstrual incapacitation, Dr. Mitchell's rest cures, and the idea that women were constantly teetering on the edge of sickness because of their inherently weak bodies became part of a centuries-long economic scam to turn healing medicine into a gold mine. But they did almost no real research on these women patients. The anecdotes in their books are nearly all one-offs, based on evidence such as measuring women's breasts to conclude that they would lack fertility.

So when Jacobi decided to head off to Paris for medical school, she did more than just enter the medical field; she set out to change it. She was interested in the kind of medicine the French were exploring because she saw the harm caused by the American medical experiment. Then she built a career proving the establishment wrong. She started with the idea of period incapacitation—Dr. Clarke's widely accepted theory, laid out in his 1873 book *Sex in Education*, that women's health was harmed by not resting during their periods, and therefore they could not be educated in the same manner as men.

Jacobi went at this theory with the scientific rigor she would become known for. Instead of just interpreting patients' diseases as she wished and using anecdotal evidence to make sweeping recommendations for society, she asked women themselves about their health and their periods. In one of the first medical surveys ever completed, she asked 1,000 individuals questions about their menstrual cycles, pain, exercise, their overall health, their education, and their work. She also collected physiological data from a smaller group of them for three months. Her conclusion? Extra rest during menstruation was not necessary for reproductive function and mental activity for women was not dangerous in the least.

Furthermore, she encouraged fellow doctors to consider *all* the women who weren't resting at all during their periods. In the research paper she wrote to accompany her study (that won her a major medical prize when she submitted it anonymously, by the way) Jacobi noted how many women around the world were working in the physically demanding textile industry. Nearly half a million in England in 1871. And one sixth of the female population over the age of ten in the US said they worked in the industry in the 1870 census. She noted in her 1876 paper that those girls were unlikely to be given every fourth week off work to rest during menstruation. "If it be said, it is necessary that women rest during menstruation, we must ask, necessary for what purpose? The preservation of life? Evidently not, since the most superficial observation shows thousands of women of all races and ages engaged in work of various degrees of severity without attempting to secure repose at the menstrual epoch."

In response, medical officials at the turn of the century, like the physical education and track coaches forty years later, simply leaned on their lazy explanation that working-class, immigrant, Indigenous, and other women of color were clearly just made of heartier, stronger, or more "barbarous" stock than affluent white women. Dr. Lucien Warner, a popular medical theorist, wrote: "The squaw of North America and the women of all races who live in a wild and barbarous state are almost entirely exempt from that class of diseases which are the special bane of their civilized and enlightened sisters . . . The African negress, who toils beside her husband in the fields of the south, and Bridget, who washes, and scrubs and toils in our homes at the north, enjoy for the most part good health, with comparative immunity from uterine disease."[13]

Jacobi stuck to what her research showed, though. She wrote. "There is nothing in the nature of menstruation to imply the necessity, or even the desirability of rest, for women whose nutrition is really normal." She went on to give the kind of insight male doctors—who seemed obsessed with quantity, length, and regularity of menstrual flow—seemed to altogether ignore. "The menstrual flow is the least important part of the menstrual process," she wrote. "And arguments for rest drawn from the complexity of the physiological phenomena involved in this should logically demand rest for women during at least twenty days out of the twenty-eight or thirty."[14]

In other words: If you're going to say periods make women too weak to do things while bleeding, then just give them the whole month off, because the reproductive cycle never stops. Jacobi went on to observe that perhaps the supposed illness found in rich white women was due to, well, looking for it. "I think, finally, it is in the increased attention paid to women, and especially in their new function as lucrative patients, scarcely imagined a hundred years ago, that we find explanation for much of the ill-health among women, freshly discovered today."[5] Jacobi published hundreds of research papers over the years, many of which were groundbreaking. And yet her accomplishments would take much more time to work their way through to the general population than the work of some of her more extreme male peers. Nearly a century later, for instance, Bobbi Gibb would be told she needed medical help because she liked to run.

After her month-long rest cure, Gilman reported that Dr. Mitchell gave her a prescription: "Live as domestic a life as possible. Have your child with you all the time. . . . Lie down an hour after each meal. Have but two hours' intellectual life a day. And never touch pen, brush or pencil as long as you live."

She tried to follow his advice, but felt she came "perilously close to losing my mind." Ultimately, she would not follow this bogus medical prescription. She would divorce, move to California. Leave her child with her father for months at a time. She would write books about feminist utopias. Start magazines. Organize for the vote for women. And publish the seminal short story *The Yellow Wall-paper*, about a woman who begins to descend into insanity when she's locked in a room by her doctor husband, seeking to cure her. The story would remain a relevant critique of gendered medicine, and inequality in marriage, for years to come. Later, gratefully, Gilman would seek treatment from Dr. Jacobi.

THE BUSHES GIBB crouched behind near the start line of the Boston Marathon in Hopkinton in 1966 had yellow flowers—forsythia. Spring had been off to a warm start, and forsythia is always the first wave of runners in the marathon of spring blooms.

On that April day, Gibb had never run a race before, she rarely ever even ran on pavement, and she didn't know you were supposed to break in running shoes before putting them to that kind of test. That morning, she'd pulled on her brother's bermuda shorts—they were too big so she tightened them with some brown string—over her black one-piece bathing suit, as sports bras weren't invented yet, and laced up her brand-new boys' running sneakers. A friend in San Diego told her the nurse's shoes she'd been wearing for years to run thousands of miles would be too heavy for 26.2 miles, but they didn't make running shoes for women. Finally, she added a blue hooded sweatshirt, to cover her long blond hair for as long as possible.

Even so, it didn't take long after jumping out from behind the bushes to join the stream of marathon-running men for many of them to recognize that she was a woman. They started to talk with her while they ran. She said she was nervous to take off the sweatshirt, in case someone tried to throw her out once her disguise was abandoned. They said they'd protect her. They said: "It's a free road."

Midway through the race, she stopped being worried about being found out. Instead, she started to worry about her feet, rubbing against the hard new shoes. Blisters bubbled up, burst, bled, and rubbed some more. She didn't drink any water or eat anything during the race. She didn't carbo load the night before. She barely had breakfast.[16] She'd never had a coach, and no one really knew you needed any of that yet anyway. She just remembered how her gym teacher had told her drinking water during exercise would give you cramps. Her blistered feet were in such pain in the last couple of miles that at one point she took off her shoes, running barefoot along the pavement to cool her raw skin, only to stop again to put them back on, because running without them hurt, too. Then, at about 3 hrs and 20 minutes, the equivalent of 7.5 minutes per mile, she crossed the finish line by Copley Square. She finished the marathon, like Stamata Revithi before her. Like so many unknown, unnamed women runners had in the meantime, and like hundreds of thousands of women would do after her. And even with no sports bra, ill-fitting new shoes, no water breaks, and the general belief that she wasn't physiologically capable of doing so, she finished ahead of two-thirds of the men.

In the days after her race, reporters mobbed her, swarming her parents' house, who, though confused at first, eventually conceded they were proud of her barrier-breaking run. Will Cloney, the race director who had denied her application to the race, told *Sports Illustrated*, using Gibb's married name: "Mrs. Bingay did not run in the Boston Marathon. She merely covered the same route as the official race while it was in progress. No girl has ever run in the Boston Marathon." Like so many before him, he ignored the evidence presented.

GIBB RAN AGAIN in 1967. Unbeknownst to her, another woman had been training for the marathon that year, too—in part because she'd heard Gibb had accomplished the feat.[17] Kathrine Switzer ran as a registered entrant. She'd applied as part of a team, with her coach and a couple other runners from Syracuse University, where she went to college. She used her initials K.V. Switzer on her application, and nowhere in the form did they ask for her sex. When BAA race officials Cloney and John "Jock" Semple got word that a woman was running the race, this time with an official race number, they sought her out on the course. Semple attempted to pull the paper number off her shirt himself. Switzer, a nineteen-year-old college student at the time, twisted away from him, while her boyfriend, a hammer thrower and track-and-field coach at her college, pushed Semple to the ground. Switzer finished about an hour behind Gibb, but she finished.

In 1968, five women ran the Boston Marathon—still unofficially. Gibb was tired that year, she told me. She hadn't been training because she'd been taking a full course load back in San Diego to fulfill her premed requirements. Still, she finished far enough ahead of the other women that she didn't realize they were there until she read about them in the paper.

THREE YEARS LATER, Boston still didn't allow registered women entrants. The world was slow to catch up to Gibb. When she went to her medical school interview after completing her bachelor's degree and all her premed requirements at the University of California, San Diego, the interview panel's reaction reminded her that those headlines she'd made hadn't changed everything after all. "They said I was too pretty to go to medical school and that I'd upset the boys in the lab," she told me. They didn't want to waste a space on her when she wouldn't be able to practice medicine after graduation, as she'd be too busy being a housewife and raising her children. "[It] was infuriating," she said.

Medicine, like running, hadn't changed all that much since the days of Mary Putnam Jacobi, but the stones Jacobi and Gibb had thrown were causing ripples, and they were coming closer and closer to shore.

OFTEN, THE STORY of women running the marathon ends somewhere around here. Gibb snuck in. Switzer got attacked. Then there's a fast forward to 1972, when Boston and New York first allowed women to officially register for the marathon.[18] Or perhaps to 1984, when the first Olympic women's marathon was held—nearly twenty years after Bobbi Gibb first jumped out of the bushes when she heard the starting gun in Hopkinton, Massachusetts. But the years in between, filled with women runners, women scientists, women doctors, women researchers, and those who began to believe what they saw, made all the difference.

In reality, the women kept running. In 1969, three women ran Boston. Sara Mae Berman was the quickest to the finish line of the three. The following year, five women snuck into the race. In 1971, three women, Switzer, Berman, and Nina Kuscsik ran.[19] Kuscsik, a mother of three from Long Island who ran often with her husband, and usually got the faster time, began petitioning the AAU to sanction women's marathons.[20] As more women ran marathons "unofficially" and some races began encouraging their presence, the AAU's rules against their registration were starting to seem sillier and sillier. The Road Runners Club of America, a race organizer, grew into an advocate for women's running. They held races with women's divisions and applied for official sanctioning. Their 1970 National Championship Marathon Race held in Atlantic City, for instance, included a women's division, with prizes for the top three women's winners. They advertised the race as sanctioned, but the AAU at the same time insisted a women's marathon could not be sanctioned.[21] The following year, in 1971, the AAU finally increased the distance women were allowed to run in official competition. Not to a marathon, though: to ten miles.

An Earth Day marathon held in New York's Central Park in 1971 organized by the Road Runners Club included women with official race numbers again. After which, one AAU official told the press the women were "not sanctioned," and for good reason. "If we just allowed women to run the marathon and one dropped dead, who would be responsible? There is a historic thing that says a properly trained man can run this thing with no after effects. There's a 2,000-year precedent," Rudy Sablo, secretary-treasurer of the Metropolitan AAU club, told *Newsday* at the time.[22]

WHILE WOMEN SNUCK into marathons on the East Coast, in southern California a college student taking a track class asked her instructor why she wasn't allowed to run around the track in competition more than once. Barbara Drinkwater, the physical education teacher, wasn't actually sure.[23] But her other job at the time—working at the Institute of Environmental Stress at University of California Santa Barbara as a data analyst and experiment designer—made her curious about the answer. Drinkwater had a PhD in sports psychology, but was starting to be interested in physiology, too.[24] So she went to the library and looked up the studies on women and long-distance running, the ones that the AAU and IAAF always pointed to to deny women's long-distance events, the ones that said that women couldn't tolerate heat, that their reproductive organs would be harmed, or that they'd become masculinized if they ran too far. Reading those studies as an experiment designer made her question their validity. Perhaps knowing, as an athlete herself, that women were likely capable of running more than one lap at a time, she was able to look for flaws in protocols and methods of those studies—and she found them.

When she'd arrived at the institute in 1969, Drinkwater found an exercise physiology textbook that stated that women hit a physical peak at age fifteen and lost aerobic exercise fitness every year after. Drinkwater realized that the women in these studies, given the time periods they were completed in, were likely sedentary, and the men they were being compared to were not. She couldn't find any research, in fact, on women who were athletes, women like herself. She began designing some of her own studies.

Her first paper, published in 1971, looked at how high school girl track athletes responded to exercise. She found that these runners had higher aerobic capacities than the general population of American children.[25] This study helped Drinkwater determine the best ways to study women runners, how to simulate track practices and events in a lab, and also provided excellent fodder for a larger hypothesis she was forming: that all the data the medical world had about women and athletics up to this point was simply wrong. Like Jacobi before her, she began to seek out her own data to correct the record. After all, if women for decades had been discouraged from even being active, let alone playing competitive sports or running long distances, how could exercise physiology know anything about the differences in aerobic capacity for women and men? Or how far women could safely run? After studying high school runners, she wanted to confront the inequalities she was seeing play out in the sports world: the fact that there was no Olympic race beyond 800 meters for women, for example. So she went to the marathoners.

LIKE MANY OTHERS at the time, Jacqueline Hansen was used to hiding the fact that she was a woman runner. Her family didn't approve. She'd run at dusk, or with her hood up so that people couldn't tell she was a girl. But in 1971, while jogging around her campus at San Fernando Valley State College, she ran into another woman running. She was shocked, since she was the only woman on her college track team (which was coached by the women's basketball coach, as there was only one women's meet per year). The other woman told her she was part of a local running club, with a coach, world-renowned runner László Tábori, and a few other women were part of it. Hansen joined, and while the learning curve of working with a real running coach was steep, she stuck it out.[26] At the end of the year, she went to the Culver City Western Hemisphere Marathon as a spectator, where a teammate of hers was competing. Even though women's marathons still weren't sanctioned by the AAU, Culver City had begun allowing women to register and offered women's division prizes anyway. Hansen had never even heard of a marathon, she told me, but figured "anybody crazy enough to run that far needed a cheerleader." Cheryl Bridges, her teammate, finished that 1971 marathon in 2 hours 49 minutes, setting a new world record for women. "She made it look so beautiful and graceful . . . and easy," Hansen told me. Then and there she wanted to run this race.

The marathon world was shifting just as Hansen was preparing to dive in. The following spring, the Boston Athletic Association announced that a group of women would run the race officially, for the first time in its seventy-six-year history.[27] Nina Kuscsik, the New York housewife and mother of three who had run the race unofficially three years prior, won the first official women's division in April.[28] That December, Hansen ran the race that had inspired her, the Culver City Marathon, and she won it.[29] A friend of hers told her that the Boston Marathon allowed women now and suggested she enter next spring. She'd never heard of the Boston

Jacqueline Hansen
running in 1973
(Jacqueline Hansen)

Marathon, but she already knew she needed to run another of these crazy long races. So a few months later she ran in the second official women's division of the Boston Marathon. She won.

Hansen, training and racing consistently and running about 340 miles a month, returned to the Culver City Marathon in 1974 and set a new world record: 2 hours 43 minutes and 55 seconds. The women running this distance knew these records would continue to fall quickly. The following year, another runner, Liane Winter, beat Hansen's world record in Boston. That October, Hansen ran the marathon in Eugene, Oregon. Before it began she told a friend she was hoping to run 6-minute miles— the equivalent of a 2-hour, 37-minute marathon. She finished about a minute off that pace, setting another new world record.

By 1976, the national running boom was in full effect, and when Hansen traveled for races, journalists and others would ask her, the reigning world record holder, if she was the favorite for the Olympics that summer. But a decade after Gibb first jumped out of those forsythia bushes, there still was no Olympic marathon. "They don't have a marathon for me," Hansen found herself telling reporters. In fact, 1972 was the first Olympics in which women were allowed to compete in the 1,500-meter race. So while women were officially, finally, running 26.2 miles in road races, women track runners were allowed to run less than *one mile* in the Olympics.

"I'm not saying I would have won the Olympics, but I deserved the chance to try," Hansen told me. "So I began to question it then. Naively I thought maybe we could do a letter campaign or a petition or something, never dreaming it would take a decade."

IN 1975, THE same year that Jacqueline Hansen set her second world record, Barbara Drinkwater was presenting some of her first research on women marathoners at a conference in New York. Hansen and many other marathoners had agreed to run in Drinkwater's lab in Santa Barbara, hooked up to oxygen masks, with needles in their arms and rectal thermometers. During the study, they'd run until they hit exhaustion in rooms that got progressively hotter, to test their heat tolerance.[30] Now a group of primarily male doctors and scientists had gathered in New York because the marathon had become so much more popular in recent years, and yet little was known about the sports medicine around it.[31] When Drinkwater presented her research, she was able to show that women marathoners were not, in fact, any more prone to heat stress than men. She also found that heat tolerance had nothing to do with gender, and everything to do with cardiovascular fitness.[32]

"We went through exactly the same procedure with them and found that they were very well able to tolerate heat stress and, in fact, we compared them to males, who worked at the same relative load and in approximately the same environments, our women runners were able to tolerate the exercise longer," she would later say of that work with the early marathon runners. "They had lower core temperatures and they had equal or lower heart rates."

HANSEN ANSWERED THE call every time that Drinkwater rang her to ask her to come to the lab. Even though it was never comfortable, she found the information valuable for her own running. And she had the sense that she was changing things. "I loved being a little dot on her graphs,"

Hansen told me. She could see, as she studied the resulting papers, that she and other women marathoners were populating new charts of what was possible for women.

But even as she and a growing number of other women runners kept running long distances, and Drinkwater and a growing number of sports medicine types kept seeking to chart the truth about women's capabilities, hand-wringing about women running long distances at the highest levels continued. That summer, in Montreal, the IOC committee heard a request for the inclusion of two new races for women for the following Games, the 3,000-meter and the marathon. They were both rejected after only brief discussion.

The women from Boston realized their own experiences weren't enough. Hansen and Kuscisk recruited a group of international runners and advocates to form the International Runners Committee. Kathrine Switzer went on to prove that more women would run marathons if there were more marathons. She headed up the Avon International Runner Circuit, a circuit that set up long-distance runs for women in nations around the world. Far from the days of just a dozen at most women joining the Boston, New York or the Culver City marathon, by 1980, Avon's international road races were booming. In Brazil, 10,000 women showed up to run in one of their races in Rio de Janeiro. In Japan in 1980, nearly 800 women ran a 5K, the first road race for women the nation had ever held—by the following year, Japan was hosting a women's marathon. Avon held three international marathons for women in three years: Atlanta, Georgia, in 1978; Waldniel, Germany, in 1979; and finally, in 1980, runners from twenty-seven countries and five continents competed in the marathon in London, which should have been enough to convince the IOC that the event had global participation.

Before the IOC was set to vote again on whether to include the marathon and a 3,000-meter race, Switzer delivered a report on the state of women's distance running to the IAAF, the international track governing body, to encourage them to support the Olympic inclusion of the women's marathon. Inside was physiological data gathered by Drinkwater and others, and the stories of women—from Gibb to Switzer to Hansen and now from all over the world—who had run the marathon and lived to tell the tale.

Meanwhile, Title IX of the Higher Education amendments, which had been signed into law in 1972 by President Richard Nixon making gender discrimination illegal in all schools that received federal funding, was having a multipronged effect. In the US, girls' sports were becoming more common, and were even mandated by the government at schools over the objections of nervous school administrators and coaches, who wondered how girls could possibly play all the sports that boys play. And graduate and medical schools were no longer allowed to deny women's admission simply because they were "too pretty," or because they might have a baby one day. During the first eight years after the passage of Title IX, the percentage of women medical school students jumped from less than 10 percent to 25 percent.[33]

The evidence was mounting.

AHEAD OF THE 1980 vote for what to include in the 1984 Olympics, to be held in Los Angeles, Arpad Csanadi, the Hungarian physician who led the IOC program commission, said that he was against the women's marathon because there could be adverse medical consequences to the competitors.[34] The Americans on the committee convinced the delegation to delay the vote on the marathon until 1981, when they would meet again in Los Angeles.

Though the Eastern European and Soviet representatives continued to argue against the women's marathon in 1981, the Americans and the IAAF seemed to have finally come to accept that the event was safe. The Organizing Committee's medical director even wrote a report to read at the board meeting that pointed to some of the research being done on women marathoners: that women were not only capable of running a marathon, but "in some respects are stronger than men."[35]

Finally, nearly twenty years after Gibb was sent to a psychiatrist because she liked to run and was told it was physiologically impossible for her to run 26.2 miles, the most important sporting body in the world had admitted that women couldn't just run 800 meters, or one mile, they could run 26.2 miles and complete one of the most difficult, grueling, *masculine* races there is.

The medical research helped change the course of the marathon, but as Drinkwater wrote ahead of the 1984 Olympic Trials for the women's marathon, it wouldn't have existed without the women who ran. "It would be nice to record that research scientists were responsible for debunking the myths inhibiting women from achieving their potential as endurance athletes, but the credit must go to the athletes themselves," she wrote. "The women who persisted in running longer distances in spite of rules, ridicule and even physical restraint proved by example that women could run the marathon." Marathons, after all, are run by individuals, each against their own clock, willpower, and body—but they are also run by a group, they are a tide pulling each person along, when one person has to drop back, or walk, or stop to stretch a tight hamstring, another will move the crowd forward, proving it can be done, inspiring the next person across the line. For every huge field of marathoners, there are hundreds who don't finish. Those who don't, often "hit the wall" around the twentieth mile.[36] In other words, it feels the most impossible just before the end. When you've put in so much work, and it just feels like you've gotten nowhere. Gibb, Switzer, Hansen, Kuscsik, and many other early women marathoners hit that wall, but they all pushed through.

THE DAY BEFORE the 2023 Boston Marathon, I had been looking in the Hopkinton town square for Gibb's sculpture "The Girl Who Ran," because the article I'd read about it online from a few years earlier said that it was to be placed near the spot where she hid in the bushes, a short distance away from the official Marathon starting line. But the town square, the

day before the marathon, was a mess of fencing and tents, trucks install-
ing time clocks, preparation for tens of thousands of runners due to arrive
the following day and then be organized into their racing positions. After
walking through the little square park a few times, weaving in and out of
the fencing, I could find only the statue of George V. Brown, the man who
fired the starting gun of the race from 1905 to 1937 (since then a member
of the Brown family has always done the job). Brown worked in athletics,
including as athletic director of the Boston Athletic Association, for some
twenty years, and was a lifelong Hopkinton resident.[37] He was the one
who moved the race start line to the small town twenty-six miles outside
of Boston a few years after the race began. This history of the event's male
competitors, stretching back to 1897, was well represented. But I couldn't
find Gibb.

The sculpture was turning out to be as elusive as the woman herself,
whom I'd been chasing all over the Boston area that day. She'd assured
me she'd have time to chat in between pre-Marathon events, but texted
me earlier to say it might be better another time, she'd forgotten how
tiring all of the Marathon weekend festivities could be. I'd caught sight
of her at an event at Copley Square in Boston earlier in the day, but she
was whisked off to the next stop by her son soon after it ended. Unable
to find her sculpture by the starting line, I stopped at the Hopkinton
Community Art Center, where I knew Gibb was scheduled to attend an
evening event. At least, I thought, I'd be able to see some of her other
sculptures on display there, even if she was too tired to speak with me.

But after I parked in the little lot and walked toward the building, I
stopped in my tracks. "The Girl Who Ran," the sculpture Gibb herself
created based on her own twenty-three-year-old self as she snuck into
the marathon, stood outside the small community gallery, a nondescript
white building. *Here you are*, I thought. After taking in the rendering, I
headed inside to see if the real Gibb was there, too. I wandered the gallery,
seeing the smaller works by Gibb, mostly figures running, movement

captured in metal, before heading to the room where Gibb was due to speak.

The room was hushed when I walked in, despite a few squirmy young children in the corner who didn't realize the significance of the speaker. Runners, marathon fans, and art enthusiasts gathered around a large table in the back room of the community art center. Several women in the room wore that year's Boston Marathon jacket—a lavender-tinged gray, with muted yellow stripes. Runners wear these jackets throughout the weekend before the marathon in Boston, with a different color scheme each year, and you can get yours embroidered with every year you race, to not-so-subtly broadcast your participation to the marathon-crazed, or to tell everyone how many times you'd already accomplished the feat.

There wasn't much structure to the event. The gallery worker introduced Gibb as a runner and as a sculptor, and asked if she might speak for a bit. The prompt was open ended. But Gibb knew what story everyone wanted to hear. She is practiced at this story. She knew from the moment she first ran the Marathon that the point was the story: a new story about women and their bodies and what they could do. The point was to finish. The point was to do a thing she could point to and say, "See here what I did." At the art-center event in Hopkinton, on a phone call with me later, in her own autobiography, in the children's book about her, in the newspaper images that run year after year to remind everyone of *how far we've come,* certain details come around again and again. Like the bermuda shorts, the bathing suit, the brand-new shoes, the sweatshirt, and the men who saw through her disguise, supporting her endeavor. She remembers, each time the story is told, to include these details.

She often begins by saying something broad, a reminder about the times, that she wanted to end "the war between the sexes." That she just didn't understand why women were told they couldn't run marathons and men were told they couldn't be in delivery rooms while their wives gave birth. (Perhaps another question might be: Why was that doctor delivering the baby always a man?) She knows the power of this story.

She'd been told by a medical professional her running was not normal for a woman. She'd been told by a racing professional she was not physiologically capable of running 26.2 miles. She'd been told by her parents she was ruining her chances of living a normal life, of finding a husband, of becoming a mother. These were truths of the time: and she proved them wrong.

She filed these little pieces of her race away, knowing, it seems, that one day, if she did her job right, they would sound unbelievable. It was as though she realized that the race that so captured her imagination, a few hundred weirdos proving their strength and endurance by running through the suburbs of Boston, would one day become something else entirely: a globally watched event including 30,000 runners, more than 10,000 of them women, as well as nonbinary racers, wheelchair racers, and para-athletes.

It's clear, even at eighty years old, that Gibb has always thought and spoken this way: collecting little images and memories that stand out as significant, connecting the everyday to the biggest of pictures. Her account of the years she spent preparing for the 1966 race is peppered with passages in italics, some that last full pages, the thoughts that fill her head as she goes on long runs: about the makeup of the universe, how life came to be, how gravity works on objects, how our brain connects our thoughts to our bodies, to the air we breathe and the water we drink and the earth we walk upon. She thought often about how our bodies *work*. Gibb saw running, as she told the psychiatrist she was sent to in her twenties, as a way to find freedom and feel at one with the planet we call home, and she saw her act of sneaking into the Boston Marathon as a way to change hearts and minds not just about what women could do in the running world, but in the world in general. "If I could change this false belief about women, I could throw into question all the other false beliefs that have been used for centuries to keep women from having full human and civil rights and developing their potentials," she'd tell me later.

Leaving the event that evening, I took in "The Girl Who Ran" again.

She is striking. But of course she is: it's Bobbi, in bronze. There's her black swimsuit, covered by baggy knee-length shorts, there are her boy's running shoes. Those details that define her life's most well-known story are undeniable. Her hair is pulled back in a low ponytail. Her hands and legs are clearly in midstride, there's movement in the muscles and tendons and bones. But her face, like in the only photo I've seen of Bobbi running the marathon, is calm. Her eyes look off to the horizon, lost in thought. You can almost see the wheels turning behind them, thinking her big thoughts about the war of the sexes, and the way the body works, and what actually makes something alive, and how she is going to finish this run, because she is going to change the world.

Despite the fact that the articles about Gibb's marathon run in 1966 called her a "shapely blonde housewife" who was definitely "not the suffragette type,"[38] and noted that men shouldn't worry because she was headed back to California and her role as housewife, she didn't follow this prescription.

She and her first husband didn't last. After being denied entrance to medical school, she got a law degree, and practiced intellectual property law for eighteen years. She got a job in a neuroscience research lab at MIT during law school, and returned there later to study potential cures for ALS. She brought her young son to work with her because daycare wasn't a thing. She kept sculpting, and painting, having studied art in her early college years. And she continued to ask questions about how the world worked. Though she ran the marathon three more times, she didn't become a professional runner or keep running races—like the majority of marathoners, she just ran on her own time, for her own self, her own joy.

Every day, she tells me later from her home in Massachusetts, she still gets that itch in her legs, telling her it's time to go, to run in the woods and see the beauty of our planet, and think about what else people don't take the time to notice.

"Little" Mary Decker, 1974,
15 years old (*Track & Field News*)

5 : But Only If You Train Like a Man

ON AN UNBEARABLY hot summer day in 2022, I arrived in Eugene,
Oregon, with my family. We'd decided to stop on our way to our annual
summer vacation spot, Ashland, Oregon, on the California border. Steve
Prefontaine was on my mind—how could he not be? His name is seemingly ever-present in the town. There's the statue of him outside the Nike
store. There's the cross-country loop trail named for him and his contri-
bution to Eugene becoming a running town. There's the Hayward Field
stadium with the annual track meet named for him. There's the rock, too,

which his car crashed into in 1975, killing him at just twenty-four years old—even at that young age, he was already a legend in his own right.

I grew up hearing about Pre. He was a few years older than my parents, who both spent their formative years in Oregon. They knew people who knew him. As far as they were concerned, Pre was one of them. The tragedy of his story hangs over this city that was his second-home, known to insiders as TrackTown, USA.

My family and I walked the perimeter of the newly remodeled track stadium, which had just that week hosted the first-ever track and field world championships in the US—there in little Eugene, population 175,000. The same spot where Pre ran and made a town, a state, a country, fall in love with track. I pushed my younger son's stroller while we peeked through fences, taking in the enormity of the stadium and sweating in the summer heat. The stadium is huge, made of shiny white metal. A behemoth television screen looms over the track. It's akin to an NFL stadium, but all for track. Athletics is serious business here, the structure confirmed, and a lot of that is due to Steve Prefontaine.

But another athlete was on my mind, too, one who still lived here in Eugene, who held more titles than Pre ever did. The only runner to collect more American records than Pre. She and Pre were friends. He was the reason she moved to Eugene in 1979, four years after his tragic, untimely death.

August 10, 1984, Los Angeles Coliseum, Olympics
MARY DECKER, THE all-American girl with her lithe body, tanned skin, blue eyes, and perfectly coifed, bouncy blond hair, is finally on her way to Olympic glory, in her hometown of Los Angeles in 1984.

Decker, the twenty-six-year-old American favorite, and Zola Budd, the South African teenager running for Britain due to a loophole in the sanctions against South Africa's apartheid, had the worlds' eyes upon them. The two runners had been set up in the press as rivals for the

Olympic gold in the 3,000-meter race, making its debut at the Games for women. [1]

By the time the pack is at the first curve, Decker's at the front of the race. While her face remains calm, she must see Budd at her shoulder. The two superstars run nearly side by side for a half a lap before the petite Budd, who famously ran barefoot, takes the lead, passing in front of Decker and pushing to the inside of the lane. Decker speeds up and tries to maintain her inside position at the same time. But with Budd firmly in front of her now, at the 1,730-meter mark, they collide. Decker's legs tangle up in Budd's for an instant, before she falls to the ground. She's immediately bereft, her face a picture of grief as she turns from the ground to see the pack of runners, and her Olympic dreams, pass her by. She's also in pain. She's pulled a hip stabilizer muscle in the fall. Neither Decker nor Budd, both favorites, medal that day.

And neither would ever live the moment down.

DECKER WAS LIVID after the race, giving an interview in which she blamed Budd directly, as though the teenager had taken Decker's medal away on purpose. Budd was vilified in the press, to the point that she needed armed security on her journey home. "Zola was taken out of the airport under a police guard because of death threats we believe came from the United States," a Heathrow airport spokesperson said.

When people think of the tragedy of Mary Decker now, they think about her young face, twisted in agony as her red uniform blaring USA across the chest lay on the bright green grass inside the Olympic track. The towering Los Angeles Coliseum arches that surround the stadium add an air of Grecian drama to the event. Her straight white teeth are bared as she seems to let out a cry of inner pain. Her styled, streaked blond hair haloing her head in the grass, dark eyelashes scrunched and teary. People remember the fall. They blame Budd for not passing Decker with enough space between them. They watch the replays for evidence that Budd tripped Decker on purpose. Some think Decker disregarded the proper technique for passing Budd once she'd taken the lead over. The fact that the race ended how it did, however, was universally tragic.

But Budd was far from Decker's biggest foe when it came to an Olympic medal. Decker would hold middle-distance track records for decades to come. There were other chances at Olympic glory. Her own body was the bigger problem. Or maybe *her body* isn't the right way to put it. Her sex—as a female athlete, and the way she was trained before anyone knew anything about how to train women athletes—was the problem.

WHEN THE PHONE rang for Decker in high school, it was often her friend, Steve Prefontaine, on the other end. Decker and Prefontaine met for the first time in 1973 while the two were competing in Europe during the summer tour season. Over the six-week trip, Decker turned fifteen, and won all but one of her races.

"Pre felt I was very talented, but that because of all the workouts I was doing and all the racing, and the pressure on someone that young, I think he was just very concerned about 'burnout'—that was the term he used," Decker told Tom Jordan for his book *Pre: The Story of America's Greatest Running Legend*.[2] Prefontaine took Mary under his wing then. On those regular phone calls he would ask how much she was running, check on how her training was going. Just before he died, he tried his best to get Decker's mother to move the family to Eugene so she could train with Bill Bowerman, the legendary coach at the University of Oregon who revolutionized the track program there and was a cofounder of Nike.

Pre, a "brand ambassador" for the fledgling shoe company (in those days, to remain qualified for the Olympics, athletes had to remain "amateurs" so couldn't be paid directly in sponsorship deals), sent her a whole box of Nike prototypes.

At the time, Oregon was the epicenter of a radical shift in the way runners (at the time, men) were being trained. Bowerman was obsessed with the idea that training wasn't actually about running as many miles as possible as fast as possible. He recognized that rest was necessary for elite athletes to recover, long before this was borne out by sport science. One of his biggest tasks was to get the runners under his direction to slow down, to not always run at 100 percent, and to take days off. But for many competitive runners, this can be a tall order. [3]

FOR DECKER, THE concept of rest, and slowing down, was an especially difficult one to grasp. She'd been essentially training like an Olympian since she was about thirteen.

Mary Decker wasn't raised on soccer teams or wearing Nike shorts sold in the girls' section like young people are today. Decker was born in 1958 before the passage of Title IX led the way to girls' sports in schools. But by 1970, she stumbled upon a burgeoning scene: recreational jogging. One Friday, while living in Huntington Beach, California, Decker and her best friend got a flier announcing that weekend's parks and recreation department activities. One of the activities was a community cross-country meet. "Neither of us knew what cross-country was. We had no idea it had anything to do with running," she told the *Los Angeles Times* decades later. But eleven-year-old Mary Decker happened onto her life's path that day. While her best friend didn't finish the three-quarter mile race, Decker won it outright. [4]

The following weekend, she entered a city race. She won. Then there was a county race. She won that, too. These wins led her to join a local track club, the Long Beach Comets.

Within a year, in 1971, she ran the fifth annual Palos Verdes Marathon. At twelve years old, she was the first woman (girl?) to cross the finish line, but perhaps that wasn't saying much—this was still a year before Boston approved women entrants. A newspaper article describing the race, and the increase in popularity for running in general in the 1970s, notes that

600 people ran this marathon, and just half of them finished, a sign of the infancy of casual running at the time. "There were people of all ages, and yes," the reporter writes, "even a few women."

This article focuses on the manliness of the marathon entrants, and the winner, who was, indeed, a young man about to be married, proving the marathon would *win you the girl*. The fact that a twelve-year-old girl not only entered and finished the marathon but beat all the other female runners and set a world record (even unofficially) for her age group merited just one sentence.[5]

At thirteen, in 1972, Decker broke a world record for her age group in the 800, 2:12.4 seconds, faster than any of the women who first ran the race in the 1928 Olympics. She also ran a sub-five-minute mile at the same age.[6] She ran times that would have qualified her for the US Olympic team that year, but she was too young to compete.

Within a couple of years, however, Decker would become known and beloved by the media. Articles would pour in about "Little Mary Decker." And this adjective, *little*, would follow her around, even as an adult.

By fourteen, her body had become an object of scrutiny, looked at under the microscope of the press: "Miss Decker is not a likely looking specimen for such achievements. She stands a fraction over 5 feet and weighs 83 pounds. She seems almost frail," an article in the *Los Angeles Times* notes.

The photo that accompanies the article shows a young girl embracing her young girlhood despite her athletic prowess. Her light brown hair is pulled into two low pigtails. Braces cover her smiling teeth. The piece makes sure to note that she loves running because she's making friends. And she's a "little gem with sewing."

Her smallness, her girlish frame, her frailty, became a media obsession. By that summer, Decker was proving herself on the international stage. In June, she won the 800 at the Pacific Conference Games in Toronto, against competitors from the US, Canada, Australia, Japan, and New Zealand. The Associated Press called her "a wispy 14 year old," and noted that at five feet and a quarter inch tall and eighty-six pounds, she is "the smallest and youngest competitor" at the event.[7] Later that summer, her pigtailed hair and braces-filled smile would grace the cover of newspapers and magazines around the country as a kind of athletic hero for democracy when she beat all the Russian competitors at the World University Games in Moscow in August. The *Los Angeles Times* (her hometown paper) trumpeted: THE GIRL WHO BEAT THE RUSSIANS— LITTLE MARY DECKER SUDDENLY VERY BIG IN WORLD OF TRACK. But the story that accompanied this sports achievement wasn't about the race at all, but about confirming Decker's young, feminine, small persona. Decker, the reporter wrote, "would like to be a typical 15 year old, bumming around barefoot in cutoff jeans." She babysits. She sews. She eats spaghetti before races. And the reporter was sure to note: She is only five feet tall. "Just a frail little thing."[8]

On the same page, just above the article on the sports page, is a reminder of the times Decker was running in: a preview of the Battle of the Sexes tennis match between Bobby Riggs and Billie Jean King, "the ferocious feminist." The article was clearly Riggs' doing. It reads like a back and forth between the two athletes, but King is never actually quoted directly, Riggs speaks for her. "She's got a bigger mouth than I have . . . She's a women's leader and she's really conscientious about that. Says she's playing for a cause. I'm the leader of the anti-lib movement and I've got to play for all those guys around the world who feel like I do. So I hate her."[9]

Such was the world of sports—and perhaps the world at large—in 1973. The "women's lib" movement was underway, but despite King's best efforts, sports remained almost entirely a boys' club.

The following summer Decker beat the Russians in the 800 again. Nearly immediately, she was faced with her first major running-related injury, a stress fracture in her right ankle. X-rays of Decker's legs after her injury showed not just the ankle injury, but multiple stress fractures.[10] Then, Decker's body changed. She went through puberty, in front of the whole world. At sixteen years old, Decker held three world indoor records: for the 800-meter, 880-yard, and 1,000-yard races. LITTLE MARY ISN'T LITTLE NOW, reported Dick Draper at the *San Mateo Times*. "Miss Decker, a 16 year old who crashed onto the track scene as a 4-6, less than 100 pounds teeny bopper and subsequently set three world standards is now a more substantial 5-5, 110."[11] Never mind that she was just about five feet when she first began running competitively, not four six, and never mind that 110 pounds was still *much smaller* than the average American woman of the same height. For the next two years, Decker could barely compete. She felt pain in her legs. Pain in her shins. Pain all the time.

This was when Steve Prefontaine tried to take Mary, seven years his junior, under his wing. "Her future could go up in smoke if she's pushed too hard," he said to *Sports Illustrated* that year. "I couldn't believe her training schedule when I saw it. She could become so sick of running that she'll want to retire at 18."[12]

But getting sick of running wasn't the problem for Decker, or for the many, many young women runners that came after her. The problem was getting sick *from* running. All those training miles, with the hormonal shifts of puberty and the pressure to remain small, light, and fit, equals a body that rebels, that breaks down piece by piece, often to the detriment of the one thing the young person wants to keep doing.

IN THE SUMMER of 1975, Prefontaine died suddenly, in the mysterious late-night car crash that claimed his life and shook the small town of Eugene and the running world in general. The calls checking on Decker, trying to keep her from training too much from a concerned, older-brother figure, trying to keep her healthy, ended.

The 1976 Olympics in Montreal loomed. Now a high school senior who'd been looking forward to this opportunity for four years since she was too young for the prior Olympiad, Decker should have had her first chance to compete on the world stage. But the qualifiers came and went. The pain in her shins was too much for her to even think of competing. She watched the Montreal games from home—teary-eyed as runners she had beaten for years won Olympic medals while she sat on her couch.

A year later, Decker was attending the University of Colorado on a running scholarship, but still in pain, unable to train, and working in a running shoe store owned by Olympian Frank Shorter. One of Shorter's friends heard of Decker's shin plight and suggested she get checked for compartment syndrome, a relatively newly diagnosed condition that he himself had just been treated for.

Many young runners experience shin splints, a kind of stabbing pain in the shins after exercise caused by the repetitive stress of impact on the tissues that attach your muscles to your shin bone. The pain is especially bad if those muscles and bones are in the midst of adolescent growth spurts. Compartment syndrome can feel similar, but worse, and is often caused in young athletes by overtraining. The muscles in your leg live in four separate compartments that connect like puzzle pieces around your tibia bone. When you run, these muscles fill with blood and expand. The tissue around each muscle typically adjusts accordingly. But with compartment syndrome, the tissue doesn't expand, instead the expanding muscle is squeezed in the too-tight sheath, to the point of pressure, pain, and even numbness.

In July, Decker's doctor diagnosed the compartment syndrome, and surgically slit the tissue around her shin muscle so it could expand again as she ran. The pain was gone, and she was racing again. But it wasn't a forever fix. The following summer, she had a second operation, slicing more of the muscle compartments in her shins. At the end of her second year at the University of Colorado, she dropped out to run professionally. She moved, finally, as Prefontaine had tried to get her to do for years, to Eugene, Oregon.

What she found there was a town obsessed with running, the storied University of Oregon (men's) track program, and the fledgling Nike company. What she also found was a boys' club. Athletics West, an organization founded by Nike in 1977, was training all the best male runners of the time. Decker, who wanted to work with Bowerman and Dick Brown, a physiologist for the team, had to go through a hazing of sorts to join. "They kind of bent the rules for me," she said years later. "It was a test to see how women would work in a team situation with men and I was only let in after a meeting where the team's members and their wives voted on whether to let me in."

In that first year in Oregon, twenty-one-year-old Decker was, essentially, back to her pre-surgically-altered self. She ran her first outdoor world record in the mile race, finishing in 4:21.68 in January. By the end of March, she'd set three more world records, in the 1,500, the mile, and the 880-yard race. That summer, even though she won the 1500 Olympic trials, she wouldn't be on her way to the Olympic podium.[13] The Soviet Union, that year's hosts, had invaded Afghanistan, and President Jimmy Carter announced the entire US Olympic team would boycott the 1980 Moscow Olympics as a result.[14]

But even if geopolitics hadn't obstructed Decker's chances that summer, it's likely another injury may have. Decker went on the typical European racing summer tour that year, but during a 3000 in Brussels, her sixth race in eighteen days, she felt a sharp pain in her heel. She dropped out two-thirds of the way through. Doctors found a minor tear in her Achilles. Another surgery. When she resumed training, the old compartment syndrome pain flared back up. Yet another surgery. She went through all of this while the rules about remaining an "amateur" to participate in the Olympics remained. While Decker and other track athletes, especially on teams like Bowerman's, had found a way to get paid via a complex loophole of trusts held in their name until they were retired from competition, her health care was funded by Athletics West. This was fortunate, as Mary was desperate, going from doctor to doctor and trying any and everything to treat the pain in her legs. Pain and injuries that seemed to stem from the thing she loved most, the thing she was the best at. But the fact remained: the more she ran, the more she got hurt.

The press never seemed to let up on her, whether she'd been through a growth spurt or not: "little Mary Decker" became "frail," "fragile," "made of glass." Her blue eyes and dark blond curled hair completed the image: she was an elite athlete, yes, but also a little porcelain doll—feminine and liable to break with too strong of a touch. By 1981 she was training more with Brown than Bowerman, but both insisted the key to Decker's success, and staying healthy, would be to keep her from overtraining.[15]

"She's genetically gifted. God went zap and her genes came together. After that it's a matter of not allowing her to overtrain and get hurt," Brown said to journalist Jason Henderson. "From the knees up, she's world-class. From the knees down, we live from day to day."

Brown's philosophy was rooted in the one Bowerman revolutionized at Oregon during the 1970s—the need for recovery, for pacing instead of pushing. Brown, a physiologist, took these ideas and evolved them. He kept Decker to less than sixty miles a week in training. She had weekly sessions with a chiropractor and daily massages to work out the scar tissue in her war-torn legs.

For a time, all of this helped. Decker's best year of her already illustrious career was 1982. She set four world indoor records at the beginning of the year and broke her own indoor mile record three separate times. That summer she blasted through the outdoor world mile record, setting a time of 4:18.08—more than two and a half seconds faster than the previous mark, held by Lyudmila Veselkova of Russia.

After five races in three weeks in Europe, she headed home to Eugene, where a 10,000 meter race was being held at Hayward Field. Mary wanted to run, but Brown was hesitant. She hadn't prepared for a race of this length specifically, and she was due a rest break. In the end, he said she could run it, as a kind of test, but only if she wore road racing shoes instead of spikes, since they were more supportive; if she dropped out if she felt any pain; and if she'd take at least a week off the track afterward, for recovery.

She ran the whole race, in heavier shoes than her competitors, and set another world record: 31:35.3, besting the previous record by 42 seconds. By the end of that year, Decker held every American record from 800 to 10,000 meters. The next year she'd just add to her totals, ending the 1983 season with thirty-eight races won, and with eight world records in just two years. Then, in the inaugural World Athletics Championships in Helsinki, Finland, at the end of the season, Decker pulled off a seemingly impossible feat, one never repeated since: she not only won gold in the 1,500, but the 3,000, too. The "Decker Double," as it came to be known, earned her *Sports Illustrated*'s third-ever Sportswoman of the Year honors. (The title is only given to one person per year, so usually it was Sports*man* of the Year, naturally.)

It was on the back of this success that the 1984 Olympics arrived in Decker's hometown, Los Angeles, and the fateful collision with Zola Budd robbed her of what many saw as the gold medal she was owed. Indeed, this was a tragedy. But by then, it was far from the only Olympic miss for Decker.

After the compartment syndrome that kept her out in 1976, the boycott in 1980, and the infamous fall in 1984, she qualified again in 1988, but finished a disappointing eighth in the 1,500 and tenth in the 3,000—some reports noted she'd been ill, but others said she'd been dealing with injuries again. Between 1989 and 1990 she went through four separate surgeries on her Achilles tendon. She came back to competition in 1991, winning a 1,500 against a national favorite,[16] only to strain her calf and be out again for weeks, missing the World Championship qualifiers.[17] But she fully planned to make the 1992 Olympic team for the 1,500, only to be edged out by three younger runners in the qualifiers; she finished

Mary Decker, left, running the 3,000 at the 1984 Olympics in Los Angeles (USOPC)

fourth.[18] She tried for the 3,000, too, but after setting the pace most of the race, she finished sixth, not enough for another Olympic trip.[19] Another missed opportunity—whether because she was dealing with her seemingly perpetually injured legs, or because at this point she was thirty-four years old and had been training intensely for more than two decades, who could say.

Two years later, Decker started working with Alberto Salazar, one of the original members of Athletics West, who had been a marathon record-breaker. Salazar was known for pushing himself in training to extremes. At twenty-three years old, he'd won the Boston Marathon, drinking almost no water and losing ten pounds in water weight during the race. At the finish line he collapsed. Paramedics had to pump six quarts of saline into his veins to revive him.[20]

Decker turned to Salazar for help—she and her surgically mutilated legs clearly weren't afraid of going to extremes—to stay injury-free long enough to have another Olympic medal chance. So Salazar and Bill Dellinger, another famed Oregon coach, took Decker on, putting her on a restrained training timeline. While all her coaches had tried over the years to keep her mileage down to help address the injuries, these two also tried to keep her from training *too hard*. "Back [in the 1980s], everything was so much more intense from the start," Decker told *Runner's World* in 1996. "This time I'm trying to get stronger as I go. That way, when I get to the intense stuff, I should be strong enough to keep from breaking down. At least, that's the theory."[21]

But just six months before the Olympic trials, she was hurting again. She'd tell multiple reporters later that it hurt just to stand up to do the dishes, let alone go for a jog. Still, somehow, by June, she qualified for the Olympic 5,000. But during the Games, Decker didn't even make it out of her first heat. She placed seventh. Months later, the International Amateur Athletic Federation would announce that her urine test at the qualifiers was above the allowed testosterone to epitestosterone level, a potential sign that she was doping with testosterone. She threatened a lawsuit, saying the test was flawed and didn't account for fluctuations in testosterone caused by menstruation, or taking the birth control pill. By the end of the year, USA Track and Field had suspended her, then cleared her name after a panel review. But the international governing body disagreed, imposing a two-year retroactive ban from when the drug test was taken, stripping her of a silver medal she won in the 1997 World Indoor Championships.

She fought back, suing the IAAF in 2000, in part because she had always been vocal about running drug-free, and in part because she felt her career wasn't quite done. Still clinging to the dream of an Olympic medal, with her eyes toward the 2000 Olympic team, when she would be forty-two years old, she tried a last-ditch effort to get her legs healthy again: a surgery that rerouted the tendons to her toes, so the lower legs suffered less impact while she ran.

"It took close to a year until I could walk straight, let alone jog," Decker said in 2013. "I went through several years of physical therapy, strength training; I tried everything. Nothing gave me the strength in my lower legs again. With tendon rerouting, I can't flex my toes. I've always been a toe runner, so it completely destroyed the way I run. I can't run. I can jog."

Even jogging, though, resulted in that old foe: stress fractures. So in 1998, Mary Decker lost her life's love, obsession, and destructive enemy. She would not make the 2000 Olympic team. She would never win an Olympic medal. She would never, really, run again.

DECKER'S CAREER RAN straight through a turning point in women's sports in the United States. That marathon she ran on a whim, at twelve years old, was just five years after Bobbi Gibb snuck into Boston. When she started running, Decker would get stared at while jogging on the road. Her coaches had her do most of her training on a track because running around the streets of Southern California when you were a girl simply wasn't done. She discovered running through a parks department cross-country run, because school-based sports programs still weren't available for girls. But Title IX passed when she was thirteen, and school sports began including girls' teams in the following years. Even still, as a professional, she had to convince the wives of the other athletes on the Eugene team that she wasn't a threat to their husbands. Nike's first shoes were made by Bill Bowerman and Phil Knight in a waffle iron—Pre sent her some of the first versions. While Gibb had to run in a swimsuit and nurse's shoes, Decker wore swooshes on her feet. By 1977, she could wear a sports bra under her racing kits, because they'd finally been invented. Though she won the first marathon she ran, as a teenager, she barely got a mention in the press. Within a matter of years, she was gracing the cover of *Sports Illustrated.*

During Decker's lifetime an entirely new running world had been born: some women, finally, were not only allowed to run, but even given some tools. Still, as physical fitness and recreational jogging became more widespread, as sports bras and running shoes were made, women were outside the norm in a very important respect: the field of sports science. Though this area of study can be dated back to ancient Greece and became widely respected in the nineteenth century, the extent of research like Drinkwater's focused on women was still miniscule, and often was focused on proving women could run, not on how they could run better, farther, or faster.

Instead, the prevailing running wisdom was based on an equation. Runners are nothing but mass trying to move, at least when it comes to physics. Mass times acceleration equals force, says Newton's Second Law of Motion. This theory has driven running coaches for decades to push an oversimplified agenda: to go faster, slim down. To follow orders, many runners, already obsessive about their performance, eat less, and run more. Soon, this became a terribly dangerous combination, especially for young women runners.

IN THE SUMMER of 1980 in Tucson, Arizona, Leslie Heywood was a state-ranked runner. She competed in those two laps around the track—the same two that Florence MacDonald and the other Olympians ran, and then were banned from running, back in 1928. She also competed at longer distances. She regularly ran dozens of miles a week. She and her teammates would log 1,000 miles every summer vacation by racking up at least ten miles a day in the desert heat.

Born less than a decade after Mary Decker, her exposure to sports reads as though she's been born into a different century. At her high school, there was a girls' cross-country team and track team. She competed at district, state, and national competitions.

But some things were still much the same. Heywood and her coaches didn't really see her as a girl athlete. In fact, they had her train with the boy's team. She was too good, they seemed to think, to be a girl. "I want her to stop thinking like a girl runner . . . Not that I want her to stop being a girl, but because I want her to work and think like an athlete. Right now she's just one of the guys," one of Heywood's coaches told the local paper.

For Heywood, though, as much as she thought of herself as separate from the girl runners, her girl-ness was never unnoticed, she writes in *Pretty Good for a Girl*, her 1998 memoir of her high school and college running days.[22] Her predatory coach certainly noticed, as did the newspaper photographers following her around with cameras at practice, snapping photos of her achievements, the nationally qualifying times at two different distances, and of her lounging in the grass in her running clothes, her blond hair loose. Leslie felt the girl-ness, too, though she tried to outrun it. Like many girl runners of the era, she treated her body like a machine that needed to shed its femininity to succeed. She pushed herself to the absolute extreme, thinking that if she cut more calories, skipped more meals, she'd be thin enough to run faster. Thin enough to look like a girl, while acting like a boy, because girls—still—weren't supposed to run, not like her, anyway.

> . . . Make us like those silly prom girls
> Who worried about Ralph Lauren dresses
> And J. Renee shoes, the way
> Their hair curled down their backs
> And coiled up the gawking men,
> The men that we, the women's track team,
> Tried so hard to be, our breasts run off
> By months and months of eleven miles
> Twelve thousand feet straight up
> Kitt Peak, our biceps
> Hard as buttons, our backs and flanks
> Muscled like horses, our skin tanned deep . . .

Decades later, Heywood would publish this poem, and many others, in a collection called *The Proving Grounds*. You can read here, in her memory, that she still has trouble associating running, muscles, her own body, with being a girl.[23]

BEFORE PUBERTY, GIRLS are usually taller, bigger, faster, and stronger than boys of their same age. But instead of celebrating those things, society often makes girls feel badly about it. Raewyn Connell, who has studied the sociology of gender for decades, wrote in her 1987 book *Gender and Power* that we define young girls as "weak" and "fragile," even when we can plainly see they're larger than their male peers before puberty. These messages can lead to girls putting in work to actually change their bodies to fit those descriptors, especially after puberty.[24] Connell's observations are from thirty-six years ago, not long after Heywood had to give up running. Her body's immune system began to flare from the damage she had done trying to be smaller and lighter while also pushing her muscles and bones and immune and nervous systems to their limits. Her doctor told her she had to stop running. He said she had mixed connective tissue disease caused by extreme stress. He said her joints looked like the joints of a fifty-year-old, when she was just nineteen. If she kept running, it was likely her vital organs would be next to shut down, he said. Heywood was in shock leaving the doctor's office. "My mother was right: I'm just a girl after all. I can't hack it," she thought at the time.

Boys, on the other hand, who are told most of their lives that bigger, stronger, and taller bodies are good and masculine, largely call puberty a positive bodily experience. Most boys' body dissatisfaction decreases as they move toward adulthood and they gain mass and size, which moves them closer to what society tells them they should look like.[25] For runners, the changes puberty brings affect boy and girl runners in opposite fashions. Young women runners start to see less improvement each year as they go through puberty, because an increase in fat stores causes sudden weight gain and a bump in estrogen can lead to less muscular definition. While young men see an increase of red blood cells, bone strength, and a big stretch in height. Young men and young women both do get faster during the years of puberty and just after, however young women runners tend to seem to be slowing down, mostly because they're often just as fast or faster than young men of the same age before puberty. Then—in relation to young men runners—they're improving less each year during their late teens. Once they get into their twenties, women runners improve faster than men do.[26] If, that is, they can stay in the game long enough to get there.

The vast majority—70 percent—of girls after puberty report a preference for being thinner, and are more vulnerable than boys to psychological stress, depression, and eating disorders.[27] They also begin to refrain from activities that they fear might make them even bigger, or stronger, or more "masculine."[28] Girls are still two times more likely than boys to quit youth sports altogether by age fourteen[29] and are more likely to be more sedentary in general than boys by age eleven.[30] While this may seem like a minor problem to some, sports and exercise during childhood and adolescence are more than just about having fun, learning to play on a team, or improving mental health (all important things!). Youth exercise actually impacts our body's size and capability of strength for the rest of our lives.

More than one-third of the human skeleton is formed during a four-year adolescent window, the two years before and after puberty. Children who engage in six minutes per day of moderate to vigorous physical activity have significantly higher bone strength by age seventeen.[31] Our bone density peaks in our twenties and generally declines from there.[32] So when girls become more sedentary at age ten than boys, they set themselves up for a lifetime of weakness—and illness.

Older women are far more likely than older men to experience osteoporosis. In fact, 80 percent of the Americans with osteoporosis are women. Women with lower peak bone density in their twenties, the girls who didn't get enough exercise in their adolescence, are more likely to develop osteoporosis as they age. Half of women over age fifty will break a bone due to osteoporosis, often in the hip or spine, which could result in serious disability or lack of mobility—that means less independence and worse health as you age. In many European countries women are in the hospital for osteoporosis more than for any other ailment.[33] Broken bones as you age also bring higher morbidity rates.[34] A broken bone can be what ends your life.

When we tell adolescent girls that they're weaker than boys, that they should restrict their exercise accordingly, that they *should* be smaller, even when they're growing, in order to keep up with the boys, we literally create bodies that are weaker than they could and should be.

When younger women do resistance training in their youth—running, jumping, playing sports, and lifting weights—they're less likely to develop osteoporosis altogether. This is one of the reasons that medical experts have pushed for girls to stay in sports, for kids to get outside and play. It's a public health win. But there's a catch.

Runners like Heywood, like Decker, like countless others, were getting in lots of exercise, but they were also likely taught that equation about mass: that they must be like birds, getting lighter so their bodies could go faster on the track. Many girl athletes, and especially runners, have been taught to focus especially on the smallness of their bodies, not just for the normal male gaze reasons, but because coaches have been telling them that's how they improve their performance. The fact of the matter is, eating disorders, more prevalent among young women than men, are even more prevalent among runners.[35] Exercise dependency—the feeling that exercise is necessary at a higher and higher level and must be chosen over family, friends, and other life commitments, otherwise symptoms of withdrawal will set in—is also more prevalent among runners.[36]

BY THE TIME Mary Decker's bones had gone through countless breaks and Leslie Heywood's running career had ended because she ran for years while starving herself, women like Barbara Drinkwater had some company in the American College of Sports Medicine. After she'd helped prove women could run the marathon in the 1970s, Drinkwater had moved to Seattle and opened her own research facility at the Pacific Medical Center in 1983. Drinkwater would take over the ACSM presidency in 1988.

While working with more and more young women athletes, she began noticing something alarming. Drinkwater had spent her career proving that girls and women were physically capable of running long distances, of playing sports, and yet they were breaking. Literally. Young women runners, gymnasts, and ballet dancers were suddenly showing up in doctor's offices and emergency rooms with bones so brittle they'd cracked under little force. Drinkwater recognized that these broken bones looked a lot like osteoporosis—which sets in for many women postmenopause—and saw a pattern. Menopause is the end of menstruation. And many young athletes had accepted missing periods as a normal part of training.

As she began to study the prevalence of amenorrhea, or a menstrual period that has stopped showing up, in young women athletes, she found that the rate of the problem was alarming. One researcher in Palo Alto had begun a study on amenorrhea in the Stanford women's track team and had to go outside the team to find a control group because every female athlete on the team was currently not menstruating.[37] Drinkwater published multiple studies that showed the correlation between the loss of the menstrual cycle and lower bone density.[38, 39] Those bone injuries that were often just written off as part of running, especially for girls, suddenly seemed to have a different cause. "When you miss six months to five years of periods, the chances are very good that the estrogen levels are low. Any time you have low estrogen, it is highly probable you're going to see bone loss," Drinkwater told the *Chicago Tribune* in 1992.[40] The question then became, why were these women's menstrual cycles stopping so often? Amenorrheic young athletes' blood work showed hallmarks of another epidemic impacting young women at the time: disordered eating.

As Drinkwater began to discuss her research with others in the community, she heard these three concerns: bone injuries, amenorrhea, and eating disorders, come up again and again and again. So she called a conference in Washington, DC, in 1992 to see if researchers, doctors, athletes, and coaches could connect the dots. "We all seemed to have the same story. It wasn't just a coincidence that these three things were occurring together," Dr. Aurelia Nattiv, a sports medicine doctor in California, said years later.[41]

The American College of Sports Medicine issued a paper defining the "Female Athlete Triad: disordered eating, amenorrhea, osteoporosis," the year after the DC conference.[42] Drinkwater, Nattiv, and the other authors noted that a focus on weight as a measure of performance is extremely common in many sports, despite the fact that continued weight loss can often lead to *poorer* performance. "The constant focus on either achieving or maintaining a prescribed weight goal may put the female athlete at risk for developing a disordered pattern of eating. This in turn may put the athlete at an increased risk of developing two associated disorders, amenorrhea and osteoporosis. Alone each disorder is worrisome and can yield considerable disability, but in combination, the triad disorders are potentially fatal," they write.

IMAGINE YOUR BODY as a circuit, sort of like a version of the Operation game board: with little bulbs illuminating over each of the many functions your body is processing even if you're just sitting there doing apparently nothing. One light bulb over your beating, pumping heart. One over your lungs as they pull oxygen in and push carbon dioxide out. Another over your brain, which helps you think, talk, and move your limbs. Another over your skeletal system, working hard to keep your body upright, strong, pulling in nutrients and building bone density from your adolescence into your mid-twenties. Another over your muscles, holding you together, keeping you stable and strong. These bulbs light up more brightly the more you use them. You glow like a Christmas tree when you are enduring a long run or a hard workout, all systems are engaged, using up energy. But when the battery doesn't have enough energy stored to keep all the lights on, it doesn't shut off every single light bulb, not right away. Instead, the circuit shuts down methodically; each light has its own breaker. Because your body has evolved to survive.

In young women, if the battery power is lacking, the first light to turn off is usually the one over your reproductive system; the wisdom of the human body goes, if this body is starving, it certainly cannot sustain a whole other life, so let's save some of that bodily energy there. Off goes the light.

If energy still is lacking, the lights begin to dim over your muscular system, causing fatigue. The brain light bulb might dim as it struggles to focus on anything except what it needs most: more energy in the form of calories. And then that bulb over your bones, building up their strength, goes out, too. Not only do your bones not gain strength, the energy already stored in the bones gets leached out to try to keep your body's most necessary functions going, so the bones become brittle.

If this energy-deprived athlete keeps up their training anyway, running for miles and miles on end, the force on the brittle bones is much more likely to cause fractures. Sometimes these miniscule breaks are caught. Sometimes they're not, and they heal wrong. Or maybe a demanding competition schedule means the breaks aren't given enough time to heal at all. The battery, nearly drained, keeps trying to turn the lights on over the systems, but they all dim: the bones, tendons, muscles, the heart, the brain, the whole system becomes fragile, out of balance, leading to more pain, more of the evolutionary response trying to tell the runner to just stop. The results are physical—injury, pain, bone breaks, loss of menstruation, lack of energy—and psychological—*why am I always injured? Why are my times getting worse? I must need to eat less. I need to get lighter. I need to run more. But I'm so hungry. Something must be wrong with me.*

AFTER THE 1992 conference, the sports science researchers who were focusing on women started to spread the word about the Female Athlete Triad, the triangle of pain hurting women athletes. But the message was easily sensationalized.

TOO MUCH TOO YOUNG ran the front page of the Sunday *San Francisco Examiner* that summer.

A *Los Angeles Times* story asked if there was A HIGH PRICE FOR GOLD? And equated the achievements of female athletes with long-term health risks. "For females training at high intensity levels, the price of a toned body and peak performance may be some potentially serious health problems." [43]

Drinkwater, Nattiv, and the others did their best to push the story of the Triad for the sake of public health. They wanted the information out there that young women athletes need to pay attention if they're losing their periods, and/or experiencing multiple stress fractures, and/or struggling with disordered eating. But the media seemed to spread another message altogether: THE FEMALE ATHLETE TRIAD: MORE PROOF THAT WOMEN AND GIRLS SIMPLY AREN'T CUT OUT FOR ATHLETICS.

The stories they chose to tell nearly always painted young women athletes, and especially long-distance runners, as outsiders, freaks, innately prone to bone breaks and missing periods. The stories seemed to say that, for girls, the act of running, of being fit and athletic and competitive, is, in fact, a precursor to bodily harm. That, sure, some exercise and sports were fine for girls, but parents should watch out that their daughters don't do *too much.*

The narrative got more extreme after the Olympic gymnast Christy

Henrich died of anorexia at twenty-two years of age in 1994. After this, there was an explosion of newspaper articles on young women athletes suffering from eating disorders.[44] The media at the time seemed to be trying to solve some kind of mystery: What kind of girl does this happen to? *Perfectionists. Runners. Gymnasts. Type As.*

The articles make me shudder. All of this blame being put on the athletes themselves, when all those athletes were doing was listening to the messages they were given. Women who grew up in the 1990s, as I did, will be familiar with the messages we received. *Girls are meant to be thin. Are you sure you want to eat that? Are you going to burn it off later? Intense athletes don't get periods. The thinner you are, the more in shape you are.*

And yet the scientific community had already figured out something so important: that losing your period wasn't normal. That thinner didn't mean faster. That bone injuries were related to amenorrhea and eating disorders. And yet, it seemed like no one was listening.

Seven years after the 1992 meeting that named the Female Athlete Triad, the *New York Times* reported that: "experts worry that many female athletes—and a fair number of doctors—hold the belief that amenorrhea is a natural side effect of high-level exercise."

And nearly thirty years later, even coaches at the highest level of the sport were still pedaling the idea that *lighter is faster* to the most elite athletes in the country, to disastrous effects.

MANY OF DECKER'S records would stand for decades. Her former coach, Alberto Salazar at Athletics West, later founder of the Nike Oregon Project, a team with a specific focus on growing American talent in middle-distance running, would continue to search for the next Mary Decker. At one point, it seemed, he found her. "Her name is Mary, oddly enough," Decker told a reporter in 2013. "He thinks she may be the one to break some of my American records in middle distance."[45]

When Mary Cain shot onto the scene in 2012 at just sixteen years old and broke the American high school girl's outdoor record in the 1,500 at the World Junior Championships, many people did compare her to Mary Decker. That same year, Cain signed with Salazar. By early 2013, she'd won gold in the mile race against a field of professionals at the US Indoor Track and Field Championships.[46]

But Cain and Decker would have more than their early success in common. Because even though Cain was born thirty-eight years later, tragedy was still a seemingly inevitable part of being a girl who could run unbelievably fast.

IN 2013, WHEN she was a junior in high school, Mary Cain ran her best event, the 1,500, with a US Junior record of 4:04.62.[47] But after two years as a professional under Salazar, she was running slower. At nineteen, she won a race in early May in 4:15.42. Salazar, though, instead of praising the win, told the *Oregonian* that Cain's slow time was due in part to the windy conditions. He said Cain, who had just completed her first year of college, but was running professionally, would "be down in the 4:07 range," by the following month.[48]

But at the end of May, Cain ran the 1,500 again, this time at the Hoka One Middle Distance Classic at Occidental College in Los Angeles, and instead of a better time, she got a worse one. She finished in 4:16.48, in twenty-fifth place. Salazar wasn't pleased.[49]

A thunderstorm rolled in right after the race, pelting the track with hard raindrops. The runners scattered, seeking shelter. Cain ended up crowding under a tent with many of the other runners, coaches, and staff. Salazar laid into her there, not about her performance, but about her weight. "He yelled at me in front of everybody else at the meet," Cain later told the *New York Times*. "He told me that I clearly gained five pounds before the race."

In fact, since she'd moved to Oregon to work with Salazar, he'd been seemingly obsessed with Cain's weight. He thought she, at five feet seven, needed to be 114 pounds. Why 114? Cain says he just insisted that was what she needed to weigh to get faster. But when she came to him, at seventeen years old, she already was fast. The fastest girl in America. She was already beating women twice her age in national races. But she needed to get thinner. Less mass meant more acceleration, right? Well, not when you've lost your period for three years, like Cain had. And broken five bones, like Cain had. And fallen into a depression so deep you're cutting yourself and considering suicide, like Cain was. Not when that mass doesn't have enough *energy* to move itself.[50]

Salazar, who had run an entire marathon decades before without drinking any water and had to be revived by paramedics at the finish line, had become a coach who pushed his athletes to similarly unhealthy extremes, all in the name of winning. But when it came to his female athletes, that didn't even work, because he ignored what the science had been clear about for thirty years. He took Cain to the doctor when she told him about her period. The doctor prescribed birth control pills. Salazar told her to take them, and to take diuretics, too, to help her shed "water weight." Despite the fact that Drinkwater and her colleagues had suggested decades earlier that using birth control pills to restart menstruation in amenorrheic athletes won't help build back bone strength—it would just mask the fact that an athlete's battery was drained.[51] The battery needs more power, or the lights will keep going out.

Cain would reveal all of this and more in 2019, to the *New York Times*, years after she'd left the Nike Oregon Project, and Salazar. But she didn't really need to reveal it, did she? Much of what she experienced happened in public, or at least around others. Once she spoke out, other athletes, trainers, and meet directors corroborated her stories. Another runner who'd worked with Salazar, Olympian Amy Yoder Begley, said she stopped training with him in 2011 because of the way he harassed her about her weight. "I was told I was too fat and 'had the biggest butt on the starting line,'" she tweeted, after Cain's story went public. Kara Goucher, an Olympian who trained with Salazar for seven years before leaving him in 2011, the year before Cain joined his team, revealed in her 2023 book that she had been sexually abused by him, as well as routinely harassed about her weight, breasts, and butt. Though Goucher worried about Cain, who had joined the team the year after she left, she didn't think she'd be able to convince her his tactics were unsafe. "I'd be coming at her just trying to convince her to trust me," Goucher told me, which she knew would be difficult when Salazar's tactics weren't so out of the ordinary in the world of track.[52]

Shortly after that May meet and public shaming in 2014, Cain called her parents. She left Oregon immediately and went home to New York. But there was no big investigation into what happened. Ken Goe, a long-time track reporter for the *Oregonian*, noted the absence of Cain in a newspaper article published in late May. "For three days last week, photographer Tom Boyd and I shadowed the Nike Oregon Project during training sessions in Provo, Utah, and Park City, Utah. During that time, Mary Cain was absent." They asked Salazar where Cain was and he gave a matter-of-fact response. "Salazar said Cain has returned to her home in Bronxville, New York, where she is continuing to train. He said they remain in communication, and she still is a team member." Goe goes on to speculate about her performance dip, that of a nineteen-year-old girl. "It's hard to know exactly what is happening here, and Salazar didn't want to discuss it at length. A freshman year of college is a time of change and transformation in many ways. My educated guess is that Cain is in the midst of the process, and it has impacted her running."[53]

OVER AND OVER and over, anyone who has paid attention to the way young women runners have been trained can see the pattern. Thirty-some years earlier, no one seemed to ask any questions when Mary Decker was experiencing stress fractures almost constantly, either. Even when the only descriptor the press could find for her was "little" or "fragile" or "glass." *Sports Illustrated*'s profile of her noted that in 1983, after her divorce, her weight fell dangerously low. But then, the research hadn't been done yet saying these might be warning signs of harm.

Instead, the press praised Decker's relationships with her coaches to the extreme, assuming they were doing all the right things, even though no one knew what those things should really be for a woman runner. While Dick Brown did urge caution in Decker's training runs, he also obsessed over certain bodily data, despite the fact that there were no studies that focused on women's performance and body-fat percentage at the time. *Sports Illustrated*'s Sportswoman of the Year profile of Decker is accompanied by multiple photos of Decker's sinewy body. In the caption of one, Brown is assessing Decker. "The coach who has become a father to Decker," it notes, "uses calipers to measure her body fat."

Nike responded to Cain's allegations in the *New York Times* article, saying in the spring of 2018 Cain tried to work with Salazar again. The statement seemed to imply: would she do that if he was so abusive?

Cain responded: "For many years, the only thing I wanted in the world was the approval of Alberto Salazar. I still loved him. Alberto was like a father to me, or even like a god. Last spring, I told Alberto I wanted to work with him again—only him—because when we let people emotionally break us, we crave their approval more than anything."

And Salazar gave a full-throated defense of his focus on weight to *Sports Illustrated* in the aftermath of the Cain allegations. "Because runner weight is inherently tied to performance for elite runners, I saw it as part of my job as an endurance sport coach to help the team's runners understand the impact weight has on performance," Salazar wrote to *SI*. "I had a lot of frank discussions about weight with all of my athletes— both women and men."[54]

That old trope again.

Salazar won't coach again. He was suspended for four years for doping violations. But even before he could complete his appeal of the decision, he received a lifetime ban from coaching from SafeSport for sexual and emotional misconduct, after Goucher testified against him.[55, 56]

But the problem facing young women runners' health isn't just about one bad coach. If it were, we wouldn't hear the stories of young women runners echo in our minds each time another one has a stress fracture, or speaks out about an eating disorder, or is told to go on birth control to restart her period. We wouldn't hear reports year after year of college track coaches using calipers or DEXA scans to measure body-fat percentage, and encouraging extra cardio for the runners over an arbitrary limit, and that they eat only "good food" during race season.[57] We wouldn't hear about how young women runners especially were pushed into disordered eating because their mostly male coaches became obsessed with not just their weights, but how they looked in their skimpy track uniforms.[58] While male and female track athletes have begun to discuss these unhealthy training methods, the extra societal pressure on women to be as thin as possible, and to keep up with their male peers' naturally lower body-fat percentages, lead to women still being more at risk than men for unhealthy eating behaviors and body image. [59]

WHEN KATE ACKERMAN was in medical school in 2000, she was competing on the US national rowing team. She and her teammates felt like they had questions about their training that they just didn't have answers to, like whether they should train differently at different times of their menstrual cycles, or if there were options for birth control that were better or worse for athletic output. This experience helped Ackerman decide she wanted to use her medical degree to help women athletes perform their best. When Ackerman began practicing medicine in 2006, she delved into the Triad and began to treat young people experiencing it. She and her colleagues published paper after paper, updating what they knew about the Triad, how many young athletes seemed to be affected,

what treatments were working, how the three symptoms were interconnected. The more researchers worked on the Triad, however, the more
they started to see that there were some problems with the terminology.

This wasn't a problem of three random curses affecting girls who
played too many sports. The syndrome was multifaceted—affecting
young women athletes, yes, but not just through bone breaks and missing periods. The problem was the whole circuit. Multiple bodily systems were harmed by insufficient energy in women, and it turns out, in
men, too. In 2015, the International Olympic Committee renamed the
syndrome: Relative Energy Deficiency in Sport (RED-S). The term, they
wrote, "points to the complexity involved and the fact that male athletes
are also affected."[60]

The renaming seemed to acknowledge that the disorder isn't just
some unique frailty and weakness of young women, some predilection
to becoming "an anorexic" or a problem that's caused by being a menstruating person. The cause was a lack of energy for the output the body is
using: it was fuel. It was food. "The cause of this syndrome is energy deficiency relative to the balance between dietary energy intake and energy
expenditure required for health and activities of daily living, growth and
sporting activities," the IOC reported.

Even though it's been decades now since the term the Female Athlete
Triad was first coined, and even though the early researchers like
Drinkwater *were* connecting the ailments of young women athletes to
the fact that they weren't fueling efficiently, this knowledge wasn't dis-
seminated well at all throughout the medical community or the (far less
regimented) sports community. While coverage about Mary Cain before
her 2019 personal essay, from *The New York Times* to *Sports Illustrated*,
noted the inherent danger in being a young elite woman runner, runners
themselves certainly weren't getting the message.

In 2013, *Sports Illustrated* introduced Cain's story this way: "In some
distant, imagined future she does historic things. Running with a long,

brown ponytail floating behind her like a vapor trail, she wins gold medals, breaks world records and restores track and field to a place where
little girls dream that someday they will be just like Mary Cain. Or in
another version of that same future, she is injured or overwhelmed and
never finds the greatness that once seemed imminent."[61]

In 2015, Elizabeth Weil wrote in the *New York Times Magazine* that
running programs had done away with the "outdated idea that the best
way to make a girl run faster is to make her skinnier, so that she carries
fewer pounds around the track. The dominant philosophy now is that
girls, like all other runners, should train to become very strong by lifting
heavy weights." Weil notes that Salazar is, in fact, zeroed in on making
sure Cain isn't overtrained, and doesn't go to any extremes, like he did to
burn out his own running career, or like Decker did, who, Salazar called
in the same article, "a racehorse that wasn't held back."[62]

These stories often also note that a performance dip, a lag, a plateau—
whatever one wants to call it—with young women runners is normal: that
pesky puberty thing that tends to slow down progress more for young
girls than for young boys. But if this information was out there and being
covered by the sports media, then why did so many focus on how quickly
Cain would go on to win the world records? Why all the hand-wringing
about her slower finishes when she was nineteen and certainly in the
middle of her plateau? Why did we assume that runners and coaches
were staying up to date on the latest sports science research based on
women?

Distance runners might be those impacted most severely by this
lack of information dissemination. Across all collegiate sports, female
cross-country athletes report the highest occurrence of stress fractures.[63]
All exercising girls and women, according to one study, have an 11 percent
chance of bone injury. But if an athlete has a missing period, an eating
disorder, or osteoporosis, the likelihood of a bone injury goes up to 15 to
21 percent. With two of the three factors, it bumps to 30 percent. With all

three, it's up to 50 percent—a coin flip of a chance that you'll break a bone from participating in a sport.[64]

Ackerman published a study in 2022—nearly thirty years after the Triad was first named—that assessed what collegiate cross-country runners, coaches, and athletic trainers knew about either the Female Athlete Triad or RED-S (today, though RED-S is more widely used in the medical community, the term *the Triad* is still used by some). The vast, vast majority of athletes (84 percent), coaches (89 percent), and athletic trainers (71 percent) in the survey reported receiving no training from their current institution on either.[65] Other studies have shown that only 13 percent of athletic trainers knew that energy deficiency was a component of the syndrome,[66] and that as few as 15 percent of coaches are even aware of the Triad or RED-S.[67]

Ackerman told me that those training women athletes are working in an information void. In that void, coaches, doctors, strength trainers, and athletes themselves will continue to fall back on societal conditioning, on the ways that we've been taught to see women's bodies: deficient, defective, frail, small.

Women athletes don't have many people telling them the truth, Ackerman says. Even today they're more often than not told "Thinner is faster. Lighter is better," advice that's based on some small studies that have shown that for young men endurance athletes, lower BMIs are correlated with speedier performance.[68] But in more recent studies that focused on women endurance athletes, the same relationship hasn't been found.[69] What some studies are finding, however, is that if a runner's lean mass (aka muscle) percentage increases, performance tends to increase, too, and a higher lean mass can also mean a *higher* overall weight. But losing weight just to lose weight, which often means losing fat *and* muscle, can lead to decreased performances, especially in women, when that diminished energy starts to impact bone mass, too.[70, 71] Overall, we just don't know if there is a magic number to attain when it comes to body fat percentage, or BMI, and experts believe it's likely different for different people. Ackerman's voice takes on a concerned edge as she tells me: "We're making a lot of guesses. And this is why . . . the research needs to happen."

One thing she has witnessed, however, is that when sufficient energy reserves become the focus of training—instead of an athlete's body size, or shape, or even speed—performance, and injury-prevention, does improve. "When [athletes] realize that, oh wow, if I do eat better and I'm not afraid of carbs and I'm eating carbs at the right time and I'm having my recovery food and I'm getting more sleep, and I'm seeing these changes, they really buy into monitoring it."

The lack of research on women athletes' performance is part of what has held that performance back, Ackerman says. "We are applying so much information to women that is based on men, that once we start doing these studies in women that are specifically for women and having results that we can then apply to women's training, I am anticipating that we will see huge improvements in performance because now there will just be more thought and science behind it. So we haven't even begun to tap the potential of female athletes."

SO MANY OF the stories of well-known women runners are tragedies. Their bodies ravaged because they weren't cared for or believed in in the same way as male athletes have always been. They've been told they need to shed their femininity in order to run fast like a boy, but also to hold on desperately to their femininity through thinness or conventional beauty in order to have any power in this world—because their athletic ability certainly won't bring them that.

It has taken so long for sports scientists to pay attention to women, to take seriously the ills affecting young women and girls and to attempt to understand their bodies. But in that ferocity of seeking answers about what makes women different from the status quo athlete (men), a false wall has been constructed: *we need this because we are so different.* Some researchers worry that pushing too hard to find differences in female athletes will spread the message that women and men are not just variations on a theme, but different species entirely. So some are developing a more nuanced theory, that while cisgender women have various physiological differences from cisgender men, physiology *isn't* the biggest driver of gender difference in sport: our culture is.

When Sheree Bekker was completing her PhD research on female athlete injury prevention, she noticed a pattern in all the many studies coming out: ACL tears are experienced four to six times more often by women athletes than they are by men and boy athletes. "The whole history of research in this space was just kind of themed to say, 'Oh well women are just prone to knee injuries. They have wider hips and they have hormones so that's why women get more knee injuries," she told me.

She and a few colleagues began discussing the phenomenon and realized that the insinuation that women's bodies were *just more breakable* rankled them, because when male athletes experienced a rash of injuries historically, researchers studied all the things that could be contributing to the problem, like training, warmups, the field, and environment. Bekker's study put forward all of the different ways in which women and girls experience gender disparity that could impact the higher incidence of ACL tears, from lack of muscle-strengthening play in their youth, to the lower quality of fields and tracks women often have access to, to the lower amounts of time women often have to rest injuries due to pay disparities and family commitments, to differences in the surgical and rehabilitation services women often receive compared to men.[72]

Since the study was published, she told me that athletes have reached out gratefully to say they now felt *seen* as people who weren't breaking because they were "just prone to injury, or weak."

RED-S and the Female Athlete Triad have come to be seen in a similarly contentious scientific frame in recent years. Some of the original

Female Athlete Triad researchers weren't pleased with the RED-S renaming, feeling that it might take the attention away from the hard-won focus on the unique issues facing *female* athletes.[73] But the reality is the Triad symptoms don't uniquely affect women and girls. Yes, the lack of a menstrual period is a symptom only affecting cisgender women and transgender and nonbinary people with uteruses, but men and boys can have many of the same disastrous effects from improper fueling: bone loss, more fractures, fatigue, disordered eating, and a plethora of other health concerns. And women runners aren't the only ones who have dealt with coaching tactics that ignore these needs, or become abusive in any manner of ways, often by obsessing over results to the detriment of seeing the whole athlete as a person. Though socialized environments can exacerbate some of these problems for women in different ways than for men, our bodies all need proper fueling for the work we want them to do.

Bekker is worried that if the idea that women athletes are so categorically different than men persists, hormones and menstruation will become the pet excuse for all issues faced by women athletes. "While I think that work is important, I do think what we are not seeing is any kind of attention being paid to the socio-cultural side."

And that side of things certainly matters. Women and girl runners from Mary Decker to Mary Cain have been kept small and weak and injury-prone because we have assumed that is what it means to be a woman runner in a man's world. But when we think about how much the smallness, weakness, and injuries could be due to the environment women and girls live in and not their own bodies, then the question becomes: How can we know for sure what it means to be a woman runner at all?

Annet Negesa running in her heat in the 800-meter race at the IAAF World Championships in Daegu, South Korea (Kerim Okten/EPA/Shutterstock)

6: But Only "Real" Women . . .

Lake Oswego, Oregon, 2023 Summit Invitational
LAKE OSWEGO HIGH School junior Mia Brahe-Pedersen bursts from the starting blocks into the 100-meter sprint in front of a packed set of stands at Oregon's 2023 Summit Invitational. She explodes into the middle lane, pushing chest-first with perfect upright posture. Two competitors to her left start quicker, but in the last twenty meters she windmills her arms and legs, pumping so quickly you can almost feel them whirring, to heave out in front of them. Just then, another runner comes up on her right shoulder. But with the finish line just steps away, Brahe-Pedersen pulls a

stride ahead, beating everyone across the finish line in 11.08 seconds—the third fastest high school girl's 100 of all time.[1]

Those three competitors she beat in the end? They were boys. Not just any boys, but the four fastest boys from the twenty-one schools competing at the meet. Her high school coach had gotten special permission to run a few mixed-gender events, largely to give Brahe-Pedersen some tougher competition. As she crosses the line first, spectators in the packed stands scream her name, "GO MIA! GO MIA!"

Maybe because Brahe-Pedersen is white, or American, or cisgender, or because she has long chestnut brown hair and a muscular, yet curvy, build, the crowd didn't question her gender when she beat those boys. They celebrated her abilities.

BY 2011, WOMEN running two laps around a track was no longer controversial in and of itself. In the media coverage of the 800, there were no more references to women collapsing, as though their lives or reproductive abilities are in danger. Women runners were not referred to as "the weaker sex" superfluously by sports reporters, at least not explicitly. And yet, the idea of the weaker, slower, sex remained an integral part of women's track and field in general, and this running event in particular.

At the IAAF World Championships in Athletics in Daegu, South Korea, that year, five heats of women runners race the 800. World-famous names like Alysia Montaño and Jenny Meadows take the starting line in sports gear made especially for them. Unlike the motley crew of high schoolers in baggy shorts who ran a few times a week after school who made up the 1928 Olympic edition of this race, these women are prepared. They wear streamlined tanks, sports bras, compression shorts or briefs to ensure the least amount of wind resistance, with running spikes designed to weigh almost nothing while gripping the rubber track enough to propel them off the starting line with force. Their muscles have been trained for years. They take protein supplements and specialty vitamins. They've received individualized coaching, and most of them spend the majority of their time running and training. Some of them are even professional full-time women runners.

The field of runners, too, looks nothing like that group of mostly white European and American women who ran in 1928; these runners are globally, racially, and physically diverse, representing twenty-five different nationalities. Their hair and skin represent as many different shades as their rainbow of racing uniforms.

For Annet Negesa, racing at the World Championships was the realization of a dream. The nineteen-year-old Ugandan girl grew up in a rural village one hour outside of the nation's capital, Kampala. She'd been running on the junior circuit for four years and was already the national record holder for the women's 800-meter and 1500-meter races. She'd achieved all of this while training on her own, running when she wasn't in school or helping to take care of her eight younger siblings. By the time she qualified for Worlds, however, the Ugandan Athletic Association had found her a coach.

A British television news segment on Negesa that ran earlier that year[2] shows footage of some of her daily life: running along dirt roads, dodging cows, and stretching under large trees. She was living at a boarding school, where she slept in a room packed with bunk beds. During the interview sections, she smiles easily at the camera, her bright white teeth flashing as she speaks. She wears a scarf wrapped around her hair, and yellow rose earrings stud her ears. The broadcaster notes that, with Negesa's times and her training regimen ramping up now that she has an official coach and is finishing up her schooling, she could become "a major force in women's middle distance running."

Negesa tells the camera in Swahili how much she looks forward to introducing herself to people on the international stage: "Whatever happens, I know that I will be training every hour I can for the Olympics next year. Everything I'm doing now will help me be ready for London. I just hope I continue to get faster so I can go to the Olympic games as an athlete to fear."

The World Championship was Negesa's first international competition outside of Africa as a senior runner. At Daegu she ran in the fifth preliminary heat and placed first. She then moved onto the semifinals, which were run in three heats. In the first semifinal heat, she drew the inside lane.

When the starting gun fires, Negesa leaps across the line. By the first curve she is outpacing the rest of the field and draws into the lead. By the 200-meter mark, she's overtaken by Eunice Sum of Kenya. The field draws closer together at the end of the first lap, but Negesa holds on to her second-place position, drafting off of Sum. She's not slowing, but the rest of the field is speeding up. By the 600-meter mark, a blond trio pounces on both African women and begin their own battle for the front: Maggie Vessey, an American, Jennifer Meadows, a Brit, and Yuliya Rusanova, a Russian. At the finish, Rusanova crosses first, followed closely by Vessey, who just edges out Meadows. Rusanova and Vessey move onto the Finals. Negesa ends up sixth of the eight runners. Her time, 2:01.51 was good, but only enough for eighteenth best overall—she wouldn't make the finals.

No matter. Negesa had gotten her first taste of worldwide competition, and she could only think of being one step closer to her goal of heading to the 2012 Olympics in London and the chance to perform better. "I was to take the Gold. That was my goal," she would tell a documentary crew years later.[3] She'd go on to win the 800 at the All Africa meet a week after Worlds—a promising sign for her chances the following year.

A few weeks before she was set to leave for London, Negesa says she got a call from an official with the International Association of Athletics Federations, which oversees all international track-and-field competition. The IAAF official said that her blood tests had come back with levels of testosterone that were too high.[4] Negesa was sent to Nice, France, where she says she met with a group of doctors, all of them white, who measured and examined her body, while speaking French, a language Negesa does not speak. She was scared, and shy and unsure of all that was happening. But she was eager to do whatever these doctors told her so that she could achieve her dream of going to the Olympics.

The doctors told her surgery would be required for her to run again. She says they told her: "You will become weaker just for a few weeks and then you can come back and continue with your running."

Negesa was sent home then, where her manager told her she wouldn't be able to participate in the Olympics. A Ugandan track federation official called her and told her to lie low during the Games. "She said don't move around, just stay at home because they were fearing of the news people coming to me and asking me why I didn't go to the Olympics," Negesa said.[5] Media reports said Negesa, one of only five Ugandan women who'd qualified for the Games, was ruled out at the last moment with an injury.[6]

Months later, in November, a Ugandan federation official and Negesa's manager brought her to a hospital in Kampala. Negesa was confused when she woke up after a surgery. She says by the way the operation was described to her, she'd been expecting something like an injection to lower her testosterone levels. But waking up, she discovered cuts on her belly. She wasn't sure what the surgery had even accomplished. No one, not any of the IAAF officials or doctors who had pushed her to get the surgery, followed up with her about her care. The goal had been to get the surgery so she would be allowed to run again. Without follow-up care, she had trouble even standing or walking for long periods of time after the operation, let alone running.

Though she'd never signed an informed consent form, she would discover later that the doctors had performed an orchiectomy, the removal of internal testes, or gonads, according to her hospital discharge papers.

Such internal reproductive organs can exist in certain intersex individuals without their knowing, if they are born with external genitalia considered female at birth. It's unlikely, given that Negesa was born in a rural part of Uganda, that she even knew she was intersex until the testosterone screening brought her to the IAAF's attention. The discharge papers also noted that while the doctor providing her care had prescribed antibiotics for post-surgery management, they had not begun a prescription for hormone replacement therapy—which is necessary after an orchiectomy to provide the hormones the body relies on for many of its integral processes, from immune response to bone growth to sleep cycles.

A letter from hospital officials dated in January 2013, two months after surgery, said that Negesa "now complains of body weakness which we attribute to the withdrawal symptoms of the gonadectomy." It also noted that Negesa's doctors "restrained from starting her on estrogen therapy awaiting further discussions between Dr. Bermon and [redacted] . . . she is keen to resume competition in athletics."

But those discussions never happened, or if they did, Negesa never heard of them. "Dr. Bermon" refers to Stéphane Bermon, the head of the medical and science division for the IAAF. Months later, the then twenty-year-old Negesa tried to get back to running at her university. But by the end of the year, the school had canceled her scholarship. She was no longer running at her previous speeds, or anywhere close to her previous fitness. She suffered from regular headaches and joint aches. Her international manager stopped responding to her in 2016. Negesa says she hadn't heard from anyone in the IAAF for seven years.

During the filming of a 2020 video by Human Rights Watch, Negesa's face has visibly changed. The easy smile is gone. Her features seem to droop. While there is some footage of her running, she looks physically and emotionally pained on the track. Her steps are plodding.

"I was no longer a person who has importance to anyone," she said later. "I was useless to people because I was no longer racing. I lost my career, I lost my [university] scholarship, I lost income, and I was no longer able to help my family financially. I lost everything."[7]

NEGESA'S BLOOD TESTS, which flagged her for this follow-up visit in France and kept her from competing in the 2012 Olympics, weren't a standard procedure for every woman runner competing in the London Games—just for ones deemed suspicious of, essentially, not being a "real woman." Track athletes are subject to anti-doping tests at any time or place in the world, but IOC blood testing to confirm sex and hormone levels was allowed by the IAAF Medical Manager "if he has reasonable grounds for believing that a case of hyperandrogenism may exist."[8] This other kind of testing has been called different things throughout history: gender verification testing, sex testing, or even femininity control.

Negesa told Human Rights Watch in 2020 that she didn't see "anyone else giving six bottles of blood like me." No one told her what the blood was going to show—what, exactly they were suspicious of. "I was wondering, why me?" she said.

Fears about women, and especially women runners, not being "real women" were reported as early as the 1920s. Recall, for instance, Hitomi Kinue, Japan's only woman entrant to the Olympics, who earned the silver medal in the 800-meter race despite not even entering it until the day of the race. Even with all of her athletic success, the Japanese media never stopped hounding her for looking so "mannish." Because she was tall. Because she was strong. Because she was fast.

In 1936, a similar situation played out when American Helen Stephens won a gold medal in the 100. Stephens had begun training in track and field at just fifteen years old in her small rural Missouri hometown. By the time she was seventeen, standing six feet tall, she'd made the 1936 Olympic team, and went from being essentially unknown to beating Stella Walsh, the fastest woman on earth.

Walsh was born Stefania Walasiewiczowna in Poland in 1911. Even

1936 Olympics, Helen Stephens, left. Stella Walsh, right. (Polish National Digital Archive)

though she immigrated to the US as a baby, she ran for Poland internationally, much to the chagrin of many Americans, as she was the fastest female sprinter in the world from 1932 to 1935.

When Stephens beat out Walsh, and two German powerhouse sprinters, Käthe Krauss and Marie Dollinger, in the final heat with an 11.5 second race that matched the world record, Polish officials publicly questioned Stephens's gender, thinking it impossible for any other woman to beat Walsh at the 100. Stephens claimed she'd been tested by a physician before the race, "who sex-tested all athletes prior to competition."[9] After the race, Dollinger, the fourth-place runner, called out what she claimed were her "masculine" competitors, including Walsh. Dollinger said she was "the only woman in the race."[10]

Concerns dating from the Victorian era about sporting activity causing *mannishness* had evolved into a very real fear that women who were *too good* at running, must, in fact, be men. Echoes of the same sentiment resounded in the 1940s when the US Women's Track and Field team suddenly was made up of majority Black women—because as the white gym teachers were insisting, white women simply weren't *masculine* enough to participate in such a sport.

At the 1966 European Athletic Championships, the IAAF determined all women athletes needed to be sex tested in some way, because, according to *Life* magazine, "There had been persistent speculation through the years about women who turn in manly performances." As a result, all women competitors at IAAF competitions had to walk naked in front of a panel of three female doctors before the competition so their breasts and external genitalia could be visually inspected. At the Commonwealth Games that year, female athletes not only had to expose themselves to doctors, they had to undergo a gynecologist's manual exam of their genitalia.

One year later, with athletes complaining about the lack of dignity in these so-called "nude parades," the IAAF determined that, at the European track-and-field championships, they would simply swab the athletes' cheeks to perform lab-based chromosome tests. These tests, the organization figured, would easily show whether a runner is a man or a woman, or in chromosomal terms: XY, or XX.

It didn't take long for a problem to show up, however. Polish runner Ewa Kłobukowska's test came back showing a Y chromosome. But she was a woman, assigned female at birth, and she had passed the previous year's nude visual inspection.

This is where it gets complicated. Because while many people believe that *sex* is dimorphic, that is, that all people biologically are either male or female, actually, we're not. And chromosome tests are just one example of how sex is far more complex.

WHEN SCIENTISTS BEGAN the Human Genome Project in 1990, their goal to "map the human genome" meant, essentially, pulling all of the little threads that make up our chromosomes apart to see which instructions (genes, or segments of DNA) were on which chromosomes, and what bases (the even smaller segments of genes), in what order, each gene was made up of—simple, right? In 2003, when the Human Genome Project announced they had accomplished the first sequencing of the human genome, it sounded kind of like they had figured everything out. The mysteries of human biology were uncovered! But the mapping was only 92 percent complete. Since then, the sequencing has been added to and patched. In the most recent announcement in the journal *Science*,[11] the sequencing had mapped 3.055 billion base pair sequences of a human genome, including nearly 200 million *new* base pairs. And yet—there are *still* gaps.

If you're one of those people who remembers things from biology class in high school, you can skip these next few paragraphs. If, like I did, you need a refresher about how DNA works, here it is. Inside the nucleus of every single one of our cells are groups of free-floating, microscopic, threadlike apparatuses: our chromosomes. These twenty-three matching pairs of linear threads are each made of tightly coiled helix-shaped DNA strands, which each have a different job to do in our bodies. If you unraveled the threads of DNA, just from *one cell* in your body, the thread would be around six feet long. That's how much data it takes to make you *you*. One of each set of your chromosomes came from the egg that became you, and the other came from the sperm that fertilized that egg. When scientists began tracking these threadlike structures, they gave each pair a number. In humans, the first twenty-two chromosome pairs are numbered, and the last pair of chromosomes are what we call the sex chromosomes, also called the X and Y chromosomes.

Every human, regardless of sex, has at least one X chromosome from an egg, then typically the sperm cell provides either an X or a Y. If a person has two Xs, then the fetus that develops will likely have gonads that become a uterus, and a vulva with a clitoris inside will form as the fetus's genitalia develops. If the fetus has one X and one Y chromosome, then the gonads will likely become testicles, and the clitoris will elongate into a penis as the genitalia develops.

Of course, there are an infinite number of ways your chromosomes turn into the body that houses you.[12] In the most recent and significant sequencing of the genome, the scientists who were part of the project were sure to note that mapping was not the same as decoding. In other words, *Time* magazine wrote: "much of what the human genome does still remains a mystery."[13]

All the same, sex chromosomes, and what exactly about our bodies makes us male or female, man or woman, or something else entirely, all that stuff you likely forgot after some high school biology test, is suddenly what the IOC and the IAAF—and society in general—are obsessed with.

Because the thing is: not everyone ends up with exactly forty-six chromosomes. That Polish sprinter, Kłobukowska, showed a Y chromosome on her cheek swab test, but had passed the visual "nude parades" inspection with no questions. Inside Kłobukowska's cells, it's believed, some of her cells had XX chromosomes floating around, but some had two Xs and a Y, so there were forty-seven chromosomes in some of her cells instead of the typical forty-six. Other people are born with forty-five chromosomes in all their cells, with just one X chromosome. Some people are XY but have a condition where the androgen receptors (proteins that hormones bind onto in order to their jobs) in their body don't function well or at all, so messages sent by testosterone and other androgens aren't processed normally. These individuals develop a vulva, and potentially a vagina. instead of a penis, but also have internal testes. Some people have XX chromosomes but for other reasons produce high levels of testosterone that they may or may not be able to process effectively.[14]

The medical terminology for people who either don't have an XX or XY chromosomal set or have a hormonal insensitivity or genitalia that's ambiguous is intersex. Some in the medical community use the term differences in sexual development (DSD) to describe the same phenomenon more specifically. It's estimated that 1 in every 2,000 babies is born with genital differences that might be noted at birth, and that about 2 percent of all people are born intersex.[15] For decades, most intersex children in countries with advanced medical care have undergone emergency genital surgery as infants. The American Medical Association Journal of Ethics wrote in 2021[16] that the standard of care for these children needed an update: "Grounded in the historical notion that gender and anatomy are linked, surgical interventions have been performed on infants to align their anatomy with their 'optimal gender,' often chosen for them based on potential for heteronormative sexual relationships. Today, intersex children continue to receive early cosmetic genital surgery at medical institutions across the United States and worldwide." Often doctors framed the need for genital surgery on intersex infants to parents as a way to "normalize" the child's anatomy.[17]

Surgeries like this date to the 1950s, when a woman wearing pants outside the home was considered abnormal, too. Intersex adults who had surgeries as children have spoken out about the physiological and psychological harm these surgeries have done.[18] In recent years, the World Health Organization,[19] twelve United Nations agencies,[20] and the Physicians for Human Rights[21] have all issued statements citing the need for all such surgeries to be delayed until an individual is old enough to make their own decision about the procedure.

In 1980, Stella Walsh, the Polish-American superstar who raised the profile of women athletes throughout the 1930s and 1940s with her overwhelming success as a sprinter, was murdered during an armed robbery. She was sixty-nine years old. Instead of being mourned as one of the most successful athletes of her day, a salacious story came out. Because she'd been the victim of a crime, Walsh's body underwent an autopsy. The autopsy report, including details about her ambiguous genitalia, was leaked to the press. When Walsh's chromosomes were examined, many of her cells were found to be XY, but some of them were just X (similar to what experts believe about Kłobukowska). Geneticists now call this condition mosaicism, a beautiful term, I think, to describe the complexity of our biology.

Perhaps it's ironic, or just sad, that Walsh, was living with a DSD, yet her Polish national federation questioned the sex of Stephens for beating Walsh in 1936. A Polish newspaper claimed that Walsh would have won the 1936 race if "she had competed only against women." The media frenzy that ensued after Walsh's death, as well as the continued lack of clarity discovered by the IOC while trying to chromosome-test every female athlete who went to the Olympics to ensure an XX profile, led to a reckoning. Too many athletes were being disqualified, and no one even knew whether these various chromosomal structures conferred an athletic advantage. Plus, it was painful and embarrassing for the women whose gender—a part of ourselves that is so deeply personal—was questioned on the world stage.

By the 1990s, the IAAF convened workshops to determine how sex verification should be carried out for national and international track-and-field competitions. After one such meeting in 1992, the group of experts, from athletes to medical geneticists, psychologists to endocrinologists, recommended the chromosomal tests should be thrown out, and that "only masquerading males" should be excluded from women's track events.[22]

But who were these "masquerading males"? In all of my research for this book, and as a journalist covering women's sporting events for years, I have come across no examples of a man pretending to be a woman to win a women's sporting competition. Zero. Between 1968 and 1999, more than 10,000 women were sex tested at the Olympics. In that time, no "masquerading males" were ever discovered trying to sneak into women's competition. I have read about a handful of cases of either transgender women who hadn't yet transitioned (far before transgender people were taken seriously by the medical community, and before gender-affirming care existed for them), or women or men who had gone through sometimes extreme levels of doping with androgens (often due to pressure from their national athletic federations) resulting in some gender ambiguity, but never have I come across a story of a man who wanted to win a sporting competition so badly he simply *pretended* to be a woman.

Still, the search for these "masquerading males" went on. The IAAF's official policy on gender verification continued to allow an investigation if another athlete or team were to challenge the sex of a competitor.[23] While this policy remained in effect throughout the early 2000s, the results of any of these investigations generally remained confidential. Until 2009.

MAINTAINING A STRICT separation by sex—two sexes—throughout the history of sport has almost always been just the way it is. This began because the ancient Greeks (and, later, the late-nineteenth-century men who wanted to emulate those ancient Greeks) believed organized sport was a way to celebrate masculinity. So women just weren't invited. (Which didn't mean, of course, that women didn't create their own sporting opportunities, as we've seen many times so far in this book.) But the justifications for continuing to separate the vast majority of organized sport into two distinct categories have changed over time.

With running, specifically, as organized sporting events such as track and cross-country and marathons finally began to allow women entry by the late twentieth century, separating participants by sex often happened because beliefs about what women could do were so radically different from beliefs about what men were capable of. Such as how it took until 1984 to get a women's Olympic marathon, for example. Later, sex separation seemed totally rational because of recognized differences in competitive results. Recall, of course, that just days after Roger Bannister broke the four-minute mile mark, Diane Leather broke the first women's five-minute mile. Men's and women's times in track events were (excuse the pun) miles apart.

So for many, sports segregation has been about the idea that women should have fair competition, and that meant against other women. But often this separation meant that women athletes were seen in a vastly different way than men athletes. They weren't considered elite. They weren't considered important. They were second string. They were the perpetual JV squad. They were a sideshow or a favor or a joke. And they still weren't strong or tough enough for certain sports. See: football, baseball, the decathlon, ski jumping, the Tour de France. We see the ramifications of this hierarchy still, today, in the way that boy's high school football teams are far more likely to get new uniforms and equipment than girls' high school soccer teams,[24] and the fact that the highest paid WNBA players make less than 2 percent of the average NBA player's salary.

And sometimes the binary separation is upheld in sport even when there are no performance gaps based on sex. Take the fact that competitive bowling, billiards, and darts are often separated by sex. In 1992, China's Zhang Shan won the gold in Olympic skeet shooting, which was not separated by sex at the time, beating her male competitors outright. The following Olympics, the international governing body for shooting

sports only held a men's event.[25] In 2000, women were allowed to participate again—in their own separate category. In big-wave surfing, Maya
Gabeira rode the biggest wave of the year in 2020, but her award from the
World Surfing Association was notably the *Women's* Biggest Wave Award
(out of only two women), and the *Men's* Biggest Wave Award wasn't noted
as smaller.[26]

In other words: separating sport by sex is not always about protecting women's opportunities—it's sometimes about protecting the gender
hierarchy.

By the late 1970s, US schools were expected to be in compliance with
Title IX. Specifically, sports departments needed to follow the law's call
to provide "equal opportunity" for girls and boys at schools that receive
federal funds. But instead of hiring coaches for girls' soccer, and basketball, and track and field, many schools fought back. Coaches and athletic
directors complained that they couldn't possibly afford to expand opportunities for girls' sports without cutting programs like boys' football.[27, 28]
So some suggested that, to be equal, they'd have to start letting girls try
out for boys' football and baseball teams,[29] and then just let the public
spin out over the idea of girls being injured by the *big, strong boys.*

This fostered another false narrative about the need to protect wom-
en's bodies from sports. Perhaps the wording no longer explicitly reflected
the fear that athletic girls would be unable to bear children, but the idea
remained the same: sports needed a softer, pinker, gentler version for
girls to remain safe. But in the 1980s and 1990s in the US, especially in
areas where girls' sports weren't flourishing, it was common for girls
to play baseball on Little League teams (after they sued for the right to
join in 1972),[30, 31] or join boys' basketball and soccer teams when there
weren't girl's teams available to play on. US women's soccer superstar
Megan Rapinoe and her twin sister Rachel grew up playing on a boy's
team in California. More than 3,000 girls in the US today play tackle
high school football—all of them on boys' teams, because there are no

girls' high school football teams in the US.[32] These girls aren't getting hurt more often in sport because they're playing with boys. Furthermore, even though the evidence of brain injury to those who play football is undeniable, millions of boys play the sport each year anyway; the physical danger for boys in sport is often just an accepted possibility, whereas exposing girls to "potential danger" caused by boys in sport is often painted as unethical.

Girls and women have undoubtedly grown many women's sports into juggernauts of their own. We live in a world post–Billie Jean King's Battle of the Sexes; post–1999 Women's World Cup; post–NCAA Women's Basketball Tournament (yes, they can actually call it March Madness, now[33]); post–US Soccer salary equity. But fear remains an integral part of women's sports, nonetheless. The fear now is that it will all go away if we don't carefully protect our opportunities from disappearing by shielding these sex categories at all times from gender interlopers who are trying to erase women athletes altogether.

Some who argue that women's sports need this kind of protection like to point out statistics such as the fact that renowned seven-time Olympic gold medalist Allyson Felix's best 400-meter time would put her in 689th place when compared to the best high school boys' records.[34] This data seems to cement the fact that because one of the best woman runners in the world couldn't beat *high school boys,* women athletes are so vastly disadvantaged that we're practically a different species when it comes to our athletic talents.

But here's the thing: If Allyson Felix's best 400-meter time puts her at 689th in high school boy's times, that would still put her in the top 0.1 percent of the high school boy track athletes in the country.[35] And even against senior national elite runners, in many countries, she'd be highly competitive. In fact, her best 400 time[36] would have won her the 2023 National Senior Outdoor Championships men's division races outright in Iceland[37] and Greece.[38] She would come in seventh place in Portugal,[39] eighth in Sweden,[40] and fourth in Serbia.[41] As seen in the way Mia Brahe-Pedersen, the Oregon high school runner, could beat the best boys in her district in a head-to-head race, the spectrum of athletic ability, even in sprinting—which continues to maintain some of the biggest sex differences we see when it comes to sport—is much less dimorphous than we've been led to believe.

AVERAGE SEX DIFFERENCES in many running events exist. Sex differences when it comes to certain athletic advantages like muscle mass, height, and VO_2 max, on average exist. At the elite levels of most running events, the best men typically outperform the best women by somewhere between 8 percent to 10 percent. Anyone can see that. But these are average differences across a vast spectrum of humanity, which is far more gray and muddled than black-and-white. When we separate everything about sport into two sex-specific categories, then insist women athletes are at risk because anyone who isn't a "real woman" holds some automatic insurmountable athletic advantage, we not only leave people out, we continue a myth about women's weakness and inferiority.

Even if we are looking just at the elite levels of running and comparing men's times to women's times, no one actually knows for sure exactly *what* in our biology causes those differences. Not yet. Just as no one could say exactly *why* Roger Bannister was able to break the four-minute mile when no one could before. As biology shows us, our bodies are all different because of a compendium of genetic and physiological and psychological factors that even the most advanced genetic science hasn't pinned down yet. The vast diversity that makes up humanity is the exact reason sports continue to be compelling in an age when, otherwise, computer models could just calculate everyone's physiological traits and do the competing for us.

Having two sex-differentiated categories very well may continue to make sense in sport forever, even as we learn more about what causes sex differences in the body and how to include people who are intersex, nonbinary, or gender-nonconforming. But *policing* sex categories certainly isn't necessary. What if we stopped acting like women's sport was in danger, and instead, we just believed that the strength and speed of women can come with all kinds of advantages and variations? What if we stopped seeing women athletes as definitively inferior to men? What if we celebrated the diversity of women athletes' bodies, including the outliers, the same way we celebrate the diversity of men athletes' bodies—especially the outliers?

IN 1869 ANTOINETTE Brown Blackwell, an American suffragist, abolitionist, and minister, told Charles Darwin he was dead wrong about his theory that female animals were less evolved, and therefore weaker, than males of the same species. She recognized that Darwin's groundbreaking work *On the Origin of Species* didn't look at female animals at all, so she wrote her own book, *The Sexes Throughout Nature*, that did. An amateur scientist, she was profoundly well read and passionate about equality in all realms. She made charts and lists of all kinds of living creatures, splitting the characteristics of the males and females. Then she compared them. She came to the opposite conclusion than Darwin had: "As a whole, the males and females of the same species, from mollusk up to man, may continue their related evolution, as true equivalents, in all modes of force, physical and psychical."

This physical equivalence was not always obvious on the surface, she wrote. Male lions, for instance, may be physically larger, but females are "more complex in structure and in functions," since their bodies were strong enough not only to hunt (female lions do the majority of the hunting), but also to reproduce and feed their young.[42]

Blackwell was right to call out Darwin, and to point out differences and complexities he hadn't bothered to notice. But we know now that the story of sex and gender difference, especially in humans, is more complex than a chart split into two binary sides.

One hundred fifty years later, undergrad Alexandra Kralick was intrigued by great ape skeletons when she was spending a lot of time at the mammals collection of the Smithsonian Museum of Natural History in Washington, DC. By the time she became a doctoral student in biological anthropology, she was curious about a mystery in the field dating back to one of Darwin's colleagues, one of the co-conceivers of the theory of evolution, Alfred Russel Wallace, who examined orangutan skeletons in the 1850s. When Wallace found a certain type of male orangutan that was fully grown, but the size of an adolescent, he suggested this smaller type of orangutan must be a different species altogether. Now, however, it's become known that some male orangutans are just much smaller, they don't all grow into the highly-dimorphous-sized male orangutans that are twice the size of females. Kralick couldn't understand why the narrative remained when it came to great ape biology that males are "consistently and substantially larger than females."[43]

These smaller males, deemed "unflanged males" by scientists in the early 2000s because they also lacked the flanges, or large cheek pads, that encircle the bigger males' faces, hadn't really been studied more than that.

During her doctoral research, Kralick ended up traveling to five countries and seeing fourteen museums with orangutan collections, matching up their orangutan skeletons and pelts to see what patterns she could find in the adult males. After comparing nearly a hundred adult orangutan skeletons, she found full-grown male orangutan body size ranged from female-sized to the biggest males with the biggest cheeks. In other words, she wrote later for *Anthropology News*, "Orangutans show us that a feature that varies according to biological sex is more complicated than a large/small dichotomy. Features typically thought of as highly sexually dimorphic can vary on a spectrum." Kralick goes on to note that peer-reviewed biology articles have used the dimorphism of apes to reinforce the believed sexual binary and dimorphism in humans, but if we start taking research like hers more seriously—examining body diversity instead of strict sex dimorphism—perhaps we can start to think differently. She hopes that "we can let go of pathologizing the bodies of those who do not fit clearly or cleanly into male or female categories in every way and instead seek evolutionary explanations that can capture the diversity of body shapes and sizes we see—whether we are speaking about apes or ourselves."

Work like Blackwell's and Kralick's shows that the way sex separates bodies into different categories is far more expansive and overlapping than the stories we've always told about it—even in science.

AT SEVENTEEN YEARS old, Caster Semenya, a teenager from a poor province of South Africa, won the gold medal in the 800-meter race at the 2008 Commonwealth Youth Games. One year later she won the same race at the African Junior Athletics Championships in a remarkable time: 1:56.72—the fastest time in the world for the season.

That year, the IAAF World Championships were to be held in Berlin, and all eyes were on Semenya. Before the meet, however, the teenage South African girl was deemed "suspicious." Without signing an informed consent, and believing she was undergoing drug testing, the IAAF asked the national federation of athletics in South Africa (ASA) to have Semenya tested by a gynecologist. Supposedly, these test results would take too long to be returned before Worlds, so ASA and IAAF allowed her to compete.[44]

She won the 800 in 1:55.45—equivalent to the thirteenth fastest women's 800 at the time. The backlash to Semenya's muscular, African, Black body, and her lightning-fast time, was not awe at a new superstar, but outrage. Two of her fellow competitors let their feelings be known to the press gathered in Berlin. An Italian competitor, Elisa Cusma, who placed sixth, told Italian reporters, "These kind of people should not run with us. For me, she's not a woman. She's a man."[45] Russian Mariya Savinova told one journalist, "Just look at her."

Perhaps these fellow competitors felt comfortable making such offensive and uncalled-for accusations because the IAAF had confirmed publicly between the semifinals and finals of the 800 that Semenya was undergoing a gender test "because of concerns she does not meet requirements to compete as a woman." This, despite the fact that sex testing was supposed to remain confidential due to the known psychological and social harm questioning someone's gender publicly can cause.

According to the Associated Press, Semenya's sex testing was called for because of her "dramatic improvement in times, muscular build, and deep voice." The BBC reported, however, that the gender tests were due to "unexpectedly high" testosterone readings taken back in South Africa.

Semenya's own mother insisted that the young runner was "a girl . . . I'm the mother of that girl. I'm the one that knows about Caster. If they want to know about Caster, tell them to come to me." And South Africa's president at the time, Jacob Zuma, said that Semenya "reminded the world of the importance of the rights to human dignity and privacy which should be enjoyed by all human beings."[46] All the same, the IAAF required Semenya complete a physical medical evaluation including reports from a gynecologist, endocrinologist, psychologist, an internal medicine specialist, and an expert on gender. They also did nothing to quiet the media reporting on her as though she were truly a man, set out to ruin women's sport for all.

Months later, in November, the South African sports ministry said that Semenya would be allowed to keep her gold medal and prize money from Worlds. However, the results of the testing, which would determine Semenya's future as a runner, were not announced. At the time, Semenya's coach, Michael Seme, told the New York Times[47] that she "is going to compete as a woman and will remain a woman until she dies."

When the newspaper asked if she would be allowed to compete without any further testing or surgery, Seme told the paper: "I don't want to talk about that. The only thing I want to say is that I'm happy Caster will retain her title as the fastest 800-meter runner in the world."

Semenya did not race again until July 2010. In a press release at the time, the IAAF said that the organization "accepts the conclusion of a panel of medical experts that she can compete with immediate effect."[48] Neither the results nor the reasons that she was now allowed to run again were detailed, which only stoked further media scrutiny about Semenya's physiology. In a 2010 *New York Times* article, for example, the reporter noted as fact that Semenya had "outward male characteristics."[49]

At the time, the IAAF nor the IOC had any rules about testosterone level limits for women competitors. The following year, the IAAF changed that.

As soon as Semenya's case began making headlines in 2009, the IAAF convened a group of experts to come up with more specific rules as to how, exactly, international running would define a woman. By May 2011, the group released two separate documents, one for women with high testosterone levels, or *hyperandrogenism*, and one for transgender women. All together, these documents said that so long as a woman was seen as legally a woman and had testosterone levels lower than 10 nanomoles per liter (nmol/L) in serum, they were allowed to compete in the women's category.

Two months later, Annet Negesa failed to make the final heat at Worlds, in her last international competition. Caster Semenya, however, was just getting back into form following her forced eleven-month hiatus from sport.

IN THE 800 final in Daegu, Janeth Jepkosgei, the Kenyan 2007 world champ, goes out hard from the gun, running the race from the front. Semenya runs from the middle of the pack, letting Alysia Johnson

Montaño and Jepkosgei run a hard first lap. At the one-minute mark Semenya is in fifth place. She begins a kick then, passing each of the runners ahead of her by the 600-meter mark. It looks as though she'll have the field beat, but in the final straightaway, Savinova, who had been running closely behind Semenya throughout her kick, surges. Savinova and Semenya are a good 10 meters ahead of the rest of the field. Semenya is in her full kick, but Savinova seems to have more in the tank—she pulls ahead with only a few meters left. She crosses first, in 1:55.87. Semenya won the silver in 1:56.35. Jepkosgei ended up third, in 1:57.42.

Savinova's time was just half a second slower than Semenya's 2009 finish—the "suspiciously fast" race that had consequently turned Semenya's life upside down, after which Savinova told the press Semenya must be a man.

One year later, Negesa was scratched from the Olympics and ushered into the surgery that ended her career, despite the fact that her supposed "natural advantage" hadn't even gotten her to the final heat in the same competition. Semenya, however, was allowed to compete at the 2012 Olympics. Many assumed that she had taken some kind of hormonal medication to lower her testosterone levels. But the new limits required by the IAAF did nothing to keep her fellow competitors, and Olympics watchers around the world, from referring to her sex skeptically, and assuming she would easily win Gold. However, Semenya had an uninspiring racing year, beginning with an injury. She ended up winning the silver medal in the 800 at the Olympics, second to Savinova, again.[50]

Funnily enough, no one questioned Savinova's extremely fast times as being "suspicious," even though she had beat Semenya on the world stage twice. Savinova is white, two inches shorter than Semenya. She also has a flat chest and sported a well-defined six pack—physical characteristics that Semenya was called out for in the media for "looking male."[51]

Today, Savinova is far less widely known as a threat to women's professional running than Semenya, even though she was secretly filmed admitting, in an interview that aired on Russian TV in 2014, to injecting testosterone and using an anabolic steroid, and consequently three years later was stripped of her Olympic gold medal and World Championship for doping. Semenya became the 2012 Olympic Gold medalist retroactively.[52]

The same year, an academic paper appeared in *The Journal of Clinical Endocrinology & Metabolism*, written by several doctors and researchers associated with the IAAF, including Stéphane Bermon, the head of their medical and science division, who Negesa claims was present for the testing she underwent in France.[53] The paper describes how this study aimed to determine whether high testosterone in four young elite female athletes would reveal a particular XY difference in sex development. The paper notes that the four athletes in question "presented as tall, slim, muscular women with a male bone morphotype, no breast development, clitoromegaly, partial or complete labial fusion, and inguinal/intralabial testes." In other words, they were intersex, with a particular DSD called 5-alpha reductase deficiency, which is a mutation on SRD5A2, a gene known to be involved in processing androgens. The paper goes on to note that "the major question is whether this condition provides unfair advantages."

The paper didn't answer this question. Instead, it reveals that these four athletes all underwent an MRI of their abdomens and pelvises and were X-rayed to determine their bone mineral density, and gene molecular analysis, as well as genomic DNA extraction. All four athletes, the paper says, "wished to maintain their female identity, and had many questions about menstruation, sexual activity, and child-bearing," suggesting they may not have known anything about their own conditions previously.

The authors noted that there's no health risk to leaving internal gonads in patients with this chromosome type, however they informed them that surgery would be required to "continue elite sport in the female category." But in addition to removing the gonads, the doctors also proposed a "partial clitoridectomy" and a "feminizing vaginoplasty," neither of which had anything to do with their testosterone levels or athletic eligibility, but were instead about fitting external genitalia into a more dimorphous sex binary. Nowhere in the paper do the authors mention offering these athletes another, less invasive or less drastic way to lower their testosterone, such as taking birth control pills. Nor does it question whether their bodies were even affected by their testosterone levels, as their particular DSD involves a gene that processes androgens.

The paper concludes by simply saying that some female athletes might have this particular genetic mutation, which might impact their testosterone levels and subsequently somehow threaten fairness in women's competition, so athletes should be screened to make sure that they don't fit this profile. What the paper does nothing to prove, however, is whether this condition confers any "unfair" advantages, or even any advantages at all.

All four of these athletes were operated on. Nowhere does the paper note their acknowledgment to be written about in a study, although this would have been a typical ethical practice. The initial examinations and recommendations were done at a hospital in France, and the paper says: "Institutional review board/Independent Ethics Committee approval for publication is not required in France."

This paper, in addition to the IAAF's 2011 testosterone rules, set off alarm bells for some in the world of endocrinology, where researchers study the intricacies of gender, chromosomes, and hormonal profiles. A group of geneticists, endocrinologists, doctors, psychiatrists, historians, and kinesiologists gathered at UCLA in 2013 for a symposium sponsored by the school's Institute for Society and Genetics in order to respond to the IAAF's most recent sex testing rules in athletics "with the objective of proposing changes to the FH [female hyperandrogenism] policy to help make it more equitable and not to repeal or replace it." A paper written from consensus of the meeting lays out several specific recommendations for updating the regulations. They note that the purpose of the regulations themselves aren't fully clear, and that the group questioned the processes of informed consent and privacy in the implementation of these rules, especially in the case of the paper about the four athletes who underwent gonadectomies.

"Our group questions the process of informed consent described by the authors and the fact that surgical recommendations for a clitoridectomy and gonadectomy were made in tandem. . . . it is not apparent that all available medical and non-medical options were presented to the athletes," the authors wrote. The group also wrote that there are difficulties in assessing athletic advantage via testosterone level alone, especially when considering many women with DSDs also are androgen resistant in some capacity. They write that "precisely defining the degree of resistance to androgens in an athlete with FH [female hyperandrogenism] will likely be a challenging task." While there are ways to assess whether a person's androgen receptors are resistant to androgens, there's no way to quantify how resistant they might be. So if any degree of androgen resistance is found, the authors recommend the athlete be eligible to compete, "regardless of the level of testosterone."

As you may have already surmised, one of the women described in the SRD5A2 study was almost certainly Negesa. She thinks she is Case 1 in the paper, but can't be sure. She was never told by the doctors that her body was going to be described in detail in an academic paper. Just as she was never given another option for lowering her testosterone levels. And no one has ever proved that her testosterone levels gave her an unfair athletic advantage.

FROM NUDE PARADES to chromosomal testing to measuring hormone levels and giving pelvic MRIs, governing bodies had been trying for decades to figure out just how to target the "suspicious" interlopers in the world of women's running. But by the time Semenya and Negesa started to make headlines, it was clear that the newest big threat to women's running had been decided: testosterone.

But testosterone levels, like chromosome tests before them, don't just come in two sizes. Major medical societies in the US, including the American Medical Association, the American Academy of Pediatrics, and Endocrine Society, have all agreed that IAAF should not subject any athletes to such invasive testing to determine their exact chromosomal structure or testosterone level, as there is no medical evidence to believe it would confer an unfair advantage.[54]

Eric Vilain, a pediatrician and professor of medicine at the University of California Irvine who took part in the UCLA symposium on the new policy, told the *New York Times* at the time that treating women with "ambiguous" sex characteristics as something to be dealt with or fixed in order to maintain a "level playing field" in sport won't work. "It's just impossible," Vilain said. "We are going to have to accept that at the fringes, there are no perfect categorizations."[55]

IN JULY 2014, Dutee Chand, an eighteen-year-old Indian sprinter, was dropped at the last moment from the roster of her nation's competitors at the Commonwealth Games. After winning two gold medals at the Asian Junior Athletics Championships the month prior, several of her competitors had requested she be tested for hyperandrogenism, according to the Indian national track confederation. Chand underwent a battery of medical exams: blood tests, visual exams of her genitalia and naked body, an MRI of her pelvis. Like Negesa, Chand was never told what the tests were for. "I was made to understand that something wasn't right in my body, and that it might keep me from playing sports," she told the *New York Times*.[56] According to Chand, the director of India's national track federation told her she was undergoing a "routine doping test" and that because no nurses were available, that would include an ultrasound examination. The Indian federation, for its part, said that Chand was given an ultrasound after complaining of "chronic abdominal pains." But they also said many of her fellow competitors at the National championships "had expressed concerns . . . about the athlete's appearance and questioned whether she should be permitted to compete in female athletics events."[57]

It wasn't long before it was leaked to the press that she was dropped from the Indian team ahead of the Commonwealth Games, and was undergoing sex testing. Soon after, Chand was contacted by Payoshni Mitra, a researcher and activist who had read the 2013 paper about the four athletes who underwent surgery to address their hyperandrogenism. Mitra urged Chand not to consent to treatment or surgery and also suggested she appeal to the Court of Arbitration for Sport—essentially the Supreme Court for cases brought against international sporting governing bodies. Because her testosterone was above the limit at that time, Chand missed the 2014 Commonwealth Games, and all following competitions until her trial was complete.

Her case was heard by the CAS the following March. But instead of specifically focusing on Chand and her medical case, the hearing became a kind of legal proceeding for testosterone itself.

Chand's team argued that her testosterone levels were a "natural genetic gift, which should not be viewed differently from other natural advantages derived from exceptional biological variation." They also noted that limiting female athletes to a specific level of testosterone but not doing the same for male athletes was sex discrimination, and that if this is truly a justified means of preserving a "level playing field" for elite female athletes, then the IAAF needs to justify that discrimination by showing data that supports the claim that testosterone levels above 10 nmol/L (the IAAF limit) are unfair in a women's category. Her team also said that there are no published scientific studies that link athletic performance with testosterone concentration in women with hyperandrogenism.

The IAAF's team contended that there was "a strong body of scientific opinion that the main cause of male athletes' power, size and strength advantages over female athletes is the significantly higher levels of testosterone that males generate during and after puberty."

But these claims are not mutually exclusive.

One endocrinology expert, Richard Holt, a professor at the University of Southampton, noted at the hearing that while the average testosterone levels for women are generally agreed to be between 0.5 nmol/L and 3 nmol/L, and men's are between 10 nmol/L and 35 nmol/L, one study showed 16.5 percent of male elite athletes had serum testosterone levels below 8.4 nmol/L, and 13.7 percent of elite female athletes had serum testosterone above 2.7 nmol/L. In other words, *averages* are just that and many athletes, in particular, show outlier numbers. He noted that the limit of 10 nmol/L for women athletes with hyperandrogenism, like Chand, was ignoring other influential factors of athletic advantage, like height, lean body mass, age, and nutrition.

Another expert witness, Sari van Anders, a neurobiology professor at Queens University, noted that testosterone levels fluctuate daily, hourly, and seasonally in men and women, and are often influenced by our social behaviors. She also noted that even women who have hyperandrogenism, and thus may have testosterone levels in the supposed "male" range, do not perform at the same level as men within that range—which is pretty obvious when you look at any of the times of the women who are being penalized by these testosterone level regulations.

When I spoke with van Anders in 2023, she told me that research into how testosterone affects women is basically "in its infancy." And that's essentially because of the story we've told about hormones since they were first discovered. Namely, that testosterone is "the male hormone" and estrogen is the "female hormone," because these hormones were found early on to have a huge impact on reproductive function and development.

In reality, everyone has varying levels of both kinds of hormones throughout their lives. And men and women can typically have very similar levels of estrogens (in fact, the normal range of the estrogen estradiol in postmenopausal women is lower than the normal range for men in general).[58]

What we do know is that estrogen helps people with uteruses menstruate and grow breasts, and testosterone helps people with sperm develop that sperm. But testosterone and estrogen also help people with all types of bodies do lots of other things, like sleep, build immunity, and develop strong muscle and bones. Beyond that, van Anders says, it's hard to say exactly what else these hormones do, especially across populations, because *most* androgen studies have been done on men, while most studies about hormones in women focus on estrogens.

Even those testifying on behalf of the IAAF during Chand's CAS hearing noted the reality of hormone data being pretty scant. They admitted that "we don't have much evidence" and there was no "definitive proof" that testosterone levels are *the* difference between male and female athletic performance. And they said that there was difficulty in understanding exactly how sensitive individuals are to their levels of testosterone.

The Court of Arbitration for Sport found in favor of Dutee Chand. They wrote in their concluding statement that "the IAAF has not provided sufficient scientific evidence about the quantitative relationship between enhanced testosterone levels and improved athletic performance in hyperandrogenic athletes. In the absence of such evidence, the Panel is unable to conclude that hyperandrogenic female athletes may enjoy such a significant performance advantage that it is necessary to exclude them from competing in the female category."

Chand was able to compete again in national and international level athletics events in July 2015, and the hyperandrogenism regulations were suspended entirely. However, the court noted that if the IAAF wanted to rewrite the hyperandrogenism rules with more data backing their decision, they'd be able to do so for a period of two years after the ruling. The court wrote that the evidence submitted should show the "actual degree of athletic performance advantage sustained by hyperandrogenic female athletes as compared to non-hyperandrogenic female athletes by reason of their high levels of testosterone." If they couldn't provide such evidence, then the hyperandrogenism regulations would be declared void entirely. In the meantime, there would be no regulation on naturally-occurring testosterone for women with DSDs, though doping with testosterone was still prohibited.

At the 2016 Rio Olympics, Dutee Chand and Caster Semenya were both eligible to compete without lowering their testosterone levels. In the 100-meter race, Chand didn't make it out of the preliminary heats. She ended up fiftieth out of the eighty runners. But no one argued that Chand's high testosterone allowed her to beat those thirty other runners. Instead, all eyes were on Semenya. In the 800-meter event, Semenya crossed the final finish line in 1:55.28. It was two seconds slower than the world record, and more than thirteen seconds slower than the men's gold medalist ran the same race earlier that week. But it was good enough for Gold, and good enough to stoke the rage of the gender police once again.

News stories insinuated that the silver medalist, Francine Niyonsaba, and the bronze medalist, Margaret Wambui, were also women with hyperandrogenism who were now competing with no need to lower their testosterone levels. They are also, all three of them, Black African women. The rest of the final field was made up of white women.[59] The times were close—2.41 seconds between the first- and sixth-place finishers (which happens to be the median difference in top six finishers for this event in the most ten recent Olympic Games). Canada's Melissa Bishop finished one stride behind bronze medalist Wambui. In the aftermath, however, the sixth-place finisher, Great Britain's Lynsey Sharp, who is white, held back tears during an interview, insinuating that the change in testosterone rules affected the outcome of the race. "I have tried to avoid the issue all year. You can see how emotional it all was. We know how each other feels. It is out of our control and how much we rely on people at the top sorting it out. The public can see how difficult it is with the change of rule but all we can do is give it our best," Sharp told the BBC.[60]

Despite the close race, the malice against the three 800-meter medalists in 2016—for, essentially, not *looking* feminine enough, and winning—was swift. A fellow runner on Team Great Britain congratulated Sharp on Twitter for "coming 3rd in women 800m." Famed marathon world record holder Paula Radcliffe told the BBC that she understood why Sharp was so upset. "However hard she goes away and trains, however hard Jenny Meadows goes and trains, they are never going to be able to compete with that level of strength and recovery that those levels of elevated testosterone brings."[61] However, many women have placed in the times that the 2016 medalists posted—sixty-nine, in fact, have run official 800 times good enough to have medaled in the race.

THE IAAF DID end up submitting new evidence to the CAS in 2017, which they said proved that quantified hyperandrogenism regulations were necessary for women with elevated testosterone levels. This evidence included another paper coauthored by the IAAF's own Bermon. The study had been published that year in the *British Journal of Sports Medicine* and analyzed hormone levels of 2,127 athletes (795 males and 1,332 females) who had competed at the 2011 and 2013 IAAF World Championships.[62]

The authors concluded that "women with the highest free testosterone levels performed 'significantly better' in the 400m, 400m hurdles, 800m, hammer throw, and pole vault." As such, the IAAF put forth new hyperandrogenism regulations in 2018 that would only apply to events where testosterone gave an "unfair advantage." So women competing in the three races noted above (and notably also the 1500-meter and mile events and not the hammer throw or pole vault, even though the former two were not mentioned in the study and the latter two were) would have to reduce their testosterone levels to below 5 nmol/L in order to compete, half the limit under the previous regulations.[63]

A separate paper submitted by IAAF, authored solely by Bermon, said that after three of those four athletes with hyperandrogenism went through gonadectomies, their times had dropped between 2 percent and 5 percent.[64] The governing body said this quantified the advantage of elevated levels of testosterone in women with DSDs. If this paper included Negesa as one of these data points, however, then it would include a woman who wasn't even provided with appropriate follow-up care and had stopped training altogether. Furthermore, a 2–5 percent change in performance is nowhere near an "unfair advantage" in sport. Athing Mu, the American who won gold in the 2021 800, turned in a performance about 16 percent faster than the slowest finisher of the 800 Olympic field that year.

Sebastian Coe, the IAAF President, a two-time Olympic Gold medalist himself, said in announcing the new regulations that "our evidence and data show that testosterone, either naturally produced or artificially inserted into the body, provides significant performance advantages in female athletes." Here, he implies that women with DSDs that give them higher-than-average *natural* levels of testosterone are akin to dopers. Their own natural bodies, lying outside of the strict sex binary, are cheating.

Dr. Bermon emphasized the new IAAF regulations were data-driven, saying: "The latest research we have undertaken, and data we have compiled, show that there is a performance advantage in female athletes with DSD over the track distances covered by this rule." Even though their own data showed no advantage for the 1,500-meter race nor the mile. Despite these issues, CAS determined the IAAF had fulfilled the target laid out two years prior in Chand's case, allowing the hyperandrogenism rules to be reinstated at that even stricter level.

Months later, several independent researchers began to question the data in these papers.[65]

Ross Tucker, an exercise physiologist who specializes in sports performance, told the *Daily Mail* in 2016[66] that he disagreed with the CAS decision to throw out the hyperandrogenism rules, and that Caster Semenya should not have been allowed to compete. But when the 2017 study and new regulations came out, Tucker and two peers—Roger Pielke, Jr., the director of the Sports Governance Center at the University of Colorado, and Erik Boye, a cell biologist at University of Oslo who has done a lot of work on anti-doping testing—began to look into the data, a common procedure for researchers with studies that come out in their field. "This is especially the case when an interested party (in this case IAAF) is sponsoring research to support a policy that it advocates," Tucker wrote on his website.[67] None of these researchers were able to replicate the results listed in the IAAF's paper.

In April 2018 Pielke requested the performance data from Dr. Bermon and the editor of the journal. Pielke told me they both refused, so he started to publicly question why they wouldn't release it. After the three researchers wrote a public letter, Bermon sent Pielke an email. "I remember it like it was yesterday," Pielke told me. It was the morning of the Fourth of July, but instead of celebrating with fireworks and parades and hot dogs, Pielke spent the whole day analyzing data, and chewing over the note included with the data. Bermon had written: "Here's some of the data. This is the version with the errors." Now that Bermon admitted to errors in his own message, Pielke was especially interested.

The three researchers found that the data used in the study's analysis did not just include some errors, it was "chock full of errors," Pielke says. In fact, they found the data used was inaccurate or anomalous up to 33 percent of the time in some events. They found instances where times were recorded more than once, for example, and the same times for one individual athlete were repeated, and times were listed when no athlete could be found who ran that time. They also included times for athletes who had been disqualified later for doping, which would certainly artificially raise testosterone levels with different results than naturally-occurring testosterone can have.[68, 69]

When the researchers reached out to the authors, Bermon replied, saying in an email to one of them that those errors "do not have significant impact on the final outcomes and conclusions of our study." However, the researchers determined that "all three outcomes change for all female athletes in the four events (included in the new regulations) upon the elimination of the previously described problematic data points." In fact, they found that in three of the events the performance difference actually changed from positive to negative, meaning that those with higher testosterone actually performed worse than those with lower testosterone, and that in the four regulated events, the difference in times between those in the highest-third testosterone and the lowest-third testosterone levels was only 1.6 percent, and only in one of those events was this even a statistically significant difference *at all*.

The researchers published a letter asking *BJSM* to retract the paper, given the erroneous data and results, and when they were told it would not be retracted, they called the *New York Times*. Pielke told the *Times* that "I think everyone can understand that if your data set is contaminated by as much as one-third bad data, it's kind of a garbage-in, garbage-out situation."[70]

Even though Tucker had, in his own words, felt "some sympathy for the IAAF" and agrees "in principle with the IAAF's attempts to regulate the boundary between women's and men's competition," he says that reviewing the actual data the IAAF used to back up the regulations was a "watershed moment" for himself. "I remember thinking, 'Is that it? This is all you got? This policy is now much weaker than the one before it.'"[71]

Sari van Anders, who had testified on the other side of the Chand case, had a similar response to the paper coauthored by Bermon. She said she was looking forward to seeing what the data, now revealed, said about the athletic advantage conferred by testosterone levels. Instead she read the paper and thought, "Oh, wow, this is terrible statistically," she told me. "I don't think my colleagues would publish this, much less use it as a basis for international policy. It's quite shocking."

Because Semenya would be required by the new rules to medically suppress her hormone levels in order to continue competing at her event, she followed in Chand's footsteps and challenged the new policy at the Court of Arbitration for Sport.[72]

Despite independent scientists across the ideological spectrum questioning the IAAF data and the fact that Semenya's times were never close to the "male range," the Court of Arbitration for Sport ruled against Semenya in May 2019. They let the new 5 nmol/L rule stand for all of the middle-distance races, which would require Semenya to medically alter her hormonal profile in order to compete.[73]

The ruling shocked many in the scientific community, especially after the IAAF paper used to underpin the new regulations had issued an official correction in Sept. 2017, and Tucker and Pielke provided expert testimony at the hearing. The IAAF itself admitted that its data was flawed during the CAS hearing. However, in its final decision, CAS wrote that "the Panel is not required to—nor does it consider it has sufficient evidence to enable it to—appraise the adequacy of the IAAF's policy-making process."[74]

Tucker was concerned by the court's decision to not weigh in on the scientific evidence underpinning the new rules, especially after they'd made the opposite point in deciding Chand's case. In a blog post after the hearing, Tucker wrote that he was troubled that women with DSD were being treated as though they were not women with elevated testosterone levels, but "biological males" because of their testosterone levels, while at the same time the very evidence the IAAF were citing showed that in 17 out of 22 events, testosterone levels made *no* difference in performance.

Pielke, who was there for the whole week of proceedings, was surprised at how "insufficient and archaic the proceedings were compared with the scale and scope and complexity of the issue," he told me.

CAS's full report on the trial and decision noted that IAAF's argument emphasized that women with DSDs like Semenya's were "biologically indistinguishable . . . in all relevant respects" from cisgender males.

"If you're going to impose on someone a new biological reality at the age of say eighteen, because they happen to be a fast female runner, then you had better be really, really sure that it's necessary," Tucker wrote. As was true of many other experts in endocrinology, medicine, and physiology alike, he did not see women born with DSDs, including Semenya, as male. Instead, he and many others called for more research into DSDs, hormone levels, and physiological performances. But the call was lost in what was soon to become an even angrier storm over who, exactly, was threatening women's sports.

IN OCTOBER 2019, five months after CAS's decision in the Semenya case, Negesa went public. She appeared in that German television documentary discussing how she had been forced into surgery by IAAF officials and was never the same. She applied for and received political asylum in Germany that year, because when news of her intersex status became public, she feared for her life should she return to Uganda, as members of the LGBTQIA community there are often subject to violence and harassment.[75]

IAAF has strongly denied Negesa was told by anyone in the organization to have surgery. "The IAAF does not advise, nor has it ever advised, an athlete on a preferred treatment route. The IAAF encourages relevant athletes to seek independent, medical advice and will, if requested, provide athletes with information on independent experts and reference centre specialists,"[76] a statement in response to the documentary read. The statement also denied Bermon ever met Negesa or was involved in her treatment. The federation and Bermon did not respond to my requests for an interview for this book.

The same year, IAAF changed its name to World Athletics, a rebrand that was meant in part to wipe the slate clean from the state-sponsored Russian doping scandal for which the IAAF president was arrested in 2015. According to InsidetheGames.biz, a news site dedicated to covering Olympic sport, "The IAAF claims the rebrand builds upon the organisation's restructuring and governance reform agenda to represent a modern, creative and positive face for the sport, while breaking away from the past."[77]

In other words, one could say that while IAAF played fast and loose with the rules for too long when it came to doping, World Athletics took unfairness extremely seriously. And they had scapegoats to prove it.

Despite coverage of Negesa's story in the *New York Times*, what she had gone through went largely ignored by the running world. I had followed Chand's and Semenya's cases closely, and I don't recall even hearing about Negesa's accusation then. Perhaps because she was a woman from a rural Ugandan village who had never won an Olympic medal and did not stand out on the starting lines of her races as particularly masculine. She did not tower over her competitors, nor were her muscles any more defined than any other elite athlete on the track. Still, Pielke tells me, her story was "just horrible." Ethically, he says, any part the IAAF played in the process would be a gross violation of medical and research ethics. These women, he points out, "didn't have any idea they were going to be research subjects." He considers Negesa's claims to be as gross a violation of medical ethics as the Tuskegee study, which allowed nearly 400 Black men living in Alabama who had syphilis to suffer the disease without treatment, and without being informed of their condition, between 1932 and 1972, simply to see what would happen. "It shows that the IAAF has some pretty clear ideas about male and female that align pretty narrowly with Western European North American stereotypes of how women should be, and how men should be," he said.

AT THE 2019 Outdoor State Open in Connecticut, a group of high school girls took their marks in the 100-meter final.[78] High school juniors Andraya Yearwood, Terry Miller, and Chelsea Mitchell, and freshman Alanna Smith were among them. Yearwood and Miller knew of each other, they'd been finishing state races in first and second place for the past year. According to ESPN reporter Katie Barnes, Mitchell said she was nervous before the race. In the preliminary heats, Miller, the previous year's state and New England champion in the 100, had run the distance in 11.64 seconds. Mitchell told Barnes, "I didn't think I could compete with that."

Smith was also dejected before the race. According to her mother, it was the first time she'd heard her daughter say "I don't have a chance," before the race began.

But before the final did begin, Miller was disqualified for a false start. Without her, Mitchell shot to the front of the pack. She won the race with a personal-best time of 11.67. She was a state champion. Smith ended up third. Yearwood placed fourth.

At the New England outdoor championships four days later, Mitchell repeated her win of the 100, Miller took the 200, and Smith took the 400. But Smith and Mitchell believed they had been wronged because Miller and Yearwood are transgender girls.

Days later, Smith, Mitchell, and Selina Soule, another high school runner who had raced against Yearwood and Miller that year, filed a federal discrimination complaint against the US Education Department's Office for Civil Rights, saying that Connecticut's law allowing high school athletes to compete according to their gender identity without restrictions violates Title IX rules. Miller and Yearwood were both cited by name in the complaint. The group of high school girls who brought the complaint, represented by the advocacy group Alliance Defending Freedom, claimed the state's policy of inclusion "cost them top finishes in races and possibly college scholarships."

They said in the complaint that "Girls deserve to compete on a level playing field" and "allowing boys to compete in girls' sports reverses nearly 50 years of advances for women under [Title IX]. We shouldn't force these young women to be spectators in their own sports."[79] Eight months later, the same group filed a federal Title IX lawsuit against the conference and multiple school boards, challenging the Connecticut Interscholastic Athletic Conference's policy, citing Yearwood and Miller again by name, and referring to them throughout the suit as "males."[80]

The case was dismissed by a district court judge as well as by the US Court of Appeals for the Second Circuit, ruling the plaintiffs lacked standing to challenge the policy and that discrimination against transgender students violates Title IX. The ADF group has appealed to the full circuit. The case will likely end up at the Supreme Court.

A new bogeyman, out to erase women's sports entirely, had been established.

In the three years since the suit was filed, twenty state houses in the United States have passed bills banning transgender athletes from participating in girls' sports. Prior to this, no states had such laws. The first passed in Idaho, in March 2020.[81] Many of these bills are titled "Save Women's Sports," or some such. The young women from Connecticut who ran against Miller and Yearwood have been referred to in, or have directly testified before, nearly all of these state legislatures.

It's easy to skim the headlines about these cases and think, yes, of course, women's sports should be *protected at all costs*. Especially if you are or have ever been a woman athlete, at any level, and fought for attention and space and funding for that sport. But this is the same language that has been used for over a century to paint women as weaker, more fragile, less able, than men. That women, as a class, are in need of protection. That we should feel lucky to have been given sport through Title IX. That we can't keep up with the boys. That women who are *too good* must be *suspicious.*

Those three girls from Connecticut who brought the lawsuit all compete on Division I college track teams, as of this writing. While they spread what is essentially a warning to fear transgender athletes in order to protect women's sports across the United States, they also compete. Miller and Yearwood, who supposedly took opportunities from them, don't run in college. Neither received athletic scholarships. Mitchell beat Miller *and* Yearwood several times during her high school career. Sometimes they beat her. That's typically how competitive sports works.

If transgender girls are truly such a widespread threat to women's sports that we need new state laws excluding them in order to protect the entire category, then why do these three girls from Connecticut need to testify in all these other states? Were there not local girls who could have spoken to their experiences? Where are all the other threats?

Meanwhile, Terry Miller and Andraya Yearwood have become pariahs, vilified in state houses across the US, simply for being girls who wanted to run track in high school. Who's protecting them?

SOCIOLOGIST JOAN FUJIMURA spent her career researching how scientists' own assumptions have shaped biomedical and genomic research. In 2006 she wrote about the scientists who were searching for the molecular genes that determined sex[82] and how the experiments they were undertaking and publishing weren't nearly as straightforward as they led people to believe. A study in *Nature* explained how a group of scientists had found the "male" gene, Sry (which sits on the Y chromosome). To test their hypothesis, they injected this DNA sequence into fertilized mice eggs and then transferred these eggs to the uteruses of female mice. Of the three XX mice who survived and had Sry incorporated into their chromosomes, two were females that produced eggs and were able to reproduce. The third was called an XX male. The mouse had a penis, but produced no sperm and was infertile. And yet the scientists who published this study claimed that the experiment showed that Sry *is* the male-determining gene. Even though many more females were produced than males, the females "were treated as the anomalies," writes Fujimura.

Fujimura calls data that gets ignored in this kind of experiment an "awkward surplus." She says that often, in science—and especially in science that is working in the realm of something like biological sex, which has so many preconceived notions around it—data that doesn't fit neatly into the anticipated results gets ignored in the final conclusions, or is never included in the experiment documentation in the first place. Think of all of the medical research done in the 1800s and early 1900s that attributed any female's malady to her uterus, or those male orangutans that didn't get as big as the ones with the puffy cheeks, so biologists just assumed they weren't fully grown. Fujimura writes that human and molecular geneticists have often used their own ingrained narratives about sex "in their experimental designs and analytic frames, thereby setting the stage for reproducing their own taken-for-granted categories of sex." In the case of the Sry mice experiment, for instance, they assumed that sex is binary and there is a gene that determines sex. So, instead of wrestling with the complexity of the actual experimental results that challenge this assumption—that perhaps there is more to how sex differences come to be and that those differences are not black-and-white—they chose to focus their conclusion on the most interesting thing to them: that one mouse that did grow a penis.

This is partially just how science works; researchers are typically very siloed in their own specialties, so what they focus on will likely be siloed, too. And because experiments almost never produce results that are universal or black-and-white, drawing any kind of conclusion can require focusing on trends or interesting anecdotes, instead of the big picture. Whether in the results or the design of the experiment itself, scientists sometimes just leave the awkward data out.

Which leads me to wonder: what if we stopped ignoring the "awkward surpluses" of data we are confronted with all the time? What if we stopped thinking of women who were especially talented runners, or who looked especially tall or muscular, or who have deep voices, as some kind of glitch in the system, or even a threat to humanity? What if we stopped trying to shove the results of these studies about testosterone levels into some preconceived notion of "male hormones" and "female hormones" and just looked at the data in front of us: that bodies are complex and sex is made up of chromosomes, gonads, hormones, receptors, genes, tissues, proteins, and other parts of the human genome we haven't even decoded yet?[83] What if we just accepted that there is no way you can simply measure a level of testosterone in a human and *know* they have an athletic advantage?

As a parent of two small children, I am supposed to teach my children a better way. I read them a picture book about gender that boils down to, essentially: gender is what you feel about yourself on the inside.

"I'm a he, right?" my four-year-old says after we read the book. "If you feel you are, you are," I say. But I can't tell if he is looking to me for confirmation because that's just what he's heard us say, or because that's how he feels. We don't dwell on it. In part because he doesn't seem that concerned. And in part because I don't know how to explain gender beyond that.

I don't know, myself, what it means that I feel like a woman inside. Do I feel nurturing? Soft? Weak? Slow? Quiet? Dependent? I don't really feel any of those things most of the time. I feel competitive. Loud. Independent. Argumentative. Angry. In fact, I often feel like I'm not fitting into the box created by society to mean "woman," at all. But still, I feel something in my deepest inner core that tells me that this is what I am.

When I speak to Sari van Anders, the neurobiologist who studies hormones, she tells me that one thing about sex hormones that has been studied pretty extensively is that high testosterone is associated with competitive behavior, and that low testosterone is associated with nurturing behavior. She says, if you look at this from believing the original story about these hormones (that testosterone is a "male" hormone and lack of it is "female"), then it fits into the idea that men are competitive, and women are nurturing. But, if you don't ignore the awkward data here, "we know that men are and can be nurturing. And we know that women can be intensely competitive," she told me. She notes studies show that when men become fathers, the more they help care for their babies, the more their testosterone levels drop. When women are pregnant, their testosterone levels jump. Why do we ignore that these levels can change, and that hormones aren't binary?

As a young person, I used to think something was genuinely wrong with me. I'd get so angry during soccer games that I'd yell, scream, curse. (I was carded more than once.) I'd hurl my body at much bigger players to get the ball, hoping I might cause a little pain. Afterward, when we inevitably lost, I'd explode. Tears chilled my reddened cheeks as I stalked off the field in a huff. Sometimes I thought I could literally feel my blood boiling under my skin. The anger from losing, the rage of wanting to win, I could feel it bubble up as soon as I began to play. Every time. Every game. After, it took hours sometimes to cool my body back down, to quit shaking and calm the bubbling rage and competitiveness inside of me. I couldn't control it.

Years of scholarship have shown that even young female athletes are aware that if they are good at sports, they need to emphasize their femininity in order to not be seen as a societal "deviant."[84] In years past, this kind of ability sometimes, as in Helen Stephens' case, meant you were accused of being a man. But also, as basically any girl who has ever shown any aptitude for a sport could tell you, there is a fear of being seen as a lesbian. In an academic paper from 2005 that interviewed several high school athletes, researchers were told about the need many of their peers had to be seen as girly when not competing. One basketball and track athlete put it like this: "If someone goes to celebrate, they have to get their hair done; they gotta put on makeup; they have to get cute . . ."[85]

These attitudes have shifted some in recent years, as gender stereotypes and the binary in general have been relaxed. Compare the looks of the women athletes who attended the ESPYs, for instance, twenty years ago, when all the women wore high heels, full makeup, and uber-feminine dresses, to today, where many of the players choose suits or more androgynous looks. These shifts have happened at the same time as more and more professional women athletes have embraced LGBTQ identities and largely been supported. But as nonbinary and transgender people are becoming more outwardly common in society in general, the fear of losing the distinction between genders grows for some—and this fear, as it was a century ago, is often directed at female athletes. Female athletes who are too competitive. Too muscular. Too good. Or just too masculine. And sports continues to be a place where people feel like it's okay to police this kind of gender deviance.

At an elementary track-and-field meet in British Columbia, Canada in 2023, a spectator stopped the competition to call out a nine-year-old girl he thought looked like a boy. He said he thought this was a girls' event, so why was there a boy competing? The girl's mother told the *New York Times* later, "My daughter is a girl, was born female, and uses she/her pronouns. She has a pixie cut."[86]

The man reportedly demanded a birth certificate to prove she was born female. A nine-year-old girl. "My daughter was physically shaking so hard, she was sobbing. She has never been exposed to queer or trans hate before. It rocked our whole family. It's shocking. Who does this to a child?"

WHEN I MEET Dr. Katherine Ackerman, at her offices in suburban Boston where the Wu Tsai Female Athlete Program has recently moved, she's a few minutes late. She walks into the office and everyone stops to hear what she has to say. "Sorry I'm late," she laughs. She'd been pulled over for answering her cell phone while driving, she explained. She tells everyone in earshot that she was able to talk her way out of the ticket. I'm not surprised. She had that certainty in the way she speaks—the thing that makes people listen. I would have let her off without a ticket, too.

Ackerman's authoritative style of speaking and her reverence for her work helped me understand how she'd gotten where she was: the director of a multidisciplinary medical clinic, the first of its kind, that focuses medical care for, and research studies on, female athletes and their unique needs. The clinic offers care from all the interconnected specialists female athletes likely need, from sport psychologists, to nutritionists, endocrinologists, orthopedists, and cardiologists. After decades of studying endocrinology and the menstrual cycle and RED-S in sport medicine, I was curious how she felt about the fear that women's sports are somehow at risk today. Since her research focused on sex differences, I wasn't sure how she would respond when I asked about transgender and intersex athletes and the concept of male natural advantages.

But Ackerman told me that actually, what's been so impactful about further developing the theory of the Female Athlete Triad into what is now known as RED-S has been that its helped not just women and girls get the help they need to be healthier and more competitive athletes, but also male athletes who were previously going totally unseen in their problems with underfueling. Because, as it turns out, there's overlap in how energy deficiencies in female athletes also show up in male athletes. And often, because of those cultural stories we tell about gender—like for instance, that girls are the only ones who have body issues or eating disorders—energy deficiency in male athletes can go undetected for longer. But underfueling can have massive negative impacts on male athletes, too, from thyroid issues to heart problems. It's a good example of how more gender equality helps everyone. And that, even across sex differences, bodies are more alike than different.

As an endocrinologist, Ackerman recognizes that the way we talk about gender has shifted in recent years away from the binary. "I'm fifty, so in the beginning this sort of blew my mind, because it's not something I grew up with," she told me. "It is pretty enlightening to watch how accepting kids are with the gender spectrum. It's been a good journey for me to see with my own children and with my patients."

At the same time, she says, conversations about the variations in the sex and gender binary from a medical and scientific perspective are getting harder. "It's just such an extreme conversation," she told me. "I have this conversation amongst friends, and we can get into really interesting dialogue and talk about the ethics and ramifications and those conversations I find enjoyable and challenging and interesting, but unfortunately, the public discourse is really extreme on one side versus the other. If you talk too much about the benefits of testosterone, performance-wise, people think you hate trans and nonbinary people, and if you talk about including trans people in sport at any level, from kids to Masters, then people think you hate women."

Ackerman, like all researchers in the field, says that testosterone *does* have an impact on sex differences. "We can't ignore the fact that testosterone has some physical benefits and how women and men diverge after puberty because of that huge testosterone surge," she tells me. However, she adds: "we don't have enough data" to establish fair and inclusive sport regulations yet when it comes to transgender and intersex athletes.

While some very small studies have been done on transgender athletes, they have been made up almost entirely of transgender women who transitioned as adults, post-puberty.[87, 88] But Ackerman's lab is trying to change that. When I spoke to her, she was just beginning a longitudinal study following kids who have decided to transition before puberty. Her lab will do regular labwork, track their hormone levels, and monitor physiological and psychological changes. This information will contribute real data to the currently mostly theoretical controversy over athletic advantages or disadvantages of young transgender kids—especially those who don't go through puberty as the sex that was assigned at their birth.

Unfortunately, studies like Ackerman's, which are necessary to begin answering questions about sex categories and sport, are getting even harder to undertake. At her office in spring 2023, she told me she was nervous about being able to recruit for the transgender study, even though they were recruiting from four separate gender clinic sites, across the country. She does not seem to be a woman who frightens easily; she mentioned that day that she's one of the only researchers willing to speak publicly about how the end of *Roe v. Wade* has made it more difficult for research such as hers on the menstrual cycle to happen.

In other words: she is not easily spooked. And yet she hesitates just a moment after telling me about the longitudinal study on trans youth before saying "this political environment, frankly, puts us a little at risk because people will be paying attention."

She's not wrong. The summer prior, Boston Children's Hospital, where her clinic is based, was inundated with threats of violence and harassment when a right-wing Twitter account began a misinformation campaign claiming certain surgeries were done on minors at the hospital's Gender Multispecialty Service.[89] Doctors received death threats. A bomb threat was called into the hospital. Phone calls, social media activity, and harassing emails flooded the hospital's communication channels. The chief of Adolescent and Young Adult Medicine at nearby Mass General for Children and Harvard Medical School, Dr. Scott Hadland, wrote that he had received personal death threats and worried for his patients, himself, and his family. "Professionals who work with LGBTQ young people, especially those who identify as LGBTQ themselves, are facing serious peril," he said in an essay in *New England Journal of Medicine*.[90] "We have seen the politicization of health care and the vilification of professionals play out before; one need only recall the everyday risk faced by our colleagues who provide abortions to understand how rhetoric can escalate to violence."

Violence is not an exaggeration. Quick on the heels of these twenty state laws banning transgender girls from playing school sports came bills that tried to erase children from outside of the gender binary altogether. As of this writing, twenty-one states have banned gender-affirming care for transgender youth. Gender-affirming care is, however, considered best practice and lifesaving care by all of the major medical organizations.

Intersex children, meanwhile, are still often subjected to invasive surgeries without their consent, essentially forcing a child who is born outside of the sex binary into it—with no regard for their future health or gender identity.

All in the service of forcing children into one or the other of the two buckets we've established as "normal."

THREE YEARS AFTER Negesa first went public with her story, filmmaker and former Olympian Phyllis Ellis released her own documentary, *Category: Woman*, which included Negesa's story, as well as Semenya's, Chand's, and Wambui's. In it, she highlights how regulations and sex suspicions have all seemed to target women from the Global South, who don't fit white, Euro-centric ideas of femininity. "If you wrote down what happened to the athletes in *Category: Woman*, it would sound like a science fiction novel," she told me by phone. "But it's real, it's real life."

In the aftermath of the IAAF controversy over testosterone levels, the 2020 Olympic Games (held in 2021 due to the Covid-19 pandemic) brought the question of sex divisions in sport into stark relief. While Caster Semenya was not allowed to compete in her preferred event, the 800, because she refused to medically lower her naturally-occurring testosterone, the first out transgender women athletes did compete at the Olympics: Laurel Hubbard, a weightlifter from New Zealand, and Chelsea Wolfe, an American BMX freestyle rider. Since 2015, the IOC had declared that transgender women athletes were allowed to compete in the female category at the Olympics so long as they had declared their gender identity as female for at least four years, and if their testosterone levels were below 10 nmol/L for at least twelve months prior to their competition and throughout their eligibility period.

Though Hubbard did not medal, and Wolfe was an alternate who did not end up competing, the fact that transgender women were competing on the world stage added tinder to the flames now raging rhetorically around trans women in sports. So in the months after, the International Olympic Committee consulted more than 250 athletes in order to write a document addressing the issue of gender diversity. Negesa was one of those athletes. She told the committee about the surgery she underwent and the downfall of her running career due to IAAF's regulations. In November 2021, the group released a "Framework on Fairness, Inclusion and Non-Discrimination on the Basis of Gender Identity and Sex Variations." The document seems to make the sporting world more equal and inclusive for those like Negesa, stating that "everyone, regardless of their gender identity, expression and/or sex variations should be able to participate in sport safely and without prejudice." It also includes a provision that notes that "eligibility criteria should be established and implemented fairly and in a manner that does not systematically exclude athletes from competition based upon their gender identity, physical appearance and/or sex variations." Restrictions from eligibility, it suggests, must be based on "robust and peer-reviewed research that demonstrates a consistent, unfair, disproportionate competitive advantage in performance and/or an unpreventable risk to the physical safety of other athletes." The release of the framework by the IOC felt like a win for inclusion. Negesa and Ellis were both proud.

But the document also gave the international sporting federations, which govern the international competitions of each sport, full sway to develop their own individual policies. The IOC hoped to offer *advice,* in other words, to those governing bodies in the form of a ten-principle approach of fairness, but they also said that they couldn't create *regulations* for sports (even though the IOC has done so in the past, such as with their 2015 transgender inclusion policy).

In March 2023 World Athletics (formerly the IAAF) announced its new eligibility policy for women with hyperandrogenism and transgender athletes. It stated that any woman with a DSD that increases her testosterone, had to lower the hormone to below 2.5 nmol/L—one-fourth of what the original regulation had been—for twenty-four months prior to competition, in order to compete in the female category in *any event*. Gone, in other words, was the supposed data-backed rule that said only middle-distance races were affected.

Transgender women were banned outright from competition.[91]

Ellis was angry when she spoke to me about the new regulations. As an Olympian in the 1980s who was subject to the blanket chromosomal sex tests, she says part of her understands why some of the women athletes from that era are so protective of the women's sport space, because they had to fight for it to exist. "Those women who advocated for Title IX . . . paved the way for a lot of us," she said. But the world has changed, she added, and women's sports exist now in a manner that was unimaginable fifty years ago. "With the Women's Sports Foundation, with all of the allies and places in the world for women's sport and the calls for equality and inclusion, how in God's name could they possibly destroy the integrity of women's sport? It's not possible."

World Athletics has ignored the awkward surplus of data in front of them. No one affected by these hyperandrogenism regulations has put up "unfair" times. In the 2021 Olympic Games, for instance, the women's 800 final would not include the 2016 medalists: Semenya, Niyonsaba, nor Wambui (who were all suspected of hyperandrogenism), yet all three medalists in 2021 would cross the line in faster times than those three did.

The new IOC framework says "robust" data indicating a "consistent, unfair, disproportionate advantage" must be used to implement exclusionary regulations like those World Athletics has written. The only data World Athletics has provided has since been corrected to show no causation between testosterone levels and performance. The World Medical Association called for physicians around the world not to participate in implementing World Athletics' discriminatory testosterone regulations in 2019, as they were not data-driven or medically necessary.[92] The United Nations said the regulations in 2020 were a potential human rights violation.[93] Despite all of this, World Athletics has doubled down on the cultural narrative that women athletes require protection from other women athletes who don't fit a narrow definition of *woman*. "In these circumstances, the Council decided to prioritise fairness and the integrity of the female competition before inclusion," the organization said in a press release.

World Athletics, like nearly half of the states in the US, have decided it can say definitively what makes a man or a woman, even when science says we don't know for sure. They've set in stone the idea that "data around physical performance" shows "male advantage." This is just the way things work. Men are just *always* going to win.

But what if they're wrong?

Jasmin Paris running the Spine Race in January 2019 (Racing Snakes Photography)

7: What About the Long Run?

January 2019, England, the Pennine Way,
Between Hadrian's Wall and Bellingham

JASMIN PARIS'S EYELIDS are heavy. She snaps to attention—and catches herself just before falling to the cold, wet ground. Paris awakens in that surreal world in-between consciousness and not. It takes her a moment before she recognizes her surroundings. Spiderwebs and dewdrops shine in an otherworldly silver that cuts through the dark. It's only 4 p.m. or so, but the sun is down. She has a pack on her back, and a headlamp lighting her way. The hood of her black rain jacket is pulled tight around her face to keep the rain and bitter wind out. Her trail-running shoes are covered in mud beneath a few layers of tights and gaiters on her legs—she's doing all she can to remain warm, and awake, and to continue to run.[1]

At some point while cataloging the facts of her surroundings, Paris remembers that she is on the Pennine Way, a trail that goes through the Pennine hills, sometimes called England's backbone, participating in an ultramarathon known as the Spine Race. Paris has been running for about 200 miles, stopping to rest for just a few hours in total since she began this trek three days earlier.

She remembers to check the GPS to see where Eugeni Roselló Solé is, the closest competitor. She left him at the last checkpoint, where he'd accidentally fallen asleep. She'd planned to sleep, too, but instead, she ate, pumped breast milk for her daughter, had a strong coffee, and took the opportunity to pull ahead.

The Pennine Way is known as one of the toughest trails in the country, running 268 miles from the town of Edale in Derbyshire all the way up to a tiny village in the Scottish borderlands called Kirk Yetholm. Inspired by the Appalachian Trail in the US,[2] it bears some similarities—and not just because the Appalachians and most of the British Isles all used to be part of the same prehistoric mountain range. For walkers and hikers in Britain, the Pennine is seen as a challenge, and like the Appalachian, you can take the whole trail in one epic go—which takes normal backpackers between two to three weeks—or you can run or hike it section by section, adding up to a lifetime accomplishment. This being Great Britain, the hills are often covered in fog, and the trails take you through moors, bogs, farmers' fields, and tiny hill towns with bed and breakfasts or little pubs with inns attached.

The Spine Race came about in 2012, developed by two arctic expedition guides looking for a way to bring the extremes of the poles to the ultramarathon- and fell-running-loving people of the UK. They decided the event could go the whole length of the Pennine Way, with competitors having just seven days to complete the 268 miles and 37,000 feet in elevation gain. They'd have to run it. They could stop and sleep whenever they'd like, but they'd have to factor that into their time, a contrast to some other multiday events that had certain sections completed each day and rest time in-between for all. For this race, each runner can have one pack transported to each of the five checkpoints along the way, but between those checkpoints would have to carry their own supplies, clothing, food, water, lamps, poles, emergency kits. Oh, and most of this must be done in darkness, as there's only about six hours of daylight here in the middle of January. Temperatures are often below freezing, skies are gray, wind and rain are frigid on the hilltops. The first year of the competition, eleven people entered (all of them men), and just three finished.[3]

Now, during the eighth annual race, as Paris tries to keep her eyes open and her body upright, she sings to herself, hoping the noise will rouse her senses. "If you wanna be my lover!" At first, she sings the songs of her youth. Then another comes to mind, "Woo woo goes the train!" She'd been playing the children's song for her thirteen-month-old daughter. She misses her terribly, and the song about the train makes her wonder how bedtime is going. Whether out of loopiness or some stroke of brilliance, she begins to use the voice she usually used for her daughter—a caring, motherly voice—to speak to herself. She tells herself to stay warm, to have some sweets to keep her blood sugar up. She puts on every last layer of clothes she has to survive the cold, dark, surreal night. "Somehow the comfort of having a caring voice made it all less hard, even if that voice was my own," she'd write later.

When Paris first sees the woman outside the farmhouse, she thinks it might be another sleep-deprivation-induced hallucination. But when the woman offers Paris some hot broth, she can't say no. She goes inside, surprised at what a treat this is. Hot broth that's thick and reviving when she'd just been cold and alone in the dark outside. She feels warm and comforted and ready to move on. The woman also gives Paris some news:

"Pavel's tweeting about you," she says. "He's excited, but he's worried you haven't had enough sleep."

Pavel was Pavel Paloncy, a kind of Spine Race hero. The Czech ultra-runner had won the Spine Race the prior year, during what some called the worst weather the race had ever seen, making him the first to win three times.[4] Organizers actually required runners to stop one night when blizzards and high wind made the route too dangerous. Pavel wasn't running this year, but he was "dot-watching," the term for what those fans of ultra running do during a race. Since ultras are typically difficult to actually attend and see in person, spectators watch the drama unfold on their screens. Each runner has a GPS tracker, and spectators can follow their little dots along the map of the course as they run. Pavel and other dot watchers could see that Paris was in a commanding lead ahead of Solé, with forty-some miles left to go, but that she'd only stopped for about three hours since the race began three days earlier.

Leaving the warm room, delicious broth, and kind woman, Paris goes back out into the cold. Her next stop is only a few more miles away: Bellingham, the last checkpoint of the race. She plans to sleep in Bellingham. But when she arrives, she can only think about how close Solé is to her, and how badly she wants to just be done with this, and to see her daughter. So instead, she gambles. She eats a meal and changes her clothes. She lays down for forty minutes. Too exhausted and too focused on her goal, though, she can't sleep. She drinks a coffee and leaves the checkpoint.

But despite her focus, she didn't actually seem to be in a hurry, one of the checkpoint coordinators, Nicki Lygo, tells me later. "Her demeanor never changed. Not from the beginning to the end. She was level, calm, polite. No hurry. There was always time to have a chat." Lygo says that Paris took a selfie with her at the checkpoint, and when she shows me this picture, she zooms in on each of their faces in turn, laughing.

"Look! I look haggard to hell, absolutely horrendous." Lygo, after all, had barely slept either, and was under loads of stress keeping the whole checkpoint volunteer system up and running. Meanwhile, she tells me, Paris looks "flawless. Like she's just driven there for a coffee." And I have to laugh, too. It's true. Paris has a genuine smile on her face, her cheeks are slightly flushed, as though she's just come in from a morning jog. Her eyes are sparkling.

Under the surface, Paris is a woman on a mission, cool and calculating. Despite how she acted with Lygo, she's trying to leave town quickly, in case Solé is coming into the checkpoint soon, she doesn't want him to catch sight of her and try to tag along.

That night is the most surreal, the darkness surrounds her as she moves through the moors. There isn't much of anything there, but in her brain's fog it feels like she's running between two giant, black walls.

Paris is so tired, so so so tired. But she knows she needs to be awake, she needs to finish. She needs to get to the little old pub and inn in Kirk Yetholm where her baby is waiting for her. She needs something to wake her up. She can feel a blister bubbling up on her big toe. Stopping for a moment, she pushes down on it—hard—to try to shock her body awake. It works, but she rips the skin off of her big toe in the process, resulting in her hopping along her route for the next few minutes.

When the sun comes up, it's brilliantly clear. The surrounding hills and trees seem to illuminate infinite shades of green for miles and miles. This is why Paris takes these runs, why she does these things that seem crazy—because she loves the earth so much. She runs out here to experience the beauty and majesty of the hills and mountains, up close, embedded, in a way so many never will. Her eyes and mind begin playing tricks on her, even in the daylight, such that everything she sees seems to change into something else. She knows somewhere in the back of her head that what she's seeing isn't reality, like when you're dreaming and you're aware that somehow you're on another plane of consciousness.

Knowing this made her hallucinations kind of entertaining. Despite the sun, the weather is bitter cold and the wind feels like ice on her face. With every layer of clothing she had in her pack now on her body, and moving as quickly as she can to keep her blood pumping, Paris starts to notice a pain in her legs each time she strides forward, a sharp jolt running up her tendons. Before she knows it, somehow that brilliant daylight is beginning to wane.

As the sun sets over the ridge that afternoon, Paris knows this image would be one of those she will remember for years to come. She tries to jog as fast as she can, but her legs are in pain, her body is depleted. Her run has become a shuffle.

When the tiny village of Kirk Yetholm, just a group of lights and a glowing finishing arch, comes into her sights, she can think only of getting to her family. Her pole-assisted hobble becomes a real run. The voices of others, many others, reach her ears. They're clapping and shouting her name. Lights and cameras are there, watching her as she crosses the arch, but she barely notices. Someone walks with her to the wall of the inn, the official end of the race—she must touch it with her own hand to mark her finish.

Paris is done. She's won the Spine Race—the first woman to do so. And she has crossed the finish line in 83 hours, 12 minutes, and 23 seconds—three and a half days since she began, with only a few hours of sleep. She's smashed the previous course record by twelve hours. She barely slept, though she did take the time to pump milk at nearly every checkpoint. At the finish line, her husband hands over her thirteen-month-old daughter, who eyes Paris skeptically until she pulls off her hood and head lamp. Paris nuzzles her baby's red, round, cold-pinched cheeks, smiling and closing her eyes.

Solé had to drop out less than four miles from the finish. He stopped and couldn't shake the cold, the medic crew had to rescue him. The second-place finisher, Eoin Keith, who has won the men's division of the race three times now and is the world-record holder for the fastest crossing of Ireland, won't arrive for fifteen more hours.[5]

KING MALCOLM III of Scotland held a race up Creag Choinnich near Braemar in 1064. He wanted to find those men best suited to be soldiers and messengers. No roads existed in the Highlands, and enemies—a neighboring clan, the English, or the Norse—were a constant threat. The Scottish clans needed a way to assemble soldiers at a moment's notice. A runner, racing through the bogs, around the boulders, carrying a wooden cross ablaze on one end and soaked in blood on the other, would shout the time and place for clansmen to assemble for a fight.

Malcolm, one of the last Gaelic kings, held his race up and down the mountain to ensure his messengers were the fastest. He gave the winner of this first race a purse full of gold and a sword as winnings. This is often called the first recorded fell race. It, and other sporting events Malcolm held, became the inspiration for the Highland Games, traditional Scottish sporting events still held today.[6]

When fell-running races in the UK resumed in the mid-1800s—for sport—women were not included. As with so many formalized sporting events, war—and its inherent maleness—was the inspiration. It's the reason that even today, we use battle terminology in sport (attack, defend, go in for the kill).

Despite its military roots, though, even from its earliest days, fell running had an amateur bent, a humbleness, an everyman sort of feel. It was man versus hill, and yet, even this sport built on supposed deep human instinct did not seem to have a place for women. That attitude echoed into the future, of course, in the exclusion of women in track, marathon running, and even early American jogging culture. *Women need not apply.* From the mid-1800s to the mid-1900s, women were turned away from fell running events throughout Britain's hills and mountains. This doesn't mean that women weren't fell running. Fell running, as a rule, is fairly free-form. You don't need to go to a track, or buy special equipment, you just have to run over fells (a term from the Old Norse word *fjall*, meaning "mountain or hill").

While a few of the fell races admitted women from time to time throughout the 1960s, most did not as a matter of course. In 1970, when the Fell Runners Association was first set up, the wife of one of the committee members wasn't even allowed to sit inside with the men while they held their first meeting. Brenda Robinson wrote later that she was "locked out of the car in the freezing car park playing with my seventeen-month-old son in the snow as dusk approached." Below the list of the first 117 members of the FRA in the organization's first newsletter, there was a footnote: "At least one enquiry has been received from a lady re membership!—How about lady members?—our constitution doesn't specify sex!"[7] The concept was apparently difficult even to comprehend.

This attitude didn't bode well for gender equality in the sport. So that even as late as 2004, Richard Askwith's *Feet in the Clouds*, a well-regarded book by the British journalist about his own obsession with the sport, refers to the act of fell running as practically the definition of masculinity itself: "I force myself to run although my legs are so shaky that I keep tripping on loose rocks . . . My thighs protest each time I lift a leg; my whole body screams each time I put a foot down. Very well: don't listen. Feelings are for girls. My mind is full of thoughts and toughness: the sheer brute willpower by which hostile mountains are sometimes tamed."[8]

When Jasmin Paris ran her first fell race four years later, she says she never felt unwelcome because of her gender. There were far more men than women, but everyone seemed to be there for similar reasons, to run, to enjoy time on the mountain, and to have cake and tea at the end of the race.

Paris never even considered herself an athlete. Growing up, she wasn't that sporty. While attending university, she tells me, she jogged every now and then for exercise. "It would be maybe twenty minutes around the park and I sort of thought that was a run," she told me.

But in her first job after graduating from veterinary school in 2008, a colleague invited her along to a local fell race. It wasn't very long, just a little hill race, she says, and she only had road-running shoes, so "I spent a lot of time falling over" and could barely catch her breath by the end. But she loved it. "I just remember thinking, These people are mad, but I feel like I fit in with them." Being out in the mountains reminded Paris of her childhood, spent hiking and backpacking with her parents and three brothers through the Peak District in England, at the southern end of the Pennines, where she grew up. They started when she was young, hill walking (the British term for hiking). Then by the time she was in her teens and twenties, the family often took long backpacking trips. "I think that's where I developed my ability to move fast across rough terrain," she says.

She joined her local fell-racing club, and started to run in the evenings with them, out in the hills. Six months later Paris ran her first ultramarathon, a 33-miler. Two weeks later, she ran a 20-mile fell race. Two weeks after that, she ran a 31-mile ultra on the Isle of Man. She was hooked, but then she had to leave.[9]

The small-animal veterinarian had a yearlong residency in Minnesota, in the US. She tried to run there, but didn't love road running. She signed up for a half-marathon because it circled a lake. "But that was the closest thing I could get to a trail race at that time," she said. When she moved back to the UK, she applied for a residency in Edinburgh so she'd be close to hills. That summer, she entered the 20-kilometer Slioch Horseshoe Race, in the Scottish Highlands. She won the women's division. Paris found she enjoyed the longer races, and kept going, often placing in the top five or ten finishers, regardless of gender category.

In 2014, six years after starting a thing for fun and continuing on just because she enjoyed it, she became the Scottish Fell Running Champion by earning the most points in three championship-level races throughout the year. In 2015 she became champion again, and she added the British Fell Running Championship. She also completed the Dragon's Back Race—a five-day, 200-mile stage race through Wales, known as one of the toughest in the UK. She finished behind just one man. Her fiancé, Konrad Rawlik, came in third. The following year she ran the Charlie Ramsay Round, a fell race that's run as a circuit, 58 miles over 24 summits and 28,500 feet of ascent in Scotland. When she won in 16 hours and 13 minutes, she set a new course record for men and women. One month later, Paris and Rawlik got married.

At the peak of her newfound sporting prowess, Paris got pregnant. She kept running and racing throughout her pregnancy, even running one fell race ten days before her daughter was born. She took a few weeks off after her baby was born, in November 2017, but remained active even in those postpartum days, slinging her baby to her belly to go for walks in the hills. Later, she'd put the baby in the stroller for a nap at the bottom of a hill and then run up and down to get her strength back up. By the spring, she competed in her first British Fell Running Championship race of the year—and won first place in the women's division. At the end of the season, less than a year after giving birth, she was named Women's British Fell Running Champion for the second time.

Still, like many new moms, she felt like she wasn't quite *back* back. Things weren't the same. She was working as a veterinarian and finishing her PhD at the University of Edinburgh and waking up multiple times a night to breastfeed and calm a crying baby. She was back to racing, but she wanted a challenge—she wanted to know she was still *herself.* So she signed up for a race she'd seen parts of but always thought was a little out of her comfort zone: the Spine Race. For the first time in her fell running career, she began to train with a coach. The only time she found to train was in the mornings, so she'd rouse herself around 5 a.m. and run the hills before work. "It wasn't easy, especially after a night of broken sleep," she remembers.

As part of her training, Paris started the weaning process, knowing that breastfeeding and a multiday ultramarathon likely wouldn't mesh. But her daughter got sick one month before the race, and all she wanted was to nurse. So when Paris was packing her drop bag for the checkpoints of the Spine Race, she included her breast pump and added an item to her to-do list at each stop.

JUST A DOZEN years before Paris's record-breaking win, the medical community doubted Paula Radcliffe's ability to run a marathon after giving birth. A century before that, half a mile was considered too far for women to run because it might damage their reproductive systems, so when Florence MacDonald had a daughter, *that* was what made headlines. One after another, women like Mickey Patterson, Diane Leather, and Bobbi Gibb have done things people didn't previously think possible for women to do. Mary Decker, Mary Cain, Caster Semenya, and Annet Negesa have been scrutinized and questioned, their bodies radically harmed or required to change to fit a mold that doesn't actually exist, simply for being women who run.

As these women proved the naysayers wrong, ideas about what women can do, how our bodies work, and what our role in this world is, have made swift progress along a parallel track. Women eschew outdated exercise advice and body ideals. Women go to college and laugh at staircases that were built for our supposedly fragile uteruses. Women are revolutionizing the medical and sports science fields by thinking about periods and about social contexts that might impact our minds and bodies without any of us realizing. Women are proving they can be construction workers and Army Rangers and mechanics and coaches. Women are speaking out about themselves, saying we don't have to look or act a certain way in order to be accepted in society. Nor do we need to be defined in opposition to men. We can define ourselves, thank you very much. And, yes, we can beat men.

Most important, women runners have proven that what is humanly possible is often beyond the scope of society's limited imaginations.

WHEN I SPOKE with Jasmin Paris in 2023, four years after she first made global headlines for beating all the men in the Spine Race and shattering the course record, she pointed to some mythological thinking in the ultra-running world. "People talk about potentially women's physiology being slightly better suited over long distance. And to be honest I'm not sure about that," she says. The veterinarian told me she's read some studies that back up the idea that women are better ultra-runners, and some that don't.

I've read many of these, too, and I could tell you here about all of the physiological studies I've read that show that women, who have more of a certain type of muscle fiber than men do,[10] may actually recover more quickly from exertion,[11] and take longer to get fatigued at similar workloads.[12] I could also point to the neurological studies that show that women aren't as affected by sleep deprivation as men.[13] And other sport-science studies that show that the farther women run, the more they can keep up with or exceed men's running speeds.[14] Still, there are plenty of physiological studies out there that show the exact opposite things. One of my favorites concludes: "Women will never outrun men in the future."[15] End. Period. Fact.

Because here's the thing about endurance running, or fell running, or just running in the mountains for days on end: Us humans, and the world we live in, are complex. And when we do extremely hard physical things and combine those with mental toughness, puzzles to solve, and a million other human decisions and errors and uncontrollable variables like equipment or the weather—like say, in school, battle, sport, work, or an ultramarathon endurance race through unmarked mountains—what we bring to the table is so much more than one aspect of our physiology. We bring our whole selves. And one study that compares the averages of women's ability to do something versus the average man's ability to do something isn't going to tell us how the race is going to end.

"You have to carry all your stuff. It's winter, so you have to keep yourself fed and warm and dry, and look after your feet. And there's just loads of other things. Fifty percent of ultra is what's in your head," Paris tells me.

And it's kind of freeing, isn't it? To think that we don't have to be constrained by what we've always thought we knew about our body and its ability just because of our sex—that we, too, can do the impossible.

January 2023, Kirk Yetholm, Scotland
JASMIN PARIS WASN'T running the 2023 Spine Race, but her name hangs in the air like a myth when I arrive in Kirk Yetholm to see "Britain's Most Brutal" in person.

After an hour-long cab ride from a train station through farmland and snow-covered hills in the Scottish borderlands, I'm dropped off at the Border Hotel, one of maybe a dozen buildings in this tiny village, all made of stone and seemingly dropped here directly from the thirteenth century. The cold wind is biting, and though I have a rain jacket on over a thick fleece, I wish I'd brought a heavier coat.

Inside Spine Race headquarters, which is just the main floor of the hotel, people are buzzing. The media team tracks runners' dots and GPS coordinates as they make their way through the brutal route. They're directing a video and photo team to certain places along the Pennine Way, and urging the Wi-Fi connection to hurry up so images for the social media posts can load. Race organizers and volunteer coordinators are communicating with checkpoints to make sure runners are arriving, departing, and in good health. Everyone seems to be comparing how much they've slept in the past few days, and since I've flown into the UK the night before on a redeye from Seattle, I feel right at home amongst the sleep-deprived, and make myself a cup of black tea when I'm told by several people to please feel free to help myself.

The first two finishers of the race had come in the night before I arrived. One of them leaves in the cab I'd arrived in (there aren't a lot of cabs out this way). The media team is thrilled because the top finishers had been on *BBC Breakfast*[16]—a popular morning program in the U.K.—a few hours earlier. Their niche sport hardly ever gets mainstream coverage, but this year's battle to the end has gained some interest. Then, the host makes a flub: he says the winner, Damian Hall, has set a new course record. But, in fact, he's only set a record for the men. An easy mistake to make, perhaps. In most sports—and certainly most races—the men's record would be the overall record. But not the Spine Race.

Because as the two leaders ran neck and neck to the bitter end the day before—they weren't just chasing each other. They were also chasing Paris. She's not there, but the course record holder gets a little dot on the tracking map, too, symbolized by a trophy that moves along at her record-breaking pace. And even as the leaders put in a grueling performance, Paris was too far ahead. Her record remained intact.

I had my eye on Claire Bannwarth from the media side of the room for most of the day, but I didn't want to bother her or, rather, wake her. She'd been the first woman to finish the race that year, crossing the finish early in the morning the day I arrived. Since then, she'd been mostly asleep, snoozing on one of two overstuffed old couches in the hotel's lobby. Every now and then someone would bring her a plate of food and she'd stir, eating before laying back, zipping up her bright blue coat once again, and pulling her knitted headband down over her eyes. She was, understandably, exhausted, only managing 1.5 or 2 hours of sleep during the entire race. She'd crossed the finish in 97 hours and 40 minutes, about fourteen hours slower than Paris but good enough for fifth overall finisher this year. (In five of the previous ten editions of the Spine Race, her time would have been good enough to win it outright).

As I watch other finishers come in throughout the day, hobbling across the finish line, their bodies seem to shut down as they walk into the hotel. The adrenaline has suddenly stopped. They're cold, shivering, and look at us as though we're mirages: people at computers, wearing nice sweaters, drinking warm tea and laughing about something on the Internet, when they've just been to the edge of human physical potential. I watched as they would get help from a medic on the other side of the room, someone to take off their shoes, to unwrap their mangled feet and soak them in a hot tub. Some asked for a beer from the pub. Some for a hot bowl of soup. Some just wanted a shower and a bed. At least one—an extremely accomplished long-distance runner—seemed horribly dazed, like he had no idea where he was or how he got there. Later, his friend asked us for some candy for him; his blood sugar had dropped and he was feeling woozy. "Does he need a medic?" The whole team jumped into action. As I saw the fragile states of these runners' bodies and minds, I worried about whether Bannwarth would even want to speak to me. I wouldn't wake her, but I did pop my head in the room as soon as I saw her eyes flit open.

Bannwarth lit up when I said I'd like to ask her about ultra racing, and women like Jasmin Paris. She says she was inspired by Paris's win. "I'm convinced that women have a place in ultra-running," she tells me in a thick French accent. Then she laughs a tiny dry laugh: "First place, in fact."

Bannwarth, like Paris, had won an ultra race outright, the Portugal 281 Ultramarathon, in 2021. "I really think that these are the kind of races that men and women can compete equally. You have just as much possibility as the men," she says before pausing to search for the right word in English, trying to explain that winning is also about more than running. "We live in a society where the place of a woman is most of the time behind the men, but it's just society that tells us this," she says. Two months after her finish at the Spine, Bannwarth won another ultra outright, the Trailcat 200 in Spain. She finished the spring 200-miler in 55 hours and 10 minutes.[17] That summer, she would venture to the US and become the first woman to win the Tahoe 200, a 200-plus mile trail run around Lake Tahoe. Just four days later, she went on to begin the 567-mile Colorado Trail in a fully self-supported run (no race crew or support team), that she completed in 9 days, 2 hours, and 50 minutes—the fastest known time of the route.[18]

SEVERAL OF THE women I speak to inside the Border Hotel bring up Paris as soon as I say I'm working on a book about women and running. Volunteers, employees, and racers alike speak of her like their own Atalanta, the mythological woman who could outrun any man.

"Have you spoken to Jasmin, yet?" they say. Or "I hadn't even heard about the Spine Race until Jasmin's story came out." One of the founders of the race told me he was proud that a woman held the official record. Many of them also said something like Paris had told me: "I've heard" or "they say" that women are better at these longer races. They often looked to me then with a questioning glint in their eye, as though perhaps I, writer of this book on women and running, might have actual data to share with them to confirm this myth.

I'd laugh then, because these were all people who have seen the truth with their own eyes. We all want confirming data, however. We want studies to prove women are superheroes and pregnancy is akin to blood doping, and that we're better at endurance or muscle recovery or strength training or sleep deprivation or what-have-you. When it comes to gender, we want the data to prove that these categories imbue our physical selves with some specific advantages or disadvantages, when really, we're all just a lot more than our sex.

The beautiful thing about Paris's Spine Race win, and about the many other women who have won ultramarathons, fell races, and sky runs out-right, is that they're not myth: they are the data. The evidence already exists, we just have to let it stand, to agree it's real and meaningful. You could explain Paris's win any one of thousands of ways. Or you could just accept that it happened and wasn't the first time and won't be the last. According to *UltraRunning* magazine, around thirty ultramarathons in North America are won by women every year. Women ultramarathoners as far back as the 1980s have been winning races outright.

Paris was a nursing mother, still used to waking up multiple times a night to feed her daughter—so yes, she was likely far more used to sleep-deprivation than her racing counterparts. She'd also been training on hills for her entire life. Despite not being a runner until more recently, she had a lifetime of experience carrying a heavy pack through moun-tains on hiking and backpacking journeys. She was competitive, she'd grown up with three brothers, and married a fellow ultrarunner (whom she beat in an ultra). She had something to run toward: her daughter, who she had missed putting to bed for three nights in a row. She'd run mul-tiple races, beating nearly all of the men, with a few close second-place finishes as well. So she had an idea of her own capability.

Paris had all it took, and she won, and her win was called impossible. Like Revithi and Radcliffe and MacDonald and Patterson and Leather and Gibb and Decker and Cain and Semenya and Negesa, who didn't achieve the "impossible" because they're Atalantas or Super Women, or cheaters, but because they're complex, multifaceted, powerful combina-tions of genes, cells, muscles, bones, joints, and brains, capable of incred-ible and unique things.

Because they're human.

ACKNOWLEDGMENTS

AS WITH ANY work that centers feminism and requires historical excavation, this book is only possible because of those who have come before me, and the stories, texts, and articles they left behind. Firstly, the runners: thank you to those feminists who ran even when they were told they couldn't—whether they called themselves feminists or not, they broke important barriers for all women. As a feminist writer and journalist, I stand on the shoulders of giants: Gloria Steinem, Betty Friedan, Simone de Beauvoir, Angela Y. Davis, bell hooks, Mary Wollstonecraft, Charlotte Perkins Gilman, and Anne Fausto-Sterling, to name just a few of those who have helped form a canon to which I humbly submit. I am hugely grateful to the many very smart researchers and academics who have helped me understand through their own publications or by patiently explained things to me in interviews over the years, including Kathryn Ackerman, Sheree Bekker, Susan K. Cahn, Cheryl Cooky, Holly Thorpe, Amira Rose Davis, Raewyn Connell, Martha Verbrugge, Sari van Anders, Robin Kietlinski, Patricia Vertinsky, Jan Todd, Jaime Schultz, Jennifer Hargreaves, Georgie Bruinvels, Stacy Sims, Phyllis Ellis, Roger Pielke Jr., Anne Blaschke, Helen Horowitz, and Tracey Salisbury. The work of all these people, and those who inspired them, appear in these pages, whether cited specifically or just through their influence on my own thinking and analysis over the years. I feel deeply grateful to have come along at a time when there is so much groundbreaking feminist thought happening in our world, and am especially happy that so many brave writers and researchers were tackling these topics long before it was widely accepted to do so.

Sarah Levitt, at Aevitas Creative Management, helped me grow this tiny seed of an idea into an entire book and bore with me as I circled around these ideas again and again and again, cheering me on the whole way. I could not have asked for a better, kinder, smarter, more patient agent.

Maddie Jones, you took a shot on this project and helped shape it into the form it's in right now with astounding attention to detail and understanding of the big and small pictures at all times. I so appreciate you and your many talents. And to the whole Algonquin team for championing this book: I'm so grateful.

To Jasmin Paris, Bobbi Gibb, Jacqueline Hansen, and Leslie Heywood, who spent personal time telling me their own stories: I greatly appreciate the trust you placed in me. To Ruth Lockley and Stuart Paul: thank you for the generous time and stories shared in Birmingham. I will remember combing through the Birchfield Harriers archives with you all fondly for years to come. Thank you, Lindsey Armstrong, for being so generous with your time and your memories of your mother (and for braving Birmingham's traffic!), she was an inspirational woman and I'm honored to share some of her story here. To Will and the Spine Race crew, thank you for being such generous hosts to a roving journalist who had never seen an ultramarathon before. Thank you, John Campbell, for sharing your memories of your mother, answering my many questions, and sending me so many documents. I hope I did her story justice.

My endless thanks to Steph Daniels and Anita Tedder, who interviewed Florence MacDonald decades ago in her nursing home and were kind enough to share the footage with me in their home all these years later. We'll get that documentary made someday! The tea and cake and stories made for a lovely afternoon. Your work has made mine possible.

Thanks to the photographers and archivists who helped me find images of many of the women in this book—especially Walt Chadwick and Jeff Johnson, who were incredibly generous, helpful, and supportive. And I am so grateful to everyone who helped me with a library card or login access to an academic site or other obscure archive when I hit digital brick walls on my research wild-goose chases. Thanks to the Smith College Archives, where Senda Berenson's papers are, and the Radcliffe Archives, which holds Charlotte Perkins Gilman's papers. Women's colleges are invaluable resources, and I'm grateful every day for my Smith College education.

To everyone who offered an anecdote or a personal story or a memory of their youth when I told them what my book was about—I appreciate all of you, and your words influenced my own.

Alexa Schnur, I truly could not have gotten this across the finish line without your keen eye for detail, and your whip-smart Smithie brain. Thank you for editing Diane Leather's Wikipedia entry in justified anger.

To every teacher who encouraged my writing: Leslee Shepler, Molly Anderson, Paulette Manuel, Laurel Anderson, and Marte Peet at Lockwood Elementary; Dave Hansen and Sherm Williamson at Bothell High; Sharon Seelig, Betsey Harries, Nancy Bradbury, and Annie Boutelle at Smith; and Honor Moore, Zia Jaffrey, and Brenda Wineapple at the New School. To anyone who told me I could write a book someday, or encouraged this wild idea in me, please keep telling writers and future writers you believe in them.

This book would not exist without Rachel, my therapist, who supported me through every overwhelming step of the process, most importantly helping me believe in myself enough to try.

Sarah and Becca and Phoebe, you provided the most excellent hospitality in Providence while I followed Boston Marathon madness (and thanks to Becca's mom for sharing her marathon memories). Thank you to the Kerwin family and Jeff and Kristen, who both generously let me bunk in their cabins for some writing-intensive alone time.

Thanks to my father-in-law, Jim Day, who is always up to chat sports with me. And for lending me a wonderful resource early on in my research in the form of a Kenny Moore tome. My love and gratitude to Jim and Paula, too, for their help wrangling my kids while I went off on multiple reporting and writing trips while writing this book. Thank you, Hal, for the kindest words of support—you're still a hell of a cheerleader.

Thank you, Latria Graham, my writing accountability buddy, for the retreat days, the daily check-ins, the pep talks, the unending support and understanding, the care packages, and the friendship. I wouldn't be here without you. I can't wait to read your book.

Sarah, Whitney, Megan, Rachel E., Jen, Ruth, Ainsley, and Allison, thank you for your writing advice, support, and friendship over the years. Hanna, thanks for helping me remember how chromosomes work. Rachel L., thank you for the writing dates, encouragement, and academic archive access. Katherine, thanks for running with me in Florence, and all the support and comfort over the years. Carly, thanks for saying you'll read this book even though it's about running.

Dad, your training runs and marathons when I was young encouraged me to embrace running, and your coaching taught me to embrace my competitiveness. Mom, thanks for telling us about your "morning runs," and for never doubting that I'd write a book. Chris, Phil, Zach, and Teddy, thanks for being such fascinating and caring beings that you sparked my interest in gender, and for countless arm wrestling matches, push-up contests, races, and pickup baseball games. Aarin, Stephanie, Jolene, and Castine, you're the best sisters I could have asked for.

Matt, your support and belief in me has made everything possible. All of it. Thank you for the commitment to me and our family—I can't imagine a better partner to have in this life. Howard and Lawrence, I love you both so much. All the time. No matter what.

NOTES

The following is a condensed list of sources for a work that took a tremendous amount of research and reporting. Any information based on personal interviews or observation is noted as such in the text. Many sources were used as references throughout the book, but are noted generally only on first reference below. Archival newspaper articles were largely sourced from Newspapers.com, and the *New York Times* Archives.

Introduction

1 Athanasios Tarasouleas, "Stamata Revithi, 'Alias Melpomeni'," *Olympic Review* XXVI–17 (1997), https://library.olympics.com/Default/doc/SYRACUSE/353009/stamata-revithi-alias-melpomeni-by-athanasios-tarasouleas?_lg=en-GB.

2 "Pierre de Coubertin's Historic Founding Text Finds Its Home at the Olympic Museum in Lausanne," press release, *IOC News*, May 21, 2022, https://olympics.com/ioc/news/pierre-de-coubertin-s-historic-founding-text-finds-its-home-at-the-olympic-museum-in-lausanne.

3 Pierre de Coubertin, "The Women at the Olympic Games," in *Pierre de Coubertin 1863–1937: Olympism. Selected Writings*, edited by Norbert Müller, translated by William H. Skinner (Lausanne, Switzerland: Comité International Olympique, 2000), 710–14.

4 Linda K. Fuller, "Olympic Access for Women: Athletes, Organizers and Sports Journalists," in Thomas L. McPhail, *The Olympic Movement and the Mass Media: Past, Present and Future Issues*, edited by Roger C. Jackson (Alberta: Hurford Enterprises, 1989), 4/9–4/18.

5 Jaime E. Schultz, *Qualifying Times: Points of Change in U.S. Women's Sport* (Champaign: University of Illinois Press, 2014), 104.

6 Martin Summers, "Manhood Rights in the Age of Jim Crow: Evaluating 'End-of-Men' Claims in the Context of African American History," *Boston University Law Review* 93 (2013): 748–49.

7 Michael A. Messner, "Sports and Male Domination: The Female Athlete as Contested Ideological Terrain," *Sociology of Sport Journal* 5, no. 3 (1988): 200, https://doi.org/10.1123/ssj.5.3.197.

8 Roger Robinson, "The Greatest Races: Women's Marathon," *Runner's World*, June 1, 2008, https://www.runnersworld.com/advanced/a20796106/the-greatest-races -womens-marathon/.

9 Shirley Climo, *Atalanta's Race: A Greek Myth* (New York: Clarion Books, 1994).

10 Reet A. Howell and Maxwell L. Howell, "The Atalanta Legend in Art and Literature," *Journal of Sport History* 16, no. 2 (1989): 132, http://www.jstor.org/stable /43609443.

11 P. Ovidius Naso, "Atalanta," in *Metamorphoses*, edited by Brookes More (Boston: Cornhill, 1922), lines 560–651.

12 "Pregnant Radcliffe Will Miss Euros," *CNN*, July 11, 2006, http://www.cnn.com /2006/SPORT/07/11/athletics.radcliffe/.

13 "Pregnant Radcliffe Vows to Keep on Competing," *The Guardian*, July 11, 2006, https://www.theguardian.com/sport/2006/jul/11/athletics.uk.

14 Pauline L. Entin and Kelly M. Munhall, "Recommendations Regarding Exercise during Pregnancy Made by Private/Small Group Practice Obstetricians in the USA," *Journal of Sports Science & Medicine* 5, no. 3 (2006): 449–58, http://ncbi.nlm.nih.gov /pmc/articles/PMC3842146/.

15 Gina Kolata, "Training through Pregnancy to Be Marathon's Fastest Mom," *New York Times*, November 3, 2007, https://www.nytimes.com/2007/11/03/sports /othersports/03runner.html.

16 Jeré Longman and Lynn Zinser, "In the End, Radcliffe and Lel Break Free to Win New York," *New York Times*, November 5, 2007, https://www.nytimes.com/2007/11/05 /sports/05marathon.html.

17 Michael Phillips, "Radcliffe Reborn with Stunning Comeback Win," *The Guardian*, November 4, 2007, https://www.theguardian.com/sport/2007/nov/05 /athletics.sport.

18 Lindsay Tanner, "Mom Did It—But Should You?," *Miami Herald*, November 9, 2007, 10A.

19 Natalie Gingerich Mackenzie, "Pacing Paradox," *Runner's World*, September 17, 2020, https://www.runnersworld.com/advanced/a20828195 /pacing-paradox/.

20 Jonathan Calvert and George Arbuthnott, with Bojan Pancevski, "Revealed: Sport's Dirtiest Secret," *Times* (London), August 2, 2015, https://www.thetimes.co.uk /article/revealed-sports-dirtiest-secret-zpnxc7ndsfp.

21 Ian Chadband, "Marathon Great Radcliffe Cleared by IAAF of Doping Claims," *Reuters*, November 27, 2015, https://www.reuters.com/article/us-athletics

-doping-radcliffe/marathon-great-radcliffe-cleared-by-iaaf-of-doping-claims
-idUSKBN0TG1SU20151127.

22 Michael Clark, "The Real Story of the Marathon," *Runner's World*,
March 24, 2003, https://www.runnersworld.com/uk/events/a760877
/the-real-story-of-the-marathon/.

Chapter 1

1 Ian Jobling, "The Women's 800 Metres Track Event Post 1928: Quo Vadis?,"
Journal of Olympic History 14, no. 1 (2006): 43–47, https://isoh.org/wp-content
/uploads/JOH-Archives/JOHv14n1m.pdf.

2 Robin Kietlinski, *Japanese Women and Sport: Beyond Baseball and Sumo*
(London: Bloomsbury Academic, 2011), 60, https://library.oapen.org/bitstream
/handle/20.500.12657/58705/9781849666695.pdf.

3 John J. Hallahan, "American Girls Have Done Remarkably Well in Olympics:
Some Distances Prove Too Much," *Boston Globe*, August 7, 1928.

4 "Miss MacDonald Sixth," *Boston Globe*, August 3, 1928.

5 "The Olympic Games: Three Records Broken," *Times* (London), August 3, 1928.

6 Jere Longman, "How the Women Won," *New York Times*, June 23, 1996, https://
www.nytimes.com/1996/06/23/magazine/how-the-women-won.html.

7 William Shire, "5 Women Track Stars Collapse in Olympic Race: Fall at End of
800 Meters—May Bar Event," *Chicago Tribune*, August 3, 1928.

8 Wythe Williams, "Americans Beaten in 4 Olympic Tests: Coach Robertson Is
Puzzled," *New York Times*, August 3, 1928.

9 John Tunis, "Women and the Sport Business," *Harper's Magazine* 159, no. 950
(July 1927): 213, https://archive.org/details/sim_harpers-magazine_1929-07_159_950/.

10 John T. McGovern, "The Story of the Ninth Olympiad," *Sportsman*,
September 1928, 96, quoted in Mark Dyreson, "Icons of Liberty or Objects of
Desire? American Women Olympians and the Politics of Consumption," *Journal of
Contemporary History* 38, no. 3 (2003): 435–60, http://www.jstor.org/stable/3180646.

11 Knute K. Rockne, "Yankees Have Another Dull Day in the Olympics: Girl Stars
Collapse," *Pittsburgh Press*, August 3, 1928.

12 Shauna Farnell, "An Olympic Hurdle: Why Is the Decathlon Only for Men?,"
New York Times, updated August 7, 2021, https://www.nytimes.com/2021/07/06/sports
/olympics/us-track-field-decathlon-women-heptathlon.html.

13 CBC Sports, "1928: Amsterdam, Netherlands," *CBC Radio-Canada*, June 15, 2012,
https://www.cbc.ca/sports/2.720/1928-amsterdam-netherlands-1.1173804.

14 Sean Ingle, "Sixty Years Ago Diane Leather Smashed World Record but Not Sex
Barrier," *The Guardian*, May 25, 2014, https://www.theguardian.com/sport/blog/2014
/may/25/diane-leather-world-record-sex-barrier-sixty-years-ago.

15 M, *A Course of Calisthenics for Young Ladies, in Schools and Families. With Some
Remarks on Physical Education* (Hartford: H. and F. J. Huntington, 1831), 77.

16   Jan Todd, *Physical Culture and the Body Beautiful: Purposive Exercise in the Lives of American Women 1800–1875* (Macon, GA: Mercer University Press, 1998), 112.

17   Florence Carpentier, "Alice Milliat: A Feminist Pioneer for Women's Sport," in *Global Sport Leaders: A Biographical Analysis of International Sport Management*, edited by Emmanuel Bayle and Patrick Clastres (Cham, Switzerland: Palgrave Macmillan, 2018), https://doi.org/10.1007/978-3-319-76753-6.

18   Mary H. Leigh and Thérèse M. Bonin, "The Pioneering Role of Madame Alice Milliat and the FSFI in Establishing International Trade and Field Competition for Women," *Journal of Sport History* 4, no. 1 (1977), 72–83, http://www.jstor.org/stable /43611530.

19   Florence Carpentier and Jean-Pierre Lefèvre, "The Modern Olympic Movement, Women's Sport and the Social Order during the Inter-War Period," *International Journal of the History of Sport* 23, no. 7 (2006): 1114, https://doi.org/10.1080 /09523360600832387.

20   "Topics of the Time: Effects of Athletics on Women," *New York Times*, August 23, 1922.

21   Colleen English, "'Beyond Women's Powers of Endurance': The 1928 800-Meter and Women's Olympic Track and Field in the Context of the United States," *Sport History Review* 50, no. 2 (2019): 187–204, https://doi.org/10.1123/shr.2018-0040.

22   "Sport: Fast Women," *Time*, February 13, 1928.

23   Ethel Perrin, "More Competitive Athletics for Women—But of the Right Kind," *American Physical Education Review* 34, no. 8 (1929): 473–74, quoted in Jaime Schultz, *Qualifying Times: Points of Change in U.S. Women's Sport* (Champaign: University of Illinois Press, 2014), 78.

24   "To Form Women's Track Team Here: Boston Swimming Club Has Made Plans," *Boston Globe*, September 22, 1923.

25   Sam Cohen, "Boston Girl Shows Grit in the Olympics," *Boston Record*, August 7, 1928, photocopy shared by John Scott Campbell with author, June 27, 2022.

26   "Roxbury Girl Fleet Half-Miler: Florence E. MacDonald Can Run 880 Yards in 2m29s, Nearly Seven Seconds under American Record," *Boston Globe*, July 13, 1928.

27   Louise Mead Tricard, *American Women's Track and Field: A History, 1895 through 1980* (Jefferson, NC: McFarland, 1996), 131.

28   "National Olympic Test Winners at Newark," *Boston Globe*, July 5, 1928.

29   Sam Cohen, "Four Hub Girls Leave for N.Y. and Olympics," *Boston Record*, July 9, 1928, photocopy shared by John Scott Campbell with author, June 27, 2022.

30   "They Showed Home Folks How They Did It in Amsterdam," *Boston Herald*, August 26, 1928.

31   James C. Whorton, "'Athlete's Heart': The Medical Debate over Athleticism, 1870–1920," in *Sport and Exercise Science: Essays in the History of Sports Medicine*, edited by Jack W. Berryman and Roberta J. Park (Urbana: University of Illinois Press, 1992), 109–30.

32   Arthur S. Draper, "Miss Bleibtrey Sets New Mark for 100-Meter Swim," *New York Tribune*, August 26 1920, quoted in Mark Dyreson, "Icons of Liberty or Objects of Desire? American Women Olympians and the Politics of Consumption," *Journal of Contemporary History* 38, no. 3 (2003): 442, http://www.jstor.org/stable/3180646.

33   Mark Dyreson, "Icons of Liberty or Objects of Desire? American Women Olympians and the Politics of Consumption," *Journal of Contemporary History* 38, no. 3 (2003): 437, http://www.jstor. org/stable/3180646.

34   "Middle Distance Star," *News and Observer* (Raleigh, NC), July 19, 1928.

35   Ethelda Bleibtrey, *Ambition Magazine*, 1923, quoted in Dyreson, "Icons of Liberty or Objects of Desire," 436.

36   Grantland Rice, "The Slightly Weaker Sex," *Collier's* 82 (September 29, 1928): 12, quoted in Dyreson, "Icons of Liberty or Objects of Desire," 455.

37   Paul Gallico, *Farewell to Sport* (New York: Knopf, 1938), 233–44, quoted in Dyreson, "Icons of Liberty or Objects of Desire," 457.

38   Jennifer Hargreaves, "The Inter-War Years," in *Sporting Females: Critical Issues in the History and Sociology of Women's Sport* (New York: Routledge, 2001), 133–34.

39   Alan J. Gould, "Olympic Events for Women May Be Eliminated: Finnish Stand Unexpected," *Saint Louis Globe-Democrat*, August 7, 1928.

40   "Women's Events to Be Retained at the Olympics," *Boston Globe*, August 7, 1928.

41   "Supports Women's Sports: Lady Heath Enthusiastic in Advocating Feminine Competition," *New York Times*, January 5, 1929.

42   "Lady Heath Will Be Speaker at A.A.U. Dinner on Monday," *New York Times*, November 15, 1928.

43   "Miss Hitomi Kinue and the Question of Womanhood," *Fujin Sekai*, July 1929, 54–69, quoted in Kietlinski, *Japanese Women and Sport*, 62–3.

44   "Miss Hitomi Kinue Passes Away Yesterday: Internationally Acclaimed Women's Track Athlete," *Asahi Shimbun*, August 3, 1931, quoted in Kietlinski, *Japanese Women and Sport*, 65.

45   "800-Meter Star's Baby Proves Star in Own Right," est. 1939, photocopy shared by John Scott Campbell with author, June 27, 2022.

46   Ivana Parčina, Violeta Šilkjak, Aleksandra Perović, and Elena Plakona, "Women's World Games," *Physical Education and Sport through the Centuries* 1, no. 2 (2014): 49–60, https://www.academia.edu/33894618/WOMENS_WORLD_GAMES.

47   Letter from Sigfried Edström to Avery Brundage, January 3, 1935), ABC, Box 42, Reel 24, Avery Brundage Collection, Archives of the International Centre for Olympic Studies, University of Western Ontario, Canada, quoted in Carpentier and Lefèvre, "The Modern Olympic Movement," 1122.

48   Ruadhán Cooke, "How Alice Milliat Brought Women into the Olympics," Raidió Teilifís Éireann, updated August 19, 2022, https://www.rte.ie/brainstorm /2022/0819/1316517-alice-milliat-womens-sport-olympics-1922/.

Chapter 2

1   Michael D. Davis, *Black American Women in Olympic Track and Field* (Jefferson, NC: McFarland, 1992), 130.

2   Cindy Himes Gissendanner, "African American Women Olympians: The Impact of Race, Gender, and Class Ideologies, 1932–1968," *Research Quarterly for Exercise and Sport* 67, no. 2 (1996): 173, https://doi.org/10.1080/02701367.1996.10607941.

3   Susan N. Lund (ed.), "Berlin Olympics, 1936: Golden Memories," *Northern Illinois University Alumni News* (Summer 1984).

4   Matt Osgood, "Sports History Forgot about Tidye Pickett and Louise Stokes, Two Black Olympians Who Never Got Their Shot," *Smithsonian Magazine*, August 15, 2016, https://www.smithsonianmag.com/history/sports-history-forgot-about-tidye-pickett -and-louise-stokes-two-black-olympians-who-never-got-their-shot-glory-180960138.

5   "Miss Didrikson, the One-Girl Track Team, Heads U.S. Squad of 18 Named for Olympics," *New York Times*, July 18, 1932.

6   Gene Mack, "Medford Is Puffed Up over Three Olympians," *Boston Globe*, July 18, 1932.

7   "Babe Didrikson Steals Show as Women's Track and Field Championships Are Staged: Fast Works," *Los Angeles Times*, July 17, 1932.

8   Harry Levette, "Tydie Pickett and Louise Stokes Were on First U.S. Track Team," *California Eagle*, August 19, 1932.

9   Doris Pieroth, *Their Day in the Sun: Women of the 1932 Olympics* (Seattle: University of Washington Press, 1996).

10   "Here Is Chart of Finals in Olympic Track, Field Show," *Asheville* (NC) *Citizen-Times*, August 8, 1932, https://www.newspapers.com/image/195703988/.

11   Alan Gould, "Americans Make New Records But Zabala Captures the Marathon: Girl Sets New Mark," *Berkshire Eagle* (Pittsfield, MA), August 8, 1932.

12   Harry Levette, "Upper-Cuts and Blocks: Race Girls Happy at Elaborate Quarters," *California Eagle*, August 19, 1932.

13   Harry Levette, "White Press Raves When Colored Girls Are Barred from Olympic Relays," *California Eagle*, August 19, 1932.

14   Don Roberts, "Roberts on Sports," *Los Angeles Evening Post-Record*, August 10, 1932.

15   Ron Grossman, "Tidye Pickett: Chicago Track Star was First African-American Female Olympian," *Chicago Tribune*, updated August 19, 2016, https://www. chicagotribune.com/opinion/commentary/ct-olympics-tidye-pickett-first-black -woman-flash-perspec-0821-jm-20160818-story.html.

16   Susan Cahn, *Coming on Strong: Gender and Sexuality in Twentieth-Century Women's Sport* (Cambridge, MA: Harvard University Press, 2000), 117.

17   Deborah Riley Draper (dir.), *Olympic Pride, American Prejudice*, Coffee Bluff Pictures, 2016.

18   Isabel Wilkerson, *Caste: The Origins of Our Discontents* (New York: Random House, 2020).

19   "Wray's Column from Berlin: A Racial Weakness?," *St. Louis Post-Dispatch*, August 1, 1936.

20   Stuart Cameron, "Owen Wins in 20.7, Gets His 'Triple'," *Wisconsin State Journal*, August 5, 1936.

21   "Tuskeegee Institute Girls Triumph in Senior and Junior A.A.U. Track," *New York Times*, June 30, 1947.

22   Jody Homer, "Pioneer from 1932 Remains Undaunted: U.S. Team's 1st Black Woman," *Chicago Tribune*, August 10, 1984.

23   Ro Brown, "The Olympics in Retrospect N.O.'s Own Audrey Patterson Tyler Set the London Olympics on Fire," *Louisiana Weekly*, July 23, 2012, http://www. louisianaweekly.com/the-olympics-in-retrospect-n-o-%E2%80%99s-own-audrey -patterson-tyler-set-the-london-olympics-on-fire/.

24   Cat M. Ariail, *Passing the Baton: Black Women Track Stars and American Identity* (Urbana: University of Illinois Press, 2020).

25   Edward Hammond Clarke, *Sex in Education: or, A Fair Chance for Girls* (Boston: James R. Osgood, 1873), 111–12.

26   Heather Munro Prescott, *Student Bodies: The Influence of Student Health Services in American Society and Medicine* (Ann Arbor: University of Michigan Press, 2007), 12–14.

27   Martha H. Verbrugge, *Active Bodies: A History of Women's Physical Education in Twentieth-Century America* (New York: Oxford University Press, 2017).

28   Susan T. Hill, *The Traditionally Black Institutions of Higher Education 1860 to 1982* (Washington, DC: National Center for Education Statistics, U.S. Dept. of Education, 1985), 22, https://nces.ed.gov/pubs84/84308.pdf.

29   Edith Naomi Hill, "Pioneers in Physical Education: Senda Berenson," *Research Quarterly of the American Association for Health, Physical Education and Recreation* 12, no. 3 (1941): 662, https://archive.org/details/sim_journal-of-physical -education-recreation-dance_1941-10_12_3.

30   Translation of "A Pioneer in Swedish Gymnastics in the U.S.A.," *Husmodern* (1922), CA-MS-00037, box 679, folder 3, Senda Berenson papers, Smith College Special Collections, Northampton, MA, https://findingaids.smith.edu/repositories/4 /archival_objects/25579.

31   Anne Blaschke, "Southern Cinderpaths: Tuskegee Institute, Olympic Track and Field, and Regional Social Politics, 1916–1955," unpublished essay, 2016, https://www. bu.edu/afam/files/2016/03/Anne-Blaschke-Southern-Cinderpaths.pdf.

32   Interviews, 1976–1981, Jessie Abbott, OH-31, Black Women Oral History Project, Schlesinger Library on the History of Women in America, Radcliffe Institute, Harvard University, Cambridge, MA, seq. 21, https://nrs.lib.harvard.edu/urn-3:rad .schl:10039841?n=21.

33   Richard Goldstein, "Alice Coachman, 90, Dies; First Black Woman to Win Olympic Gold," *New York Times*, July 14, 2014, https://www.nytimes.com/2014/07/15 /sports/alice-coachman-90-dies-groundbreaking-medalist.html.

34   Theodore Caplow, Louis Hicks, and Ben J. Wattenberg, "Education: Female Graduates," in *The First Measured Century: An Illustrated Guide to Trends in America, 1900–2000* (Washington, DC: AEI Press, 2000), https://www.pbs.org/fmc /book/3education2.htm.

35   Anne McDaniel, Thomas A. DiPrete, Claudia Buchmann, and Uri Shwed, "The Black Gender Gap in Educational Attainment: Historical Trends and Racial Comparisons," *Demography* 48, no. 3 (2011): 895, https://www.jstor.org/stable/41237816.

36   "Negro Women Boost U.S. Track Hopes," *Chicago World*, June 5, 1948.

37   John Scheibe, "Tyler Is Still Going All Out to Help U.S. in Olympics," *Los Angeles Times*, August 9, 1983.

38   Scoop Kennedy, "An Olympian Slip Docks Here," *New Orleans Item*, June 2, 1950.

39   Joel W. Smith, "Surveying the Sports Front: Alumni Bowl Again Provides Setting for Tuskeegee Relays," *Alabama Tribune*, May 9, 1947.

40   Tracey M. Salisbury, "First to the Finish Line: The Tennessee State Tigerbelles 1944–1994," PhD diss., University of North Carolina at Greensboro, 2009.

41   Nolan Thaxton, "A Documentary Analysis of Competitive Track and Field for Women at Tuskegee Institute and Tennessee State University," PhD diss., Springfield College, 1970, 66, quoted in Salisbury, "First to the Finish Line," 65.

42   "Negro Girls Take Nine out of Eleven Places on Olympic Womens U.S. Track Team," *St. Paul* (MN) *Reporter*, July 23, 1948.

43   "Women Set Two AAU Marks in Olympic Trials: Speedy Half Mile," *Los Angeles Times*, July 13, 1948.

44   Geraldine Hill, "U.S. Women Nervous on Eve of Olympics," *Dunkirk* (NY) *Evening Observer*, July 28, 1948.

45   Michael Grace, "1948 USA Olympic Team Sails on the SS America," *Cruising the Past*, April 1, 2022, https://www.cruiselinehistory.com/1948-usa-olympic-team-sails -on-the-ss-america/.

46   Geraldine Hill, "U.S. Women Nervous on Eve of Olympics," *Dunkirk* (NY) *Evening Observer*, July 28, 1948.

47   "Olympics: Rain Hampers Vaulters," *Boston Globe*, August 2, 1948.

48   Bob Considine, "New Women's 100 Meter Champ," *San Francisco Examiner*, August 3, 1948.

49   "The Story of the Fanny Blankers-Koen—The Female Athlete of the 20th Century: On the Line," *Olympics*, YouTube, January 12, 2017, https://www.youtube .com/watch?v=hOaqL_oY2P0&ab_channel=Olympics.

50   "The Incredible Dominance of Fanny Blankers-Koen: Olympic Records," *Olympics*, YouTube, December 28, 2013, https://www.youtube.com/watch?v=_Y _GoH-b3QE&ab_channel=Olympics.

51 Gayle Calbot, "High Tower Diving Easy Prize for Lee: Diving Monopoly," *St. Louis Globe-Democrat*, August 6, 1948.

52 "Matthias Scores Decathalon Win: Quarter-Milers Win," *The Tennessean*, August 7, 1948.

53 Robert Murel, "Decathalon Plum Falls to Matthias; Simmons Drops Back to Third: Triple Winner," *Daily News* (NY), August 7, 1948.

54 Paula Parker, "Mickey Aims Her Missile at the Olympics: Mickey: Ambitious Plans for the Olympics," *Los Angeles Times*, April 4, 1983.

55 Margaret E. Bernstein, "That Championship Season," *Essence*, July 1984, 58–133.

56 Ryan Whirty, "1948: New Orleans' Audrey Patterson Makes Olympic History," *NOLA.com*, updated July 7, 2021, https://www.nola.com/300/1948-new-orleans-audrey -patterson-makes-olympic-history/article_fb5ffe65-c42a-5b6f-b93f-964f9db9967a.html.

57 Steve Perkins, "New Orleans' Olympic Star 'Easing Out' for Helsinki," *New Orleans Item*, April 27, 1952.

58 National Women's Law Center and the Poverty and Race Research Action Council, "Finishing Last: Girls of Color and School Sports Opportunities," 2015, https://nwlc.org/wp-content/uploads/2022/03/final_nwlc_girlsfinishinglast _report.pdf.

Chapter 3

1 Roger Bannister, *The Four Minute Mile* (New York: Dodd, Mead, 1981).

2 "British Girl Breaks One Record; Then Achieves World Fame: Diane First to Beat Elusive 5-Minute Mile," *Sunday Dispatch* (London), May 30, 1954.

3 Gareth Rogers, *Fleet and Free: A History of Birchfield Harriers Athletics Club* (Stroud, Gloucestershire: Tempus, 2005).

4 W. O. Alexander and Wilfred Morgan (eds.), "Dorette Nelson/Neal," in Wilfred Morgan, *The History of Birchfield Harriers: 1877–1988* (Birmingham: Birchfield Harriers, 1988), 82.

5 Dick Knight, "These Girls Will Spare Nothing for Perfection: Says Dick Knight," *Evening Despatch* (Birmingham, UK), May 13, 1954.

6 "Work as Usual, Then 5-Minute Mile Attempt," *Evening Post* (Bristol, UK), May 24, 1954.

7 "British Girl Breaks One Record."

8 "Champions in the Making—But Team Spirit Counts: A Champion by Chance," *Birmingham Weekly Post*, May 7, 1954.

9 "Sports Highlights: Sept. 30," *Manchester Evening News*, January 1, 1954.

10 Triton, "Bill Gray and Fred Green Midland Athletes of Year: Diane Outstanding," *Sports Argus* (Birmingham), January 2, 1954

11 Triton, "Keen Competition for Midland Six Mile: Can Diane Succeed?," *Sports Argus* (Birmingham), May 22, 1954.

12   "Diane Is After the 5-Min Mile," *Manchester Evening News*, May 25, 1954.

13   "Diane Leather to Try for Five-Minute Mile in Women's Track Meet,"
Alabama Journal, May 26, 1954.

14   Dick Knight, "Give Diane Every Help Next Time," *Evening Despatch*
(Birmingham), May 27, 1954.

15   "Sports Round-up: Nervous Diane," *Birmingham Evening Mail*, May 27, 1954.

16   "Birmingham Girl Sets Up World Record for Women's Mile," *Birmingham Post*,
May 27, 1954.

17   "Diane Names Her Target: She Hopes to 'Do a Bannister' Today," *Birmingham
Gazette*, May 26, 1954.

18   "A Fraction of a Second Foils Diane: But She's Still the Fastest Miler," *Birmingham
Gazette*, May 27, 1954.

19   Milton Marmor, "Scientific Story: Bannister's Oxygen Supply, Nerve Were Big
Factors in Record Mile," *Chattanooga Daily Times*, May 30, 1954.

20   Alex Hutchinson, *Endure: Mind, Body, and the Curiously Elastic Limits of
Human Performance*, revised and updated (New York: William Morrow, 2018), 340.

21   Hassane Zouhal, Abderraouf Ben Abderrahman, Jacques Prioux, Beat Knechtle,
Lotfi Bouguerra, Wiem Kebsi, and Timothy D. Noakes, "Drafting's Improvement of
3000-m Running Performance in Elite Athletes: Is It a Placebo Effect?," *International
Journal of Sports Physiology and Performance* 10, no. 2 (2015): 147–52, https://doi.org
/10.1123/ijspp.2013-0498.

22   "Want to Win? Create a Rival," *NYU: Stern*, July 8, 2014, https://www.stern.nyu
.edu/experience-stern/faculty-research/want-to-win-create-a-rival.

23   John Detrixhe, "It Took 43 of the World's Fastest Runners to Break the 2-Hour
Marathon Barrier," *Quartz*, October 13, 2019, https://qz.com/1727150/breaking
-marathon-barrier-required-43-world-class-runners.

24   "Briton Beats Women's Mark," *Chattanooga Daily Times*, May 30, 1954.

25   "Woman Miler Breaks 5-Minute Time Barrier," *Press and Sun-Bulletin*
(Binghamton, NY), May 30, 1954.

26   "Next: A Five Minute Mile," *Buffalo News*, May 28, 1954.

27   Jason Daley, "Five Things to Know about Roger Bannister, the First Person
to Break the 4-Minute Mile," *Smithsonian Magazine*, March 5, 2018, https://www.
smithsonianmag.com/smart-news/five-things-know-about-roger-bannister-first
-person-break-four-minute-mile-180968344/.

28   "Diane Leather Has Tea with Lord Mayor," *Birmingham Gazette*, June 4, 1954.

29   Ann Taylor Allen, *Feminism and Motherhood in Western Europe 1890–1970:
The Maternal Dilemma* (New York: Palgrave Macmillan, 2005), 141, https://archive
.org/details/ann-taylor-allen-feminism-and-motherhood-in-western-europe-1890-1970
-the-materna.

30   Sundari Anitha and Ruth Pearson, "The Inter-war Years: 1918–1939," *Striking*

Women: Women and Work, 2013, https://www.striking-women.org/module/women
-and-work/inter-war-years-1918-1939.

31   Virginia Nicholson, "The 1940s: 'Britain's Wartime Women Gained a New
Sense of Power'," *The Guardian*, February 3, 2018, https://www.theguardian.com
/lifeandstyle/2018/feb/03/1940s-britains-wartime-women-gained-a-new-sense-of-power.

32   Prime Minister's Office and Ministry of Defence, "The Women of the Second
World War," *Gov.uk*, April 16, 2015, https://www.gov.uk/government/news/the-women
-of-the-second-world-war.

33   Peter Thompson, "Leather, Former World Record-Holder, Dies," *Museum of
World Athletics*, September 8, 2018, https://worldathletics.org/heritage/news/diane
-leather-obituary.

34   Karen Messing, *One-Eyed Science: Occupational Health and Women Workers*
(Philadelphia: Temple University Press, 1998).

35   Karen Messing, "A Feminist Intervention That Hurt Women: Biological
Differences, Ergonomics, and Occupational Health: Une intervention féministe
qui a nui aux femmes: différences biologiques, égalité, ergonomie et santé au travail,"
New Solutions: A Journal of Environmental and Occupational Health Policy 27, no. 3
(2017): 310, https://doi.org.10.1177/1048291117724800.

36   David Epstein, *The Sports Gene: Inside the Science of Extraordinary Athletic
Performance* (New York: Current, 2014), 108.

37   Mindy Weisberger, "Shattering the Myth of Men as Hunters and Women as
Gatherers," *CNN*, June 30, 2023, https://www.cnn.com/2023/06/30/world/women-roles
-hunter-gatherer-societies-scn/index.html.

38   Kathleen Sterling, "Inventing Human Nature," in *Ideologies in Archaeology*,
edited by Randall H. McGuire and Reinhard Bernbeck (Tucson: University of Arizona
Press, 2011), 192.

Chapter 4

1   Bobbi Gibb, *Wind in the Fire: Anniversary Edition* (Cambridge, MA: Institute
for the Study of Natural Systems Press, 2016).

2   Betty Friedan, *The Feminine Mystique*, 50th anniversary edition (New York:
W.W. Norton, 2013), 7.

3   Gloria Steinem, "After Black Power, Women's Liberation," *New York Magazine*,
April 4, 1969, https://nymag.com/news/politics/46802/.

4   Joan Steitz, "Women Physicians over the Centuries," *Yale Medicine Magazine*,
Spring 2018, https://medicine.yale.edu/news/yale-medicine-magazine/article/
women-physicians-over-the-centuries/.

5   Anne Walling, Kari Nilsen, and Kimberly J. Templeton, "The Only Woman in the
Room: Oral Histories of Senior Women Physicians in a Midwestern City," *Women's
Health Reports* 1, no. 1 (2020): 279–80, https://www.liebertpub.com/doi/10.1089
/whr.2020.0041.

6 "Resources to Infuse Equity: Title IX Before and After," *EquityOnline*, https://www2.edc.org/womensequity/resource/title9/before.htm (accessed August 23, 2023).

7 Patricia A. Vertinksy, *The Eternally Wounded Woman: Women, Doctors, and Exercise in the Late Nineteenth Century* (Manchester: University of Manchester Press, 1989).

8 Charlotte Perkins Gilman, *The Living of Charlotte Perkins Gilman: An Autobiography* (Madison: University of Wisconsin Press, 1991).

9 Judith A. Allen, *The Feminism of Charlotte Perkins Gilman: Sexualities, Histories, Progressivism* (Chicago: University of Chicago Press, 2009) .

10 Susan Wells, "Mary Putnam Jacobi: Medicine as Will and Idea," in *Out of the Dead House: Nineteenth-Century Women Physicians and the Writing of Medicine* (Madison: University of Wisconsin Press, 2001), 153.

11 Barbara Ehrenreich and Deirdre English, *For Her Own Good: Two Centuries of the Experts' Advice to Women*, 2nd ed. (New York: Anchor Books, 2005).

12 Maya Dusenberry, *Doing Harm: The Truth about How Bad Medicine and Lazy Science Leave Women Dismissed, Misdiagnosed, and Sick* (New York: HarperCollins, 2018).

13 Lucien C. Warner, *A Popular Treatise on the Functions and Diseases of Woman* (New York: Manhattan Publishing, 1874), 109, quoted in Ehrenreich and English, *For Her Own Good*, 125–26.

14 Mary Putnam Jacobi, *The Question of Rest for Women during Menstruation: The Boylston Prize Essay of Harvard University for 1876* (New York: G.P. Putnam's Sons, 1877), 227, quoted in Vertinsky, *Eternally Wounded Woman*, 142.

15 Mary Putnam Jacobi, "On Female Invalidism," in *Root of Bitterness: Documents of the Social History of American Women*, edited by Nancy F. Cott (New York: E.P. Dutton, 1972), 207, quoted in Ehrenreich and English, *For Her Own Good*, 105.

16 SI Staff, "A Game Girl in a Man's Game: Boston Was Unprepared for the Shapely Blonde Housewife Who Came Out of the Bushes to Crush Male Egos and Steal the Show from the Japanese," *Sports Illustrated*, May 2, 1966, https://vault.si.com/vault/1966/05/02/a-game-girl-in-a-mans-game.

17 Kathrine Switzer, *Marathon Woman: Running the Race to Revolutionize Women's Sports* (New York: Carroll and Graf, 2007).

18 Joan S. Hult, "The Female Endurance Runner: A Modern Quest for Visibility," in *Female Endurance Athletes*, edited by Barbara L. Drinkwater (Chicago: Human Kinetic, 1986), 28.

19 Jacqueline Hansen, "The Women's Marathon Movement: Or, We've Run a Long Way, but Haven't We Been Here Before?," *Marathon and Beyond*, January/February 2012.

20 Sidney Fields, "Only Human: Marathon Housewife," *Daily News* (NY), July 8, 1971.

21 "Sara Berman Scores Victory in Marathon," *Boston Globe*, October 26, 1970.

22   Marilyn Goldstein, "Women Show Spirit in Park Marathon," *Newsday* (Nassau, NY), March 22, 1971.

23   "Dr. Barbara Drinkwater, Ph.D., FACSM - ACSM President 1988–1989," ACSM, *YouTube*, March 19, 2014, https://youtu.be/qZcodWw3qLI?si=5mhBV9pedxCi56Jf.

24   "In Memoriam: Passing of Barbara Drinkwater," *National Academy of Kinesiology*, https://nationalacademyofkinesiology.org/in-memoriam/ (accessed August 28, 2023).

25   Barbara L. Drinkwater and Steven M. Horvath, "Responses of Young Female Track Athletes to Exercise," *Medicine and Science in Sports* 3, no. 2 (1971): 61.

26   Jacqueline Hansen, *A Long Time Coming: Running through the Women's Marathon Revolution* (Scotts Valley, CA: CreateSpace, 2013).

27   "After Years of Running Girls Down, Marathon Allows Official Entries," *Colorado Springs Gazette-Telegraph*, May 30, 1972.

28   Ira Berkow, "Nina the Long Distance Runner," *Times Herald* (Port Huron, MI), July, 11, 1972.

29   Randy Harvey, "Long Distance Calling: Jacqueline Hansen Connects with Lazlo Tabori to Break Running Barriers," *Los Angeles Times*, November 28, 1988.

30   "Women Can Tolerate Heat, UCSB Researchers Claim," *Goleta Sun*, October 17, 1979.

31   "Marathons Subject of Debate," *Rutland Daily Herald* (VT), October 21, 1976.

32   B. L. Drinkwater, I. C. Kupprat, J. E. Denton, and S. M. Horvath, "Heat Tolerance of Female Distance Runners," *Annals of the New York Academy of Sciences* 301, no. 1 (1977): 777, https://doi.org/10.1111/j.1749-6632.1977.tb38246.x.

33   "Figure 12. Percentage of U.S. medical school graduates by sex, academic years 1980-1981 through 2018–2019," *Diversity in Medicine: Facts and Figures 2019, Association of American Medical Colleges*, August 16, 2019, https://www.aamc.org/data-reports/workforce/data/figure-12-percentage-us-medical-school-graduates-sex-academic-years-1980-1981-through-2018-2019.

34   "Olympic Panel Approves '84 Women's Marathon," *Capital Times* (Madison, WI), February 24, 1981.

35   "IOC Votes to Include Women in Marathon Races," *Casper* (WY) *Star-Tribune* , February 24, 1981.

36   Jakim Berndsen, Aonghus Lawlor, and Barry Smyth, "Exploring the Wall in Marathon Running," *Journal of Sports Analytics* 6, no. 3 (2020): 173, https://content.iospress.com/articles/journal-of-sports-analytics/jsa200354.

37   Marvin Pave, "Sculpture to Honor Marathon Legacy," *Boston Globe*, February 24, 2008.

38   Bob Court and Jack Kendall, "Marathon Mrs. to Run Tandem with Mr. in '67: Plenty of Spectators Saw Marathon Mrs.," *Record-American* (Boston, MA), April 22, 1966.

Chapter 5

1   Jason Henderson, *Collision Course: The Olympic Tragedy of Mary Decker and Zola Budd* (Edinburgh: Birlinn, 2016).

2   Tom Jordan, *Pre: The Story of America's Greatest Running Legend, Steve Prefontaine* (Emmaus, PA: Rodale Books, 2012).

3   Kenny Moore, *Bowerman and the Men of Oregon: The Story of Oregon's Legendary Coach and Nike's Co-Founder* (Emmaus, PA: Rodale, 2006).

4   Robyn Norwood, "An Illustrious Track Record: Mary Decker Slaney Is Nothing Less Than a Legend, and Still Striving," *Los Angeles Times*, December 17, 1994.

5   Mike Braham, "Marathon: An Affair on the Hill," *Redondo* (CA) *Reflex*, May 26, 1971.

6   Earl Gustkey, "Girl, 14, Tenacious in Pursuit of Track Career," *Los Angeles Times*, March 13, 1973.

7   "Little Mary Decker, 14, among 20 Yank Winners," *Associated Press*, June 29, 1973.

8   Dave Distel, "The Girl Who Beat the Russians: Little Mary Decker Suddenly Very Big in World of Track," *Los Angeles Times*, August 21, 1973.

9   Charles Maher, "The Selling of a Tennis Match," *Los Angeles Times*, August 21, 1973.

10   Cynthia Gorney, "Mary Decker," *Washington Post*, March 26, 1980, https://www.washingtonpost.com/archive/sports/1980/03/26/mary-decker/e034a9cc-d1f5-4942-91e4-43f8b84389a2/.

11   Dick Draper,"Little Mary Isn't Little Now," *Times*, January 14, 1975.

12   Anita Verschoth, "Mary, Mary, Not Contrary : Only 15, Little Miss Decker Has Gained Poise to Match Her Status," Sports Illustrated, April 22, 1974, https://vault.si.com/vault/1974/04/22/mary-mary-not-contrary.

13   Reid English, "Decker, Scott Own 1,500," *Statesman Journal* (Salem, OR), June 30, 1980.

14   "Athletes Differ in Boycott Views," *Arizona Republic*, April 14, 1980.

15   Kenny Moore, "She Runs and We Are Lifted," *Sports Illustrated*, December 26, 1983, https://vault.si.com/vault/1983/12/26/she-runs-and-we-are-lifted.

16   Dennis Georgatos and Associated Press, "Slaney Holds off Plumer to Notch First Track Victory in Two Years," *Herald*, May 26, 1991.

17   Cleve Dheensaw, "Decker-Slaney Competing in Victoria Tonight," *Times-Colonist* (Victoria, BC), August 11, 1991.

18   Bruce Jenkins, "Plumer Was Ready to Give Slaney One Final Shot at Olympic Glory," *San Francisco Chronicle*, July 4, 1992.

19   Gil LeBreton, "Gil LeBreton's Olympic Notebook," *Fort Worth Star-Telegram*, June 23, 1992.

20   Nicholas Thompson, "The Running Life," *New Yorker*, May 14, 2012, https://www.newyorker.com/books/page-turner/the-running-life.

21   Matt Slater and Samuel Smith, "Questions Mount over Alberto Salazar's Links to Mary Slaney," *BBC Sport*, June 12, 2015, https://www.bbc.com/sport /athletics/33096367.

22   Leslie Heywood, *Pretty Good for a Girl* (Minneapolis: University of Minnesota Press, 1998).

23   Leslie Heywood, *The Proving Grounds: Poems* (Pasadena, CA: Red Hen Press, 2005), 33.

24   R. W. Connell, *Gender and Power* (Stanford, CA: Stanford University Press, 1987), 80–87.

25   Reut Agam, Snait Tamir, and Moria Golan, "Gender Differences in Respect to Self-Esteem and Body Image as Well as Response to Adolescents' School-Based Prevention Programs," *Journal of Psychology & Clinical Psychiatry* 2, no. 5 (2015), https://doi.org/10.15406/jpcpy.2015.02.00092.

26   Thomas Haugen, Paul A. Solberg, Carl Foster, Ricardo Morán-Navarro, Felix Breitschädel, and Will G. Hopkins, "Peak Age and Performance Progression in World-Class Track-and-Field Athletes," *International Journal of Sports Physiology and Performance* 13, no. 9 (2018): 1122–29, https://doi.org/10.1123/ijspp.2017-0682.

27   Linda Smolak and J. Kevin Thompson, *Body Image, Eating Disorders, and Obesity in Youth: Assessment, Prevention, and Treatment* (Washington, DC: American Psychological Association Press, 2009), chap. 3.

28   Rachel M. Calogero, Michael S. Boroughs, and J. Kevin Thompson, "The Impact of Western Beauty Ideals on the Lives of Women: A Sociocultural Perspective," in *The Body Beautiful*, edited by V. Swami and A. Furnham (London: Palgrave Macmillan, 2007), 259–98, https://doi.org/10.1057/9780230596887_13.

29   Don Sabo and Phil Veliz, "Go Out and Play: Youth Sports in America," *Women's Sports Foundation*, October 1, 2008, http://files.eric.ed.gov/fulltext /ED539976.pdf.

30   World Health Organization, "New WHO-Led Study Says Majority of Adolescents Worldwide Are Not Sufficiently Physically Active, Putting Their Current and Future Health at Risk," *World Health Organization*, November 22, 2019, https://www.who.int /news/item/22-11-2019-new-who-led-study-says-majority-of-adolescents-worldwide -are-not-sufficiently-physically-active-putting-their-current-and-future-health-at-risk.

31   Kathleen F. Janz, Elena M. Letuchy, Trudy L. Burns, Julie M. Eichenberger Gilmore, James C. Torner, and Steven M. Levy, "Objectively Measured Physical Activity Trajectories Predict Adolescent Bone Strength: Iowa Bone Development Study," *British Journal of Sports Medicine* 48, no. 13 (2014): 1032–36, https://doi.org /10.1136/bjsports-2014-093574.

32   Adam D. G. Baxter-Jones, Robert A. Faulkner, Mark. R. Forwood, Robert L. Mirwald, and Donald A. Bailey, "Bone Mineral Accrual from 8 to 30 Years of Age: An Estimation of Peak Bone Mass," *Journal of Bone and Mineral Research* 26, no. 8 (2011): 1729–39, https://doi.org/10.1002/jbmr.412.

33 "Epidemiology," *International Osteoporosis Foundation*, April 16, 2020, https://www.osteoporosis.foundation/health-professionals/fragility-fractures/epidemiology.

34 Thach Tran, Dana Bliuc, Louise Hansen, Bo Abrahamson, Joop van den Bergh, John A. Eisman, Tineke van Geel, Piet Geusens, Peter Vestergaard, Tuan V. Nguyen, and Jacqueline R. Center, "Persistence of Excess Mortality Following Individual Nonhip Fractures: A Relative Survival Analysis," *Journal of Clinical Endocrinology and Metabolism* 103, no. 9 (2018): 3205–14, https://doi.org/10.1210/jc.2017-02656.

35 Monica Klungland Torstveit, Jan H. Rosenvinge, and Jorunn Sundgot-Borgen, "Prevalence of Eating Disorders and the Predictive Power of Risk Models in Female Elite Athletes: A Controlled Study," *Scandinavian Journal of Medicine & Science in Sports* 18, no. 1 (2007): 108–18, https://doi.org/10.1111/j.1600-0838.2007.00657.x.

36 Laura Di Lodovico, Ségolène Poulnais, and Philip Gorwood, "Which Sports Are More at Risk of Physical Exercise Addiction: A Systematic Review," *Addictive Behaviors* 93 (2019): 257–62, https://doi.org/10.1016/j.addbeh.2018.12.030.

37 Joan Ryan, "Too Much, Too Young: Elite Young Female Athletes Pay Heavy Price for Success," *San Francisco Examiner*, July 12, 1992.

38 Barbara L. Drinkwater, Karen Nilson, Charles H. Chesnut III, William J. Bremner, Sydney Shainholtz, and Molly B. Southworth, "Bone Mineral Content of Amenorrheic and Eumenorrheic Athletes," *New England Journal of Medicine* 311, no. 5 (1984): 277–81, https://doi.org/10.1056/nejm198408023110501.

39 Barbara L. Drinkwater, Karen Nilson, Susan Ott, and Charles H. Chesnut III, "Bone Mineral Density after Resumption of Menses in Amenorrheic Athletes," *Journal of the American Medical Association* 256, no. 3 (1986): 380, https://doi.org/10.1001/jama.1986.03380030082032.

40 Monica Yant, "The Female Athlete Triad," *Chicago Tribune*, July 1, 1992.

41 Linda Villarosa, "Dangerous Triad: Three-Fold Ailment Stalks Some Female Athletes," *New York Times*, June 29, 1999.

42 Kimberly K. Yeager, Rosemary Agostini, Aurelia Nattiv, and Barbara Drinkwater, "The Female Athlete Triad: Disordered Eating, Amenorrhea, Osteoporosis," *Medicine & Science in Sports & Exercise* 25, no. 7 (1993): 775–77, https://journals.lww.com/acsm-msse/citation/1993/07000/the_female_athlete_triad__disordered_eating,.3.aspx.

43 Shari Roan, "A High Price for Gold?: Now That Female Athletes Are Pushing Their Bodies More They Find Peak Performance Can Also Bring Long-Term Health Risks," *Los Angeles Times*, August 9, 1992.

44 Alan Bavley, "Anorexia among Athletes: Young Gymnast's Death Highlights Growing Problem," *Kansas City Star*, July 28, 1994.

45 Michael Voepel, "Mary Decker, an American Idol," *ESPN*, August 12, 2013, https://www.espn.com/espnw/nine-for-ix/story/_/id/9561818/espnw-nine-ix-mary-decker-was-early-idol-female-sports-fans.

46 Peter Gambaccini, "High Schooler Mary Cain Wins National Outdoor Mile Title," *Runner's World*, March 3, 2013, https://www.runnersworld.com/races-places/a20842941/high-schooler-mary-cain-wins-national-indoor-mile-title/.

47   Ken Goe, "Mo Farah Wins the 5,000 at the Oxy High Performance Meet, but Mary Cain Steals the Show," *Oregonlive*, May 18, 2013, https://www.oregonlive.com /trackandfield/2013/05/mo_farah_wins_the_5000_at_the.html.

48   Ken Goe, "Alberto Salazar Says Mary Cain's Goal Is to Be Race-Fit by June," *Oregonlive*, May 2, 2015, https://www.oregonlive.com/trackandfield/2015/05/saturday _morning_news_notes_li_24.html.

49   Peter Gambaccini, "Teen Star Mary Cain Returns Home amid Disappointing Track Season," *Runner's World*, March 2, 2022, https://www.runnersworld.com/news /a20804475/teen-star-mary-cain-returns-home-amid-disappointing-track-season/.

50   Mary Cain, Lindsay Crouse, and Alexander Stockton, "I Was the Fastest Girl in America, until I Joined Nike," *New York Times*, August 4, 2023, https://www.nytimes .com/2019/11/07/opinion/nike-running-mary-cain.html.

51   Barbara L. Drinkwater (ed.), *Women in Sport: Volume VIII of the Encyclopaedia of Sports Medicine* (Hoboken, NJ: Wiley Blackwell, 2000), 386.

52   Maggie Mertens, "Kara Goucher Says She Is the Woman behind the Sexual Abuse Allegations against Alberto Salazar," *Sports Illustrated*, March 14, 2023, https:// www.si.com/more-sports/2023/03/14/kara-goucher-book-sexual-abuse-allegations -against-alberto-salazar.

53   Ken Goe, "Mary Cain Takes a Break from the Nike Oregon Project," *Oregonlive*, May 27, 2015, https://www.oregonlive.com/trackandfield/2015/05/mary_cain_takes_a _break_from_t.html.

54   Chris Chavez, "Inside the Toxic Culture of the Nike Oregon Project 'Cult,'" *Sports Illustrated*, October 18, 2022, https://www.si.com/track-and-field/2019/11/13 /mary-cain-nike-oregon-project-toxic-culture-alberto-salazar-abuse-investigation.

55   Kevin Draper and Matthew Futterman, "Disgraded Running Coach Was Barred for Life for Alleged Sexual Assault," *New York Times*, January 31, 2022, https://www. nytimes.com/2022/01/31/sports/alberto-salazar-sexual-assault.html.

56   Kara Goucher, *The Longest Race: Inside the Secret World of Abuse, Doping, and Deception on Nike's Elite Running Team* (New York: Simon and Schuster, 2023).

57   Ken Goe, "Women Athletes Allege Body Shaming within Oregon Ducks Track and Field Program," *Oregonlive*, October 25, 2021, https://www.oregonlive.com /trackandfield/2021/10/women-athletes-allege-body-shaming-within-oregon-ducks -track-and-field-program.html.

58   Alanis Thames and Jonathan Abrams, "Female College Athletes Say Pressure to Cut Body Fat Is Toxic," *New York Times*, November 14, 2022, https://www.nytimes .com/2022/11/10/sports/college-athletes-body-fat-women.html.

59   Paul Krebs, Christopher R. Dennison, Lisa Kellar, and Jeff Lucas, "Gender Differences in Eating Disorder Risk among NCAA Division I Cross Country and Track Student-Athletes," *Journal of Sports Medicine* 2019 (February 3, 2019): 1–5, https://doi.org/10.1155/2019/5035871.

60   Margo Mountjoy, Jorunn Sundgot-Borgen, Louise Burke, Susan Carter, Naama Constantini, Constance Lebrun, Nanna Meyer, Roberta Sherman, Kathrin Steffin, Richard Budgett, and Arne Ljungqvist, "The IOC Consensus Statement: Beyond the Female Athlete Triad—Relative Energy Deficiency in Sport (RED-S)," *British Journal of Sports Medicine* 48, no. 7 (2014): 491–97, https://doi.org/10.1136/bjsports-2014-093502.

61   Tim Layden, "Here Comes Mary Cain," *Sports Illustrated*, December 19, 2019, https://vault.si.com/vault/2013/07/01/here-comes-mary-cain.

62   Elizabeth Weil, "Mary Cain Is Growing Up Fast," *New York Times*, December 6, 2019, https://www.nytimes.com/2015/03/08/magazine/mary-cain-is-growing-up-fast.html.

63   Katherine H. Rizzone, Kathryn E. Ackerman, Karen G. Roos, Thomas P. Dompier, and Zachary Y. Kerr, "The Epidemiology of Stress Fractures in Collegiate Student-Athletes, 2004–2005 through 2013–2014 Academic Years," *Journal of Athletic Training* 52, no. 10 (2017): 966–75, https://doi.org/10.4085/1062-6050-52.8.01.

64   Michelle T. Barrack, Jenna C. Gibbs, Mary Jane De Souza, Nancy I. Williams, Jeanne F. Nichols, Mitchell J. Rauh, and Aurelia Nattiv, "Higher Incidence of Bone Stress Injuries with Increasing Female Athlete Triad–Related Risk Factors," *American Journal of Sports Medicine* 42, no. 4 (2014): 949–58, https://doi.org/10.1177/0363546513520295.

65   Melissa T. Lodge, Kathryn E. Ackerman, and Jessica Garay, "Knowledge of the Female Athlete Triad and Relative Energy Deficiency in Sport among Female Cross-Country Athletes and Support Staff," *Journal of Athletic Training* 57, no. 4 (2021): 385–92, https://doi.org/10.4085/1062-6050-0175.21.

66   Emily Kroshus, J. D. DeFreese, and Zachary Y. Kerr, "Collegiate Athletic Trainers' Knowledge of the Female Athlete Triad and Relative Energy Deficiency in Sport," *Journal of Athletic Training* 53, no. 1 (2018): 51–59, https://doi.org/10.4085/1062-6050-52.11.29.

67   Braeden T. Charlton, Sara Forsyth, and David Clarke, "Low Energy Availability and Relative Energy Deficiency in Sport: What Coaches Should Know," *International Journal of Sports Science & Coaching* 17, no. 2 (2022): 445–60, https://doi.org/10.1177/17479541211054458.

68   Adrien Sedeaud, Andy Marc, Adrien Marck, Frédéric Dor, Julien Schipman, Maya Dorsey, Amal Haida, Geoffroy Berthelot, and Jean-François Toussaint, "BMI, a Performance Parameter for Speed Improvement," *PLoS One* 9, no. 2 (2014): e90183, https://doi.org/10.1371/journal.pone.0090183.

69   Adelaide Cooke, "Body Composition of Female Collegiate Track and Field Athletes," honors thesis, State University of New York at Albany, 2019.

70   Yuka Tsukahara, Suguru Torii, Fumihiro Yamasawa, Jun Iwamoto, Takanobu Otsuka, Hideyuki Goto, Torao Kusakabe, Hideo Matsumoto, and Takao Akama, "Changes in Body Composition and Its Relationship to Performance in Elite Female Track and Field Athletes Transitioning to the Senior Division," *Sports* 8, no. 9 (2020): 115, https://doi.org/10.3390/sports8090115.

71 Lucy Hicks, "For Young Female Athletes, Losing Weight May Not Improve Performance," *Science*, July 29, 2020, https://www.science.org/content/article /young-female-athletes-losing-weight-may-not-improve-performance.

72 Joanne L. Parsons, Stephanie E. Coen, and Sheree Bekker, "Anterior Cruciate Ligament Injury: Towards a Gendered Environmental Approach," *British Journal of Sports Medicine* 55, no. 17 (2021): 984–90, https://doi.org/10.1136/bjsports-2020-103173.

73 Mary Jane De Souza, Nancy I. Williams, Aurelia Nattiv, Elizabeth Joy, Madhusmita Misra, Anne B. Loucks, Marion P. Olmstead, Michelle Barrack, Rebecca J. Mallinson, Jenna C. Gibbs, et al., "Misunderstanding the Female Athlete Triad: Refuting the IOC Consensus Statement on Relative Energy Deficiency in Sport (RED-S)," *British Journal of Sports Medicine* 48, no. 20 (2014): 1461–65, https://doi.org/10.1136/bjsports-2014-093958.

Chapter 6

1 Rachel Bachman, "The High School Sprint Phenom Who Beat Her Prom Date," *Wall Street Journal*, May 14, 2023, https://www.wsj.com/articles/mia-brahe-pedersen -oregon-girl-sprinter-mixed-gender-cce279f7.

2 "Uganda's Former 800m Star: Annet Negesa," *Trans World Sport*, YouTube, March 11, 2020, https://www.youtube.com/watch?v=ec8H8TeTkfA.

3 *Category: Woman*, Orama Filmworks, Proximity Film, and TVO, 2022, https:// www.categorywomandoc.com/.

4 Geneva Abdul, "This Intersex Runner Had Surgery to Compete. It Has Not Gone Well," *New York Times*, November 19, 2020, https://www.nytimes.com/2019/12/16 /sports/intersex-runner-surgery-track-and-field.html.

5 Kyle Knight, "They're Chasing Us Away from Sport," *Human Rights Watch*, December 4, 2020, https://www.hrw.org/report/2020/12/04/theyre-chasing-us-away -sport/human-rights-violations-sex-testing-elite-women.

6 "Blow for Uganda as Injury Rules Negesa Out of 2012 London Olympics," *Uganda Radionetwork*, July 30, 2012, https://ugandaradionetwork.net/story/blow -for-uganda-as-injury-rules-negesa-out-of-2012-london-olympics.

7 Amanda Shalala, "Intersex Runner Annet Negesa Fighting for Everyone's Right to Compete in Sport," *ABC News*, March 11, 2023, https://www.abc.net.au/news /2023-03-12/intersex-runner-annet-negesa-seeks-equal-rights-in-sport/102069710.

8 International Association of Athletics Federations, "IAAF Regulations Governing Eligibility of Females with Hyperandrogenism to Compete in Women's Competition," May 1, 2011, https://www.sportsintegrityinitiative.com/wp-content /uploads/2016/02/IAAF-Regulations-Governing-Eligibility-of-Females-with -Hyperandrogenism-to-Compete-in-Women%E2%80%99s-Competition-In -force-as-from-1st-May-2011-6.pdf.

9 Jaime Schultz, *Qualifying Times: Points of Change in U.S. Women's Sports* (Carbondale: University of Illinois Press, 2014), 106–7, https://doi.org/10.5406 /illinois/9780252038167.001.0001.

10   Rob Tannenbaum, "The Life and Murder of Stella Walsh, Intersex Olympic Champion," *Longreads*, October 19, 2022, https://longreads.com/2016/08/18/the-life -and-murder-of-stella-walsh-intersex-olympic-champion/.

11   Sergey Nurk, Sergey Koren, Arang Rhie, Mikko Rautiainen, Andrey V. Bzikadze, Alla Mikheeno, Mitchelle R. Volger, Nicholas Altemose, Lev Uralsky, Ariel Gershman, et al., "The Complete Sequence of a Human Genome," *Science* 376, no. 6588 (2022): 44–53, https://doi.org/10.1126/science.abj6987.

12   Roseanne F. Zhao, "The Y Chromosome: Beyond Gender Determination," *Genome.gov*, May 30, 2014, https://www.genome.gov/27557513/the-y-chromosome -beyond-gender-determination.

13   Alice Park, "The Human Genome Is Finally Fully Sequenced," *Time*, April 1, 2022, https://time.com/6163452/human-genome-fully-sequenced/.

14   Robert W. Ritchie, John Reynard, and Torn Lewis, "Intersex and the Olympic Games," *Journal of the Royal Society of Medicine* 101, no. 8 (2008): 395–99, https://doi .org/10.1258/jrsm.2008.080086.

15   Anne Fausto-Sterling, *Sexing the Body: Gender Politics and the Construction of Sexuality* (London: Hachette UK, 2000).

16   Nat Mulkey, Carl G. Streed, and Barbara Chubak, "A Call to Update Standard of Care for Children with Differences in Sex Development," *AMA Journal of Ethics* 23, no. 7 (2021): E550–56, https://doi.org/10.1001/amajethics.2021.550.

17   Stefan Timmermans, Ashelee Yang, Melissa Gardner, Catherine E. Keegan, Beverly M. Yashar, Patricia Y. Fechner, Margarett Shnorhavorian, Eric Vilain, Laura A. Siminoff, and David E. Sandberg, "Does Patient-Centered Care Change Genital Surgery Decisions? The Strategic Use of Clinical Uncertainty in Disorders of Sex Development Clinics," *Journal of Health and Social Behavior* 59, no. 4 (2018): 520–35, https://doi.org/10.1177/0022146518802460.

18   Kimberly Mascott Zieselman, "I Was an Intersex Child Who Had Surgery. Don't Put Other Kids through This," *USA TODAY*, August 10, 2017, https://www.usatoday .com/story/opinion/2017/08/09/intersex-children-no-surgery-without-consent -zieselman-column/539853001/.

19   World Health Organization and Human Reproduction Programme, "Sexual Health, Human Rights and the Law," *World Health Organization*, n.d., 26–27.

20   Office of the High Commissioner for Human Rights, "Ending Violence and Discrimination against Lesbian, Gay, Bisexual, Transgender and Intersex People," joint statement of ILO, UNHCHR, UNESCO, UNFPA, UNHCR, UNICEF, UNODC, UN Women, WFP, WHO, and UNAIDS, September 2015, http://www.ohchr.org /Documents/Issues/Discrimination/Joint_LGBTI_Statement_ENG.PDF.

21   "Unnecessary Surgery on Intersex Children Must Stop," *Physicians for Human Rights*, October 20, 2017, https://phr.org/news/unnecessary-surgery-on-intersex -children-must-stop/.

22   Louis J. Elsas, Arne Ljungqvist, Malcolm A. Ferguson-Smith, Joe Leigh Simpson, Myron Genel, Alison S. Carlson, Elizabeth Ferris, Albert de la Chapelle,

and Anke A. Ehrhardt, "Gender Verification of Female Athletes," *Genetics in Medicine* 2, no. 4 (2000): 251, https://doi.org/10.1097/00125817-200007000-00008.

23   Arne Ljungqvist and Joe Leigh Simpson, "Medical Examination for Health of All Athletes Replacing the Need for Gender Verification in International Sports," *Journal of the American Medical Association* 267, no. 6 (1992): 850, https://doi.org /10.1001/jama.1992.03480060096038.

24   Jacob Richman and Alexandra Gopin, "Title IX at 50: Girls Are Still Fighting for Equality in High School Sports," *Just Women's Sports*, April 12, 2022, https:// justwomenssports.com/reads/title-ix-50-anniversary-girls-high-school-sports/.

25   "Zhang Shan: The Only Female Shooter to Win Gold in a Mixed Competition," *Olympics.com*, July 5, 2020, https://olympics.com/en/news/zhang-shan-the-only-female -shooter-to-win-gold-in-a-mixed-competition.

26   Maggie Mertens, "This Woman Surfed the Biggest Wave of the Year," *Atlantic*, September 12, 2020, https://www.theatlantic.com/culture/archive/2020/09/maya -gabeira-surfed-biggest-wave-year/616216/.

27   Rena Vicini Koier, "Dialing Title IX . . . 'She's Away from Her Desk' A Familiar Refrain," *Lexington* (KY) *Herald*, August 7, 1977.

28   Margaret Roach and Times News Service, "Title IX Sparks Sporting Progress," *Rutland* (VT) *Daily Herald*, September 29, 1977.

29   Rena Vicini Koier, "Softball for Girls a Test for Title IX," *Lexington* (KY) *Herald*, August 7, 1977.

30   "Kim Is Little League Star," *Springfield* (OH) *News-Sun*, July 8, 1975.

31   Douglas E. Abrams, "The Twelve-Year-Old Girl's Lawsuit That Changed America: The Continuing Impact of Now v. Little League Baseball, Inc. at 40," *Virginia Journal of Social Policy & the Law* 20, no. 2 (2012): 241.

32   "Number of Participants in 11-Player Football in High Schools in the United States from 2009/2010 to 2021/2022, by Gender," *Statista*, Sepember 2022, https:// www.statista.com/statistics/267955/participation-in-us-high-school-football/.

33   Emery Winter, "The NCAA Women's Basketball Tournament Only Became Part of March Madness Last Year," *KVUE ABC*, March 16, 2023, https://www.kvue .com/article/news/verify/sports-verify/march-madness-not-used-for-ncaa-womens -basketball-tournament-until-2022-mens-tournament-only-in-2021/536-6430e604 -5ab7-484c-9c8b-bb222bcc120c.

34   Steve Magness, "There's Good Reason for Sports to Be Separated by Sex," *Atlantic*, September 29, 2022, https://www.theatlantic.com/culture/archive/2022/09 /why-elite-sports-should-remain-separated-by-sex/671594/.

35   "High School Sports: Everything You Need to Know," *NCSA College Recruiting*, n.d., https://www.ncsasports.org/articles-1/high-school-sports.

36   "400 Metres Women," *World Athletics*, n.d., https://worldathletics.org/records /all-time-toplists/sprints/400-metres/outdoor/women/senior.

37 "Icelandic Championships, 28–30 Jul 2023, Men's 400m," *World Athletics*, n.d., https://worldathletics.org/competition/calendar-results/results/7198334?eventId =10229631&gender=M.

38 "Greek Senior CE Championships, 23–24 Jul 2022, Combined Events—B, Men's 400m," *World Athletics*, n.d., https://worldathletics.org/competition/calendar-results /results/7184762?eventId=10229631&gender=M.

39 "Portuguese Championships, 29–30 Jul 2023, Men's 100m," *World Athletics*, n.d., https://worldathletics.org/competition/calendar-results/results/7201511.

40 "Swedish Championships, 28–30 Jul 2023, Men's 100m," *World Athletics*, n.d., https://worldathletics.org/competition/calendar-results/results/7193429.

41 "Serbian Championships, 29–30 Jul 2023, Men's 400m," *World Athletics*, n.d., https://worldathletics.org/competition/calendar-results/results/7194567?eventId =10229631&gender=M.

42 Rebekkah Rubin, "The Woman Who Challenged Darwin's Sexism," *Smithsonian Magazine*, November 9, 2017, https://www.smithsonianmag.com/science-nature /woman-who-tried-take-down-darwin-180967146/.

43 Alexandra Kralick, "When Ape Sex Isn't Simple," *Anthropology News*, March 14, 2023, https://www.anthropology-news.org/articles/when-ape-sex-isnt-simple.

44 Nathan Q. Ha, Shari L. Dworkin, María José Martínez-Patiño, Alan D. Rogol, Vernon Rosario, Francisco J. Sánchez, Alison Wrynn, and Eric Vilain, "Hurdling over Sex? Sport, Science, and Equity," *Archives of Sexual Behavior* 43, no. 6 (2014): 1035–42, https://doi.org/10.1007/s10508-014-0332-0.

45 Linda Robertson, "Semenya Case Reveals Gender Identity Crisis," *Miami Herald*, August 27, 2009.

46 Robyn Dixon, "Semenya and Bolt: Questions Inevitably Follow When People Break New Ground: For Many South Africans, the Controversy over Caster Semenya's Gender Is Really Just Racism," *Vancouver Sun*, August 22, 2009.

47 Jeré Longman, "South African Runner's Sex-Verification Result Won't Be Public," *New York Times*, November 20, 2009, https://www.nytimes.com/2009/11/20 /sports/20runner.html.

48 "Caster Semenya May Compete," *World Athletics*, July 6, 2010, https:// worldathletics.org/news/iaaf-news/caster-semenya-may-compete.

49 Lynn Zinser, "South African Runner Is Cleared to Compete as Woman," *New York Times*, July 7, 2010, https://www.nytimes.com/2010/07/07/sports/07semenya.html.

50 Joanna Harper, *Sporting Gender: The History, Science, and Stories of Transgender and Intersex Athletes* (Lanham, MD: Rowman & Littlefield, 2019), 139.

51 Shane Miller, "'Just Look at Her!': Sporting Bodies as Athletic Resistance and the Limits of Sport Norms in the Case of Caster Semenya," *Men and Masculinities* 18, no. 3 (2014): 293–317, https://doi.org/10.1177/1097184x14561336.

52 Marissa Payne, "Russian Runner Who Admitted on Video to Doping Is Stripped of Olympic Gold," *Washington Post*, November 27, 2021, https://www.washingtonpost .com/news/early-lead/wp/2017/02/10/russian-runner-who-admitted-to-doping-on -video-is-stripped-of-olympic-gold/.

53   Patrick Fénichel, Françoise Paris, Pascal Philibert, Sylvie Hiéronimus, Laura Gaspari, Jean-Yves Kurzenne, Patrick Chevallier, Stéphane Bermon, Nicolas Chevalier, and Charles Sultan, "Molecular Diagnosis of 5A-Reductase Deficiency in 4 Elite Young Female Athletes through Hormonal Screening for Hyperandrogenism," *Journal of Clinical Endocrinology and Metabolism* 98, no. 6 (2013): E1055–59, https://doi.org /10.1210/jc.2012-3893.

54   Lindsay Parks Pieper, "The New Olympic Policy That Undoes a Half-Century of Bigotry," *Washington Post*, November 29, 2021, https://www.washingtonpost.com /outlook/2021/11/29/new-olympic-policy-that-undoes-half-century-bigotry/.

55   Gina Kolata, "Gender Testing Hangs before the Games as a Vexing Mess," *New York Times*, January 16, 2010, https://www.nytimes.com/2010/01/16/sports /olympics/16ioc.html.

56   Juliet Macur, "Fighting for the Body She Was Born With," *New York Times*, October 6, 2014, https://www.nytimes.com/2014/10/07/sports/sprinter-dutee-chand -fights-ban-over-her-testosterone-level.html.

57   "Dutee Chand v. AFI & IAAF, Partial Award, 24 July 2015," *Jus Mundi*, n.d., https://jusmundi.com/en/document/decision/en-dutee-chand-v-athletics-federation -of-india-afi-international-association-of-athletics-federations-iaaf-partial-award -friday-24th-july-2015-1.

58   Sari M. Van Anders, "Gender/Sex/Ual Diversity and Biobehavioral Research," *Psychology of Sexual Orientation and Gender Diversity*, November 10, 2022, https:// doi.org/10.1037/sgd0000609.

59   Mark Critchley, "Rio 2016: Fifth-Placed Joanna Jozwik 'Feels like Silver Medallist' after 800m Defeat to Caster Semenya," *The Independent*, August 22, 2016, https://www. independent.co.uk/sport/olympics/rio-2016-joanna-jozwik-caster-semenya-800m -hyperandrogenism-a7203731.html.

60   "Tearful Lynsey Sharp Says Rule Change Makes Racing Caster Semenya Difficult," *The Guardian*, September 16, 2020, https://www.theguardian.com/sport /2016/aug/21/lynsey-sharp-caster-semenya-rio-2016-olympics.

61   Andy Bull, "Caster Semenya Wins Olympic Gold but Faces More Scrutiny as IAAF Presses Case," *The Guardian*, February 21, 2018, https://www.theguardian.com /sport/2016/aug/21/caster-semenya-wins-gold-but-faces-scrutiny.

62   Stéphane Bermon and Pierre-Yves Garnier, "Serum Androgen Levels and Their Relation to Performance in Track and Field: Mass Spectrometry Results from 2127 Observations in Male and Female Elite Athletes," *British Journal of Sports Medicine* 51, no. 17 (2017): 1309–14, https://doi.org/10.1136/bjsports-2017-097792.

63   "IAAF Introduces New Eligibility Regulations for Female Classification," press release, *World Athletics*, April 26, 2018, https://worldathletics.org/news/press-release /eligibility-regulations-for-female-classifica.

64   Stéphane Bermon, "Androgens and Athletic Performance of Elite Female Athletes," *Current Opinion in Endocrinology, Diabetes and Obesity* 24, no. 3 (2017): 246–51, https://doi.org/10.1097/med.0000000000000335.

65   Roger A. Pielke, Ross Tucker, and Erik Boye, "Scientific Integrity and the IAAF Testosterone Regulations," *International Sports Law Journal* 19, nos. 1–2 (2019): 18–26, https://doi.org/10.1007/s40318-019-00143-w.

66   Nick Harris, "Caster Semenya Is Running Right into an Ethical Minefield as Rio Olympics Looks Sure to Reignite Fierce Debate over 'Intersex' South African," *Mail Online*, August 6, 2016, https://www.dailymail.co.uk/sport/othersports/article-3727317 /Caster-Semenya-running-right-ethical-minefield-Rio-Olympics-looks-sure-reignite -fierce-debate-intersex-South-African.html.

67   Roger Pielke Jr., Ross Tucker, and Erik Boye, "Letter to BJSM Reinforcing Call for Retraction of IAAF Research on Testosterone in Women," *Science of Sport*, August 2, 2018, https://sportsscientists.com/2018/08/letter-to-bjsm-reinforcing-call -for-retraction-of-iaaf-research-on-testosterone-in-women/.

68   Roger A. Pielke, Ross Tucker, and Erik Boye, "Scientific Integrity and the IAAF Testosterone Regulations," *International Sports Law Journal* 19, nos. 1–2 (2019): 18–26, https://doi.org/10.1007/s40318-019-00143-w.

69   "Olympic Officials Should Tell Women 'High T' Is No Hurdle," *Scientific American* 315, no. 2 (2016): 8, https://doi.org/10.1038/scientificamerican0816-8.

70   Jeré Longman, "Did Flawed Data Lead Track Astray on Testosterone in Women?," *New York Times*, November 2, 2021, https://www.nytimes.com/2018/07/12 /sports/iaaf-caster-semenya.html.

71   Ross Tucker, "The Semenya Decision: Full CAS Report Brief Thoughts," *Science of Sport*, December 2, 2022, https://sportsscientists.com/2019/06/the-semenya -decision-full-cas-report-brief-thoughts/.

72   Jeré Longman, "Caster Semenya Will Challenge Testosterone Rule in Court," *New York Times*, June 18, 2018, https://www.nytimes.com/2018/06/18/sports/caster -semenya-iaaf-lawsuit.html.

73   Jeré Longman and Juliet Macur, "Caster Semenya Loses Case to Compete as a Woman in All Races," *New York Times*, May 2, 2019, https://www.nytimes.com/2019 /05/01/sports/caster-semenya-loses.html.

74   "Arbitral Award Delivered by the Court of Arbitration for Sport: Mokgadi Caster Semenya v. International Association of Athletics Federations," *Court of Arbitration for Sport*, May 1, 2019, https://www.tas-cas.org/fileadmin/user_upload /CAS_Award_-_redacted_-_Semenya_ASA_IAAF.pdf.

75   Ben Rumsby, "Intersex Ex-Athlete Annet Negesa 'Relieved and Happy' to Be Granted Asylum in Germany," *Telegraph*, December 5, 2019, https://www.telegraph .co.uk/athletics/2019/12/05/intersex-ex-athlete-annet-negesa-relieved-happy-granted -asylum/.

76   "IAAF Response to False Claims Made by Athlete Regarding DSD Treatment," *World Athletics*, n.d., https://worldathletics.org/news/press-release/iaaf-response -to-false-claims-made-by-athlete.

77   Duncan Mackay, "IAAF Officially Changes Name to World Athletics," *Inside the Games*, November 15, 2019, https://www.insidethegames.biz/articles/1087059 /world-athletics-officially-changes-name.

78 Katie Barnes, "The Battle over Title IX and Who Gets to Be a Woman in Sports: Inside the Raging National Debate," *ESPN*, June 23, 2020, https://www.espn.com/espnw/story/_/id/29347507/the-battle-title-ix-gets-woman-sports-raging-national-debate.

79 "Complaint Targets Transgender HS Track Athletes," *ESPN*, June 20, 2019, https://www.espn.com/high-school/story/_/id/27015115/complaint-targets-transgender-hs-track-athletes.

80 "Soule et al v. CT Association of Schools et al," *American Civil Liberties Union*, August 18, 2023, https://www.aclu.org/cases/soule-et-al-v-ct-association-schools-et-al.

81 Rachel Savage, "Idaho Becomes First U.S. State to Ban Trans Athletes," *Reuters*, March 31, 2020, https://www.reuters.com/article/us-usa-lgbt-lawmaking/idaho-becomes-first-u-s-state-to-ban-trans-athletes-idUSKBN21I2AF.

82 Joan H. Fujimura, "Sex Genes: A Critical Sociomaterial Approach to the Politics and Molecular Genetics of Sex Determination," *Signs* 32, no. 1 (2006): 49–82, https://doi.org/10.1086/505612.

83 Arthur P. Arnold, "A General Theory of Sexual Differentiation," *Journal of Neuroscience Research* 95, nos. 1–2 (2016): 291–300, https://doi.org/10.1002/jnr.23884.

84 Rachel Roth, "Gender Negotiations of Female Collegiate Athletes in the Strength and Conditioning Environment: A Qualitative Analysis," MS thesis, Southern Illinois University, 2013.

85 Natalie Adams, Alison Schmitke, and Amy Franklin, "Tomboys, Dykes, and Girly Girls: Interrogating the Subjectivities of Adolescent Female Athletes," *Women's Studies Quarterly* 33, no. 1/2 (2005): 17, https://www.jstor.org/stable/40005499.

86 Dan Bilefsky, "Man Who Questioned 9-Year-Old Athlete's Gender Spurs Outrage," *New York Times*, June 15, 2023, https://www.nytimes.com/2023/06/14/world/canada/girl-athlete-trans-gender.html.

87 Joanna Harper, "Race Times for Transgender Athletes," *Journal of Sporting Cultures and Identities* 6, no. 1 (2015): 1–9, https://doi.org/10.18848/2381-6678/cgp/v06i01/54079.

88 Joanna Harper, Emma O'Donnell, Behzad Sorouri Khorashad, Hilary McDermott, and Gemma L. Witcomb, "How Does Hormone Transition in Transgender Women Change Body Composition, Muscle Strength and Haemoglobin? Systematic Review with a Focus on the Implications for Sport Participation," *British Journal of Sports Medicine* 55, no. 15 (2021): 865–72, https://doi.org/10.1136/bjsports-2020-103106.

89 Dialynn Dwyer, "Boston Children's Hospital Inundated by Harassment Campaign over Trans Health Services," *Boston.com*, August 17, 2022, https://www.boston.com/news/local-news/2022/08/17/boston-childrens-hospital-inundated-by-harassment-campaign-over-trans-health-services/.

90 Scott E. Hadland, "Professionals as Targets in the Culture Wars," *New England Journal of Medicine* 387, no. 7 (2022): 584–85, https://doi.org/10.1056/nejmp2205560.

91 "World Athletics Council Decides on Russia, Belarus and Female Eligibility," press release, *World Athletics*, March 23, 2023, https://worldathletics.org/news/press -releases/council-meeting-march-2023-russia-belarus-female-eligibility.

92 "WMA - Reiterates Advice to Physicians Not to Implement IAAF Rules on Classifying Women Athletes," *WMA*, May 2, 2019, https://www.wma.net/news-post /wma-reiterates-advice-to-physicians-not-to-implement-iaaf-rules-on-classifying -women-athletes/.

93 UN High Commissioner for Human Rights, "Intersection of Race and Gender Discrimination in Sport : Report of the United Nations High Commissioner for Human Rights," *United Nations Digital Library*, June 15, 2020, https://digitallibrary .un.org/record/3872495?ln=en.

Chapter 7

1 Jasmin Paris, "Spine Race," *Talking of Fells* (blog), January 6, 2020, http:// jasminfellrunner.blogspot.com/2020/01/spine-race.html.

2 Kelly Bastone, "Hiking England's Pennine Way," *Backpacker*, March 9, 2009, https://www.backpacker.com/stories/hiking-england-s-pennine-way/.

3 Nick Van Mead, "Montane Spine Race: 268 Miles of Pain," *The Guardian*, November 22, 2013, https://www.theguardian.com/lifeandstyle/the-running-blog /2013/nov/22/montane-spine-race-268-miles-running-pain.

4 "Runner Pavel Paloncy Attempts to Break 268-Mile Pennine Way Record," *inov-8*, n.d., https://www.inov-8.com/us/pennine-way-pavel-paloncy.

5 Dan Bailey, "Jasmin Paris Wins Montane Spine Race 2019," *UKclimbing*, January 16, 2019, https://www.ukclimbing.com/news/2019/01/jasmin_paris_wins _montane_spine_race_2019-71824.

6 Steve Chilton, *It's a Hill, Get over It* (Sheffield, UK: Sandstone Press, 2013), 27.

7 Steve Chilton, *Voices from the Hills: Pioneering Women Fell and Mountain Runners* (Sheffield, UK: Sandstone Press, 2023), chap. 2.

8 Richard Askwith, *Feet in the Clouds: A Tale of Fell-Running and Obsession* (London: White Lion Publishing, 2005), 4.

9 Damian Hall, "A Love Affair: An Interview with Jasmin Paris," *IRunFar*, January 16, 2020, https://www.irunfar.com/a-love-affair-an-interview-with-jasmin-paris.

10 Robert C. I. Wüst, Christopher I. Morse, Arnold De Haan, David A. Jones, and Hans Degens, "Sex Differences in Contractile Properties and Fatigue Resistance of Human Skeletal Muscle," *Experimental Physiology* 93, no. 7 (2008): 843–50, https:// doi.org/10.1113/expphysiol.2007.041764.

11 R. Celes, L. E. Brown, M. C. C. Pereira, F. P. Schwartz, V. A. R. Junior, and M. Bottaro, "Gender Muscle Recovery during Isokinetic Exercise," *International Journal of Sports Medicine* 31, no. 12 (2010): 866–69, https://doi.org/10.1055/s-0030-1254156.

12 Sandra K. Hunter, "The Relevance of Sex Differences in Performance Fatigability," *Medicine and Science in Sports and Exercise* 48, no. 11 (2016): 2247–56, https://doi.org/10.1249/mss.0000000000000928.

13   Jeryl Y. L. Lim, Johanna Boardman, Jeff Dyche, Clare Anderson, David L. Dickinson, and Sean P. A. Drummond, "Sex Moderates the Effects of Total Sleep Deprivation and Sleep Restriction on Risk Preference," *Sleep* 45, no. 9 (2022), https://doi.org/10.1093/sleep/zsac120.

14   David P. Speechly, Sheila R. Taylor, and G. G. Rogers, "Differences in Ultra-Endurance Exercise in Performance-Matched Male and Female Runners," *Medicine and Science in Sports and Exercise* 28, no. 3 (1996): 359–65, https://doi.org/10.1097/00005768-199603000-00011.

15   Beat Knechtle and Pantelis T. Nikolaidis, "Sex Differences between Women and Men in Running," in *The Running Athlete*, edited by G. L. Canata, H. Jones, W. Krutsch, P. Thoreux, and A. Vascellari (Berlin: Springer, 2022), 35–41, https://doi.org/10.1007/978-3-662-65064-6_6.

16   "BBC Breakfast News with Damian Hall and Jack Scott | This Morning," *Facebook*, January 19, 2023, https://www.facebook.com/watch/?v=858321388768685.

17   Jonathan Turner, "Four-Midable! Spine Heroine Bannwarth Stars Again to Extend Incredible Run," *RUN247*, March 4, 2023, https://run247.com/running-news/trail/claire-bannwarth-trailcat-200-2023.

18   Micah Ling, "The Unstoppable Claire Bannwarth Just Set a New Self-Supported FKT on the Colorado Trail," *Trail Runner Magazine*, August 21, 2023, https://www.trailrunnermag.com/people/news/claire-bannwarth-fkt-colorado-trail/.

INDEX